The Life and Adventures of
WILLIAM COBBETT

*The Life
and Adventures of*

WILLIAM
COBBETT

RICHARD INGRAMS

HarperCollins*Publishers*

HarperCollins*Publishers*
77–85 Fulham Palace Road,
Hammersmith, London w6 8jb
www.harpercollins.co.uk

Published by HarperCollins*Publishers* 2005

3

A catalogue record for this book
is available from the British Library

isbn 0 00 255800 9

Set in PostScript Monotype Bulmer and Modern Extended by
Rowland Phototypesetting Ltd, Bury St Edmunds, Suffolk
Printed and bound in Great Britain by
Clays Ltd, St Ives plc

In memory of Paul Foot,
lifelong friend and supporter

CONTENTS

PLATES

William Cobbett in 1800. Engraved by Francesco Bartolozzi after a painting by J.R. Smith. *(Private Collection)*

The house at Farnham where Cobbett was born in March 1763. *(ARPL/Topfoto)*

Cobbett gathering evidence against his officers with the help of Corporal Bestland. No. 4 in Gillray's sequence 'The Life of William Cobbett'. *(Private collection)*

The court martial that never was. No. 6 in the Gillray sequence. *(Private collection)*

Second Street, Philadelphia, in about 1790. *(Topfoto)*

William Windham. Portrait by Sir Thomas Lawrence. *(University College, Oxford)*

The Westminster election of 1806, as seen by Gillray. *(The British Museum – DG10619; detail)*

The court of Kings Bench sitting in Westminster Hall. Engraved by Rudolph Ackermann from a painting by Rowlandson. *(Private Collection/The Stapleton Collection/Bridgeman Art Library)*

An execution at Newgate in 1809. *(Hulton Archive/Getty Images)*

Cobbett's daughter Anne. Silhouette made in Philadelphia in 1818. *(Reproduced courtesy of Lady Lathbury)*

Mary Russell Mitford. *(Hulton-Deutsch Collection/CORBIS)*

John Cartwright. Etching by Adam Buck. *(National Portrait Gallery, London)*

Henry 'Orator' Hunt. Watercolour c.1810 by Adam Buck. *(National Portrait Gallery, London)*

Admiral Lord Cochrane, Earl of Dundonald. Portrait by P.E. Stroehling. *(National Maritime Museum, London)*

Francis Place. Portrait by Samuel Drummond. *(National Portrait Gallery, London)*

Dr Benjamin Rush. *(Courtesy Winterthur Museum. Gift of Mrs Julia B. Henry)*

William Wilberforce. Mezzotint by William Say, after Joseph Slater. *(National Portrait Gallery, London)*

The Reverend Thomas Malthus. Engraving by John Linnell. *(Bettmann/CORBIS)*

Henry, Lord Brougham. Portrait by Sir Thomas Lawrence. *(National Portrait Gallery, London)*

Henry Addington, First Viscount Sidmouth. From a drawing by Catterson Smith, drawn on stone by R.J. Lane. *(Mary Evans Picture Library)*

George Canning. Portrait by circle of Sir Thomas Lawrence. *(Christie's Images)*

Spencer Perceval. Portrait by George Francis Joseph, 1812. *(National Portrait Gallery, London)*

Lord Castlereagh. Pencil drawing by Sir Francis Leggatt Chantrey, 1820. *(National Portrait Gallery, London)*

Cobbett in about 1816. Pencil drawing by Adam Buck. *(Private Collection/Bridgeman Art Library)*

Queen Caroline, wife of George IV, by James Lonsdale. *(Guildhall Art Gallery, Corporation of London/Bridgeman Art Library)*

Nancy Cobbett in about 1830, by an unknown artist. *(Museum of Farnham. Reproduced courtesy of Lady Lathbury)*

Cobbett enters Parliament in 1833. Detail from 'March of Reform' by the political cartoonist 'H.B.' (John Doyle). *(Private collection)*

The newly elected Cobbett takes his seat on the front bench, by Doyle. *(The British Museum – 1856-5-10-377)*

The reformed House of Commons, by Sir George Hayter, 1833. *(National Portrait Gallery, London)*

TEXT ILLUSTRATIONS

INTRODUCTION

I N HIS *Old Man's Diary* (1984) A.J.P. Taylor writes: 'Every now and then someone asks as a sort of parlour game, "Who do you think is the greatest Englishman?" I have never been at a loss for an answer. Samuel Johnson of course . . . Johnson was profound. He was moral. Above all he was human . . . still I have a qualm. There comes to my mind not perhaps the greatest Englishman but certainly the runner-up. This is William Cobbett.'

Yet it is undeniable that Cobbett, nominated for second place by the most readable, most popular historian of our day, is a little-known figure. Some people know him vaguely as the author of *Rural Rides*. A great many more have never heard of him. Politics aside, you might expect him to be held up to schoolboys as an example of how to write fine, clear English. But he is not. I myself had never read a word of his until I was in my thirties, and then it was thanks to G.K. Chesterton. His short biography published in 1926 inspired me to seek out Cobbett's books, but it proved a difficult task, *Rural Rides* being the only one that was easily available. I was helped in my search by a friendly bookseller, the late David Low (recommended to me by another lover of Cobbett, Michael Foot), who supplied me with a number of books and, when he retired, gave me his copy of the invaluable bibliography by M.L. Pearl, which is much more than just a list of books and contains a huge amount of information about Cobbett's life and times. Thanks to these acquisitions I was able to compile an anthology of Cobbett's agricultural writing, *Cobbett's Country Book*, published in 1974 by David & Charles (in the person of the late James MacGibbon).

More recently I have been greatly assisted by Brian Lake of Jarn-dyce Books, with the result that I have been able to do my researches for the present book mainly at home. I could not, however, have managed without that great institution the London Library, which stocks in its basement all eighty-eight volumes of Cobbett's *Political Register*. Though most of the *Register*, like all topical journalism, is of little interest to modern readers, it still contains buried in its pages much of Cobbett's best and most lively writing.

The bulk of Cobbett manuscripts, including family letters, is held by Nuffield College, Oxford, and I am grateful to the Warden and Fellows for permission to quote from this material.

In addition my thanks are due to the following for their assistance: Tariq Ali, John Bradburne, David Chun and Molly Townsend of the Cobbett Society, Clare Cowan, Charles Elliott, Michael Foot, Paul Foot, Rose Foot, Chris Hillier of the Museum of Farnham, Peter Jay, William Keegan, Hilary Lowinger, Sharon Maurice of the Fitzwilliam Museum, Cambridge, Lucy Mulloy, Nick Parker, Helen Richardson, Chris Schuler, Bridget Tisdall, E.S. Turner and A.N. Wilson. My thanks are due to Lady Lathbury for permission to reproduce the portrait of Nancy Cobbett and the silhouette of her daughter Anne. I am especially grateful to my friends Jeremy Lewis and Piers Brendon, both of whom read the manuscript in draft form and made a great many helpful corrections and suggestions.

Lastly I would like to thank Deborah Bosley, not only for her typing skills, but for her continual encouragement and support.

RICHARD INGRAMS
January 2005

Original drawing for a medallion of William Cobbett

1

A SWEET OLD BOY

'I MYSELF ONLY SAW this extraordinary character but once,' a contributor to *Blackwood's Magazine* wrote. 'He is perhaps the very man whom I would select from all I have ever seen if I wished to show a foreigner the beau ideal of an English yeoman. He was then, I shall suppose at least fifty years of age but plump and as fresh as possible. His hair was worn smooth on his forehead and displayed a few curls, not brown then but probably greyish by this time, about his ears. His eye is small, grey, quiet and good-tempered – perfectly mild. You would say "there is a sweet old boy – butter would not melt in his mouth." I should probably have passed him over as one of the innocent bacon-eaters of the New Forest.'[1]

A very similar picture is painted by a better-known witness, William Hazlitt: 'The only time I ever saw him he seemed to me a very pleasant man: easy of access, affable, clear-headed, simple and mild in his manner, deliberate and unruffled in his speech, though some of his expressions were not very qualified. His figure is tall and portly: he has a good sensible face, rather full with little grey eyes, a hard, square forehead, a ruddy complexion, with hair grey or powdered: and had on a scarlet broad-cloth waistcoat, with the flaps of the pockets hanging down, as was the custom of gentleman farmers in the last century, as we see it in the pictures of Members of Parliament in the reign of George I.'[2]

The best likenesses of Cobbett confirm the picture given by these two acute observers. The cartoonist John Doyle, who did many drawings of him – they are not really caricatures – shows him (in old age) a kindly-looking, half-smiling, slightly stooping figure. No one looking at these drawings or reading the descriptions quoted would guess that this 'sweet old boy' was one of the most extraordinary characters in English history, the most effective, most savage and most satirical political journalist of his or any other age.

Cobbett himself is almost our only source for his earliest years. In 1796, when he was living in Philadelphia, he wrote an account of his origins to counter allegations being put about by his enemies that he was a British spy. Though the memoir had a political purpose, it is an honest, straightforward story, as one would expect from someone who always considered himself to be a happy man. There may be some omissions, but there are no deliberate falsehoods.

William Cobbett was born at Farnham in Surrey in March 1763, the third of four sons of George Cobbett, a farmer (and at one time the landlord of the Jolly Farmer Inn, which still stands on the A289 road, now renamed the William Cobbett). He never met his paternal grandfather, but one of his earliest memories was of staying with his widowed grandmother: 'It was a little thatched cottage with a garden before the door. It had but two windows; a damson tree shaded one, and a clump of filberts the other. Here I and my brothers went every Christmas and Whitsuntide to spend a week or two and torment the poor old woman with our noise and dilapidations. She used to give us milk and bread for breakfast, an apple pudding for our dinner and a piece of bread and cheese for supper. Her fire was made of turf, cut from the neighbouring heath, and her evening light was a dish dipped in grease.'

Cobbett's physical and mental energy, his eagerness to be always doing something, would seem to have been with him from the beginning. 'I do not remember the time,' he writes, 'when I did not earn my living. My first occupation was driving the small birds from the turnip seed and the rooks from the peas. When I first trudged a field with my wooden bottle and my satchel swung over my shoulders, I was hardly able to climb the gates and stiles and at the end of the day to reach home was a task of infinite difficulty. My next employment was weeding wheat and leading a single horse at harrowing barley. Hoeing peas followed and hence I arrived at the honour of joining the reapers in harvest, driving the team and holding the plough. We were all strong and laborious and my father used to boast that he had four boys, the eldest of whom was but fifteen years old, who did as much work as any three men in the Parish of Farnham. Honest pride and happy days.'

Cobbett was not quite such an obedient and dutiful son as this account suggests. His elder brother Tom, who later recounted his memories to Cobbett's third son James Paul, remembered him as a lively, rather rebellious boy – 'the foremost in enterprise when anything was on foot, not remarkable for plodding, but rather the contrary, with great liveliness of spirit having a proneness to idle pursuit and to shirk steady work and an obstinate resolution for what he was bent on . . . He must have promised to turn out rather an ungovernable than a tractable youth. When sent to mind the pigs he would throw off a part of his upper clothes and stray away after some business that better suited his taste.'[3]

Tom also remembered that Bill (as he called him) used to like listening to their father reading bits out of the newspaper of an evening. Cobbett's daughter Anne records: 'It was tiresome for the other three boys to have to keep quiet the while but Bill used oftentimes to listen and pay attention to the reading and the others wondered how he could do it. And I've often thought it all very dull work, sitting there in their chimney corner obliged to refrain from their own fun.' Bill was especially interested in speeches from Parliament, and would

remind his father of who the various speakers were. Anne also remembered her father telling her how he used to make speeches aloud when
by himself, 'And go out after dark and do so. He said he recollected
being on the Common, waving his arms about, and making speeches
to the furze bushes.'[4]

It is tempting to read something into the fact that in his own
account of his boyhood Cobbett makes scarcely any mention of his
mother. The explanation is that to an exceptional degree Cobbett was
from the beginning self-centred and self-sufficient. Most of us rely on
others close to us, whether friends or family, for help, advice and
support. But even as a boy Cobbett did not seem to need other
people. Throughout his life he depended almost entirely on his own
impressions, his own judgement, his own researches and conclusions.
So, in his little autobiography Cobbett is the only character in full
colour; the others are monochrome, sometimes not even named. The
fact that he makes no mention of his mother and cannot remember
his three brothers' ages is an indication of how little they impinged
on his thoughts and needs.

Cobbett left home three times in the course of his boyhood,
according to his own account, from no other motive but a love of
adventure. His brother Tom, however, suggested that their father was
partly to blame. 'George Cobbett,' James Paul recorded, 'was not of
a gentle disposition, but subject to violent fits of temper, and we have
reason to believe that the harshness of the parent was the cause of the
son's first quitting home.' More than once in *Rural Rides* Cobbett
refers, in a light-hearted way, to his father's having beaten him – he
told how once, as 'a very little boy' he had seen a cat 'as big as a
middle-sized spaniel dog go into a hollow elm tree, for relating which
I got a great scolding, for standing to which I at last got a beating,
stand to which I still did'. (It seems as if the father had got into the
habit of picking on Bill, perhaps because he was the most daring of
the four brothers. 'One summer evening,' James Paul writes, 'he and

his brothers being all together in their sleeping room, one of them noticed the figure of a crocodile printed in the corner of a large map which their father had hung against the wall and exclaimed "How ugly he looks". William said "Aye, don't he? I'll cut his head off." The others called out "No, Bill, don't, father will be so angry." But that did not stop him. He jumped out of bed, took his knife from his pocket and made a dash at the map, cutting into it right across the crocodile's neck. Their father, when he came to see, said whichever of them did the mischief he was sure "Bill had a hand in it." ')

Cobbett was only eleven when, inspired by what a fellow gardener told him while they were working together in the grounds of Farnham Castle, he set off on foot to see Kew Gardens 'with only thirteen half pence in his pocket'. It was as he was trudging through Richmond on his way to Kew that he caught sight of Swift's *Tale of a Tub* (price 3d*) in a bookseller's window. 'The title was so odd that my curiosity was excited. I had the 3d, but, then, I could have no supper.' He bought the book, went without his supper and read on until it grew too dark. There was something about it which made an indelible impression upon him, so much so that he carried it with him wherever he went, and when he lost it some years later in a box that fell into the sea on his way to North America, the loss gave him 'greater pain than I have ever felt at losing thousands of pounds'. Why should this satire of Swift's, directed at the various Christian Churches, have made such an impact on this half-educated farmer's son, aged only eleven? It is, like all Swift's work, highly sophisticated – even abstruse – full of subtleties, Latin tags and literary allusions which must have gone over the boy's head. One can only surmise that what so impressed him, causing what he later called 'a birth of intellect', was simply the flow – even the flood – of words, phrases piled on top of one another, broken up with digressions and parentheses, all

* According to the Office of National Statistics, the modern (2004) equivalent of £1 in 1810 is £49.67.

5

producing a kind of verbal intoxication, the effect of which was later to bear fruit in Cobbett's own writing, similarly vigorous and fluent but more direct and down-to-earth, unencumbered by Swift's vast baggage of learning.

Did Cobbett remember in later life one particular passage from this book which had such a special bearing on his own career?

> It is but to venture your lungs, and you may preach in Covent Garden against foppery and fornication, and something else; against pride and dissimulation, and bribery, at Whitehall; you may expose rapine and injustice in the inns of court chapel; and in a city pulpit be as fierce as you please against avarice, hypocrisy and extortion . . . But on the other side, whoever should mistake the nature of things so far as to drop but a single hint in public, how such a one starved half the fleet, and half poisoned the rest; how such a one, from a true principle of love and honour, pays no debts but for wenches and play; how such a one has got a clap and runs out of his estate; how Paris, bribed by Juno and Venus, later to offend either party, slept out the whole cause on the bench; or, how such an orator makes long speeches in the senate, with much thought, little sense, and to no purpose; whoever, I say, should venture to be thus particular, must expect to be imprisoned for *scandalum magnatum*; to have challenges sent to him; to be sued for defamation; and to be brought before the bar of the house.

In the autumn of 1782, when Cobbett was nineteen, he went to stay with an uncle who lived near Portsmouth. Here, from the top of Portsdown, he saw the sea for the first time – 'and no sooner did I behold it than I wished to be a sailor. I could never account for this sudden impulse, nor can I now,' he wrote. 'Almost all English boys feel the same inclination: it would seem that, like young ducks, instinct leads them to rush at the bosom of the water.' (It is perhaps worth noting that Tom Paine, whose career in so many ways prefigured

Cobbett's, felt the same urge, and like Cobbett was rescued before he signed away his freedom.)

Luckily for Cobbett, when he managed to board a ship in Portsmouth dock the captain, the Hon. George Berkeley, assuming that he was running away from a pregnant girlfriend, persuaded him 'that it was better to be led to Church in a halter to be tied to a girl that I did not like, than to be tied to the gang-way or, as the sailors call it, married to Miss Roper'. Cobbett blushed at this, which only confirmed Berkeley's opinion. But it was not enough to deter Cobbett, and when he was on shore again he applied to the Port Admiral to be enrolled. However, his request was turned down – 'and I happily escaped, sorely against my will, from the most toilsome and perilous profession in the world'. But the experience had given him a glimpse of another world beyond the farm, and he was never able afterwards to resume his work there with equanimity.

Cobbett called his little autobiography *The Life and Adventures of Peter Porcupine*, an indication that he saw some similarity in his early career to a traditional romance or fairy tale, at the beginning of which the young hero sets out from home in search of fame and fortune. 'It was on the sixth of May 1783,' he writes, 'that I, like Don Quixote sallied forth to seek adventures. I was dressed in my holiday clothes in order to accompany two or three lasses to Guildford fair. They were to assemble at a house about three miles from my home, where I was to attend them; but, unfortunately for me, I had to cross the London Turnpike Road. The stage-coach had just turned the summit of a hill and was rattling down towards me at a merry rate. The notion of going to London never entered my mind till this very moment, yet the step was completely determined on, before the coach came to the spot where I stood. Up I got and was in London about nine o'clock in the evening.' (The account is contradictory as, according to the second sentence, Cobbett had not originally set out to seek adventures but with the more mundane intention of going to Guildford

7

fair – which suggests that his leaving home was possibly not so impulsive as he would like us to believe.)

Looking back on his life, Cobbett records in two separate contexts that he had always been not only happy, but also lucky. So, arriving in London without baggage and only the small amount of money he had saved for the fair, he was befriended by a hop-merchant who had had dealings with his father and who had travelled up to London with him on the coach. This benefactor, whose name Cobbett (typically) omits, took him into his own house and in the meantime wrote to Cobbett Senior, who in turn wrote to his son ordering him to return home at once. 'I am ashamed to say,' Cobbett writes, 'that I was disobedient. It was the first time I had ever been so, and I have repented of it from that moment to this. Willingly would I have returned, but pride would not suffer me to do it. I feared the scoffs of my acquaintances more than the real evils that threatened me.'

Cobbett's friend the hop-merchant reluctantly accepted that the young man was not going home, and eventually got him a job working for a lawyer acquaintance in Gray's Inn (he is identified only by his surname of Holland). 'The next day,' Cobbett writes, 'saw me perched upon a great high stool in an obscure chamber in Grays Inn, endeavouring to decipher the crabbed draughts of my employer.' He was to work nine months in the lawyer's office, 'from five in the morning till eight at night and sometimes all night long'. In the process he acquired the ability to write quickly and neatly in a clear hand – something that was to stand him in good stead later on (considering the speed at which he wrote, his manuscripts are not only legible but invariably clean, with minimal corrections). He was also able, thanks to this legal training, to write in a beautiful copperplate script.

It was the only benefit of his brief spell in Gray's Inn. Otherwise he looked back on it as the least pleasurable period of his life. The office was gloomy and dark and the hours long. Sunday was the only break, and it was on a Sunday that when walking in St James's Park he saw a poster appealing for recruits to the Royal Marines. Once again he acted on impulse, and without saying anything to his friends reported to Chatham where he accidentally enrolled not in the Marines but in the 54th Regiment, commanded by Lord Edward Fitzgerald and bound for service in New Brunswick, a province of Canada.

The pay was poor (2d a day) and the food barely adequate, but Cobbett enjoyed the army life mainly because he liked soldiers, and he formed many close friendships in the ranks (it was as a result of defending soldiers that he would be imprisoned in 1810). In addition, while stationed at Chatham he had time to embark on a crash course of self-education. He read voraciously all the books in the local library – novels, history, poetry and plays – and in the process absorbed enough knowledge of literature to be able, when the time came for him to write, to quote widely and to good effect. He learned by heart Oliver Goldsmith's *Deserted Village* and *The Traveller*. From the start, his journalism is studded with references to the Bible, the plays of Shakespeare, the poems of Milton, Pope and many others, all of which he must have read during his army days. But stylistically it was Swift who most influenced him, as he influenced Paine and Hazlitt. Following Swift, these writers broke with the Johnsonian tradition of writing only for an educated audience (Swift used to read his books to his servants to make sure they were intelligible to the ordinary man). After his obsessive reading of *A Tale of a Tub* Cobbett must have read most of Swift's works. It is no accident that his auto-biography begins with an admirable quotation from Swift which he applies to himself: 'The Celebrated Dean of St. Patrick somewhere observes that a man of talents no sooner emerges from obscurity than all the blockheads are instantly up in arms against him.' Cobbett would also seem to have studied mathematics and geometry to a level at which he was able, when in Canada, to write a handbook on those subjects for teaching soldiers.

But it was the nowadays neglected subject of English grammar that especially absorbed him during his time at Chatham. Thanks to skills acquired in Gray's Inn, Cobbett was taken on as a copyist by the Commandant of the Garrison Colonel (later General) Hugh Debbieg. Cobbett does not say as much (and does not even spell his name correctly), but Debbieg (1731–1810) was a very distinguished engineer and soldier who had served in France and Canada and had been in charge of the defences of all public buildings during the Gordon riots in London in 1780. Recognising Cobbett's exceptional abilities, he urged him to improve himself in the business of writing, promising him promotion in exchange. Debbieg gave him a popular handbook, *A Short Introduction to English Grammar* by Robert Lowth, and he proceeded to learn the entire book by heart, by writing it out three times, reciting it to himself in its entirety when on guard duty. 'The edge of my berth, or that of the guard-bed was my seat to study in; my knapsack was my bookcase; a bit of board lying in my lap was my writing desk . . . I had to read and to write amidst the talking, laughing, singing, whistling and brawling of at least half a score of the most thoughtless of men, and that too in their hours of freedom from all control.'

Cobbett eventually won his promotion from Debbieg and became a corporal, 'which brought me a clear two-pence per diem and put a very clever Worsted Knot on my shoulder too'. Corporal Cobbett sailed with his regiment in 1785, and after landing in Nova Scotia, where he remained for a few weeks, proceeded to St John in New Brunswick. It was, according to the traveller Isaac Weld, 'a garrison town' containing 'about fifty miserable wooden dwellings and barracks'. Cobbett was to be stationed there for six months before moving a hundred miles up the St John River to Fredericton. In his account of these years he says very little about his military duties, which suggests that they were never very arduous. There was a great deal of drinking: 'Rum was seven pence a quart . . . and not one single man, out of three or four hundred was sober for a week – except myself.'

The regiment's role was supposedly to guard the frontier with America – an almost impossible task. New Brunswick was a sparsely populated province (a haven for British and French settlers and native Indians, and a refuge for loyalist Americans fleeing from the south), and consisted of huge forests with hardly any roads. Journeys had to be made on the network of rivers and lakes that crisscrossed the land, by canoe in summer and by sledge in the long, hard winter.

I was stationed on the banks of the great and beautiful river St. John [Cobbett wrote], which was more than a mile wide and a hundred miles from the sea. That river, as well as all the creeks running into it on both sides, were [sic] so completely frozen over every year by the Seventh of November or thereabouts that we could skate across it and up and down it, the next morning after the frost began, while we could see the fish swimming under the ice upon which we were skating. In about ten days the snow came; until storm after storm, coming at intervals of a week or a fortnight, made the mass, upon an average, ten feet deep; and there we were nine days out of ten, with a bright sun over our heads, and with snow, dry as hair powder, screeching under our feet. In the month of April, the last week of that month, the melting of the snow turned the river into ice again. Soon after this, symptoms of breaking-up began to appear, the immense mass of ice was first loosened near the banks of the river . . . and you every now and then heard a crack at many miles distance, like the falling of fifty or a hundred or a thousand very lofty timber trees coming down all together, from the axes and saws of the fellers . . . Day after day the cracks became louder and more frequent, till by and by the ice came tumbling out of the mouths of the creeks into the main river, which, by this time, began to give way itself, till, on some days, toward the latter end of May, the whole surface of the river moved downwards with accelerating rapidity towards the sea, rising up into piles as high as [The Duke of Wellington's] great fine house at Hyde Park Corner, wherever the ice came in contact with an

island of which there were many in the river, until the sun
and the tide had carried the whole away and made the river
clear for us to sail upon again to the next month of November;
during which time, the sun gave us melons in the natural
ground, and fine crops of corn and grass.

Such conditions were hardly suitable for conventional soldiering.
There was nothing much to do except drill, and in the winter even
this was impossible. Cobbett spent a great deal of time exploring the
forests, hunting bears, skating and fishing. As always, he made a
garden, and meanwhile he continued resolutely with his course of
self-education. He studied more geometry, he learned French, he
designed and built a barracks for four hundred soldiers 'without the
aid of a draughtsman, carpenter or bricklayer, the soldiers under me
cut down the timber and dug the stones'. He later boasted that to
stop soldiers deserting to the United States he trekked a hundred
miles through uncharted forests in order to show potential deserters
that they could be pursued. Such was his overall proficiency that he
became a clerk to the regiment: 'In a very short time the whole of the
business in that way fell into my hands; and, at the end of about a
year, neither adjutant, paymaster or quarter-master, could move an
inch without my assistance.' Cobbett was so punctual, so reliable, so
industrious that after only a few months he was promoted to sergeant
major over the heads of thirty longer-serving sergeants. 'He would
suffer no chewing of tobacco while they were on parade,' his son
James wrote, 'but would go up to a man in the rank and force him to
throw it from his mouth.'[5]

From this vantage point, Cobbett formed a view of the army and
its officer class which has been shared before and since by many
who have served in the ranks. Being sergeant major, he writes,
'brought me in close contact at every hour with the whole of the
epaulet gentry, whose profound and surprising ignorance I discovered
in a twinkling'. He realised how much the higher ranks relied on the

non-commissioned officers like himself to carry out the vital tasks of the regiment, leaving them free 'to swagger about and get roaring drunk'. The only officer for whom he maintained any respect was the young Lord Edward Fitzgerald, a charming and romantic Irish aristocrat who would be cashiered for attending a revolutionary banquet in Paris in 1792. Fitzgerald, who while in Canada had lived for some time with an Indian tribe, the Bears, was wounded while helping to lead the Irish Rising of 1798 and died (aged only thirty-five) in Newgate, where Cobbett himself was to be imprisoned a few years later.

Cobbett's insistence on his own superiority, his greater sense of duty and his industriousness might well have made him unpopular with his fellow soldiers, but this does not seem to have been the case. He formed many friendships in the regiment, and in the process developed an overall view of the injustices of the society he lived in. 'Genius,' he wrote later, 'is as likely to come out of the cottage as out of the splendid mansion, and even more likely, for, in the former case, nature is unopposed at the outset. I have had, during my life, no little converse with men famed for their *wit*, for instance; but, the most witty man I ever knew was a private soldier. He was not only the most witty, but *far* the most witty. He was a Staffordshire man, he came from WALSALL and his name was JOHN FLETCHER. I have heard from that man more bright thoughts of a witty character, than I have ever heard from all the other men, and than I have ever read in all the books that I have read in my whole life. No coarse jokes, no puns, no conundrums, no made up jests, nothing of the *college* kind; but real, sterling sprightly wit. When I have heard people report the profligate sayings of SHERIDAN and have heard the House of Commons roaring at his green-room trash, I have always thought of poor Jack Fletcher, who if he could have put his thoughts upon paper, would have been more renowned than Butler or Swift.'[6] 'How often,' Cobbett wrote of another of his soldier friends, 'has my blood boiled with indignation at seeing this fine, this gallant, this honest, true hearted and intelligent young man, standing with his hand to his hat before some worthless and stupid sort of officer, whom nature seemed to have designed to black his shoes.'[7]

It was Cobbett's sympathy for his fellow soldiers which, combined with his contempt for the officer class, led to his first confrontation with the establishment. From his experience as sergeant major and his control over the regimental accounts he observed that corruption was rife. The quartermaster, in charge of issuing provisions to the men, was keeping a large proportion for himself while, in particular, four officers – Colonel Bruce, Captain Richard Powell, and Lieutenants Christopher Seton and John Hall – were making false musters of NCOs and soldiers and selling for their own profit the men's rations of food and firewood. Such practices were rife throughout 'the system', as Cobbett was to discover later. Corruption of one kind or another was the norm at all levels of politics, the Church, the armed services and the press, and when Cobbett voiced his indignation to his fellow NCOs they urged him to keep quiet, on the grounds that these things were widespread. When he persisted he realised that he could achieve nothing as a serving soldier, and would be in danger of extreme punishment from a court martial. His only hope lay in pursuing the issue following his discharge on his return to England. The evidence of fraud lay in the regiment's books, but how was it possible to protect it, when the books could easily be tampered with or rewritten before any hearing took place? Operating long before the invention of the photocopier, Cobbett decided to make copies of all the relevant entries, stamping them with the regimental seal in the presence of a faithful helper and witness, Corporal William Bestland: 'All these papers were put into a little box which I myself had made for the purpose. When we came to Portsmouth there was talk of searching all the boxes etc, which gave us great alarm; and induced us to take all the papers, put them in a bag and trust them to a custom-house officer, who conveyed them on shore to his own house, where I removed them a few days later.'

Today such evidence would be given to the authorities, and it would be up to them to undertake a prosecution. But here it was left to Cobbett, once the Judge Advocate (Sir Charles Gould) had given his approval, to act as prosecutor single-handedly, without assistance of any kind from lawyers. And from the beginning it was clear that the authorities were dragging their feet. The first indication came when Cobbett was informed that some of the charges he had alleged against the three accused (one of the four, Colonel Bruce, had since died) were to be dropped. He then learned that the court martial would take place not in London as he had requested, but in Portsmouth, where the regiment was now stationed and where it would be much easier for the accused to prejudice the proceedings. Faced with more prevarication by the Judge Advocate, Cobbett wrote personally to the Prime Minister William Pitt the Younger, with the result that the venue was changed to London, much to the annoyance of the accused officers.

By now Cobbett would have been aware of the way the wind was blowing; and there were two more important questions to be settled. The first was the need to secure the regimental account books in order to prevent any possible tampering before the trial – 'Without these written documents nothing of importance could be proved, unless the non-commissioned officers and men of the regiment could get the better of their dread of the lash.' The second was to guarantee the demobilisation of Cobbett's key witness Corporal Bestland so as to forestall any threat of retaliation by the military. Cobbett had given the Corporal his word that he would not call him as a witness – 'unless he was first out of the army; that is to say, out of the reach of the vindictive and bloody lash'.

Yet Bestland, probably under suspicion of collaborating with Cobbett, was still in the ranks. By now considerably alarmed, Cobbett wrote to the Secretary at War pointing out the various obstacles that had been put in his way and making it clear at the same time that unless his key witness (not named) received his discharge he would abandon the prosecution. He had no reply. The court martial was due to convene on 24 March 1792, and on the twentieth Cobbett went to Portsmouth in an effort to discover what had happened to the regimental accounts. He found that, contrary to what he had been told, they had not been 'secured' at all, and were still in the possession of the accused officers. More alarming was his chance meeting on his way to Portsmouth with a group of sergeants and the regiment's music master, all of them on their way up to London – though none had served with him in America. On returning to London he was told by one of his allies, a Captain Lane, that the men had been dragooned into appearing as witnesses at the trial, where they would swear that at a farewell party which Cobbett had given prior to leaving the regiment he had proposed a Jacobin-like toast to 'the destruction of the House of Brunswick' (i.e. the Royal Family). Lane warned him that if this completely false allegation were to be upheld, he could well be charged and deported to Botany Bay in Australia. So, at very short notice, Cobbett decided not only to abandon the court martial but to flee to France.

Afterwards his enemies were to make much of his flight, accusing him of cowardice. But there can be no disputing that he did the only thing possible in the circumstances. If he had not been tried for treason he might have faced charges of sedition, or even a private prosecution from the three officers. One important factor which would have weighed heavily with him – though he never mentioned it in his subsequent lengthy defence of his actions – was that he had recently married. His bride was Anne Reid, daughter of an artillery sergeant, a veteran of the American War of Independence who had served with Cobbett in New Brunswick. When Cobbett first saw Anne she was only thirteen:

I sat in the same room with her for about an hour, in company with others, and I made up my mind that she was the very girl for me. That I thought her beautiful was certain, for that I had always said should be an indispensable qualification: but I saw in her what I deemed marks of that sobriety of conduct, which has been by far the greatest blessing of my life. It was the dead of winter, and, of course, the snow several feet deep on the ground, and the weather piercing cold. In about three mornings after I had first seen her, I had got two young men to join me in my walk; and our road lay by the house of her father and mother. It was hardly light, but she was out in the snow, scrubbing out a washing tub, 'That's the girl for me', I said, when we had got out of her hearing.

Six months after this meeting Cobbett was posted to Fredericton, and in the meantime the Artillery were due to be posted back to England. Worried that Anne might fall into bad company on her return to 'that gay place Woolwich', he sent her 150 guineas which he had saved so that she would be able to be independent of her parents – 'to buy herself food, clothes, and to live without hard work'. When Cobbett arrived back in England four years later he found his wife-to-be working as a servant girl in the house of a Captain Brissac. Without saying a word she pressed the money, untouched, into his hands. They were married on 5 February 1792 by a curate, the Reverend Thomas, in Woolwich, and found lodgings in Felix Street, Hackney. The following month they left for France, leaving no forwarding address, and when court officials tried to locate Cobbett they could find no trace of him.

The newlyweds settled in the village of Tilque, near St-Omer in Normandy. Cobbett was delighted by France: 'I went to that country full of all those prejudices that Englishmen suck in with their mother's milk against the French and against their religion; a few weeks con-vinced me that I had been deceived with respect to both. I met everywhere with civility, and even hospitality, in a degree that I had never been accustomed to.'

Unfortunately for the Cobbetts their arrival in France had coincided with a turbulent period in that country's history. When they
set out for Paris in August they heard news of the massacre of the
Swiss Guard at the Tuileries Palace and the arrest of the King and
Queen. Cobbett decided to head for Le Havre and sail to America,
but they were stopped more than once, and Anne, who was so indignant that she refused to speak, was suspected of being an escaping
French aristocrat. Eventually, however, they reached Le Havre, and
after about a fortnight were allowed to board a little ship called the
Mary, bound for New York. The voyage was a stormy one, the ship
'was tossed about the ocean like a cork'. The poultry on board all
died and the captain fed the Cobbetts a dish called samp, made from
ground maize. After forty-six days the *Mary* at last docked in New
York. Anne, who was pregnant and had had to flee from two different
countries in the course of six months, had by now become accustomed
to what being married to Cobbett was going to be like.

2

OFF to PHILADELPHIA

COBBETT'S CAREER changed course round certain clearly defined turning points. One such was the chain of events by which he became a journalist, one of the most famous and prolific in history. He had arrived in America with his pregnant wife in October 1792 and settled in Wilmington, a small port on the Delaware about thirty miles from Philadelphia. In February 1794 he moved into Philadelphia itself – the national capital and centre of American social and political life, the scene of the first meetings of Congress and the drafting of the Constitution in 1787. Founded by the Quaker William Penn on the west bank of the Delaware River in the 1680s, Philadelphia had expanded rapidly; by Cobbett's time the population numbered about thirty thousand, and included people of many nationalities and religions; and, since the Revolution, a large number of French refugees. Penn had designed the city on a grid pattern with wide streets of red-brick houses, the effect of which was somewhat monotonous. 'Philadelphia,' wrote a French visitor, the Chevalier de Beaujour, 'is cut like a chess board at right angles. All the streets and houses resemble each other, and nothing is so gloomy as this uniformity.'[1]

Cobbett and Nancy (as he called Anne) rented a modest house in the Northern Liberties district at no. 81 Callowhill Street. The climate, especially in summer, was extreme. 'The heat in this city is excessive,' wrote Dr Alexander Hamilton in 1774, 'the sun's rays being reflected with such power from the red brick houses and from the street

19

pavement which is brick. The people commonly use awnings of painted cloth or duck over their shop doors and windows and, at sunset, throw buckets full of water upon the pavement which gives a feasible cool.' Health was another problem: during Cobbett's time there were two serious outbreaks of yellow fever in the city, resulting in thousands of deaths. He himself remained unimpressed not only by Philadelphia, but by America in general.

'The country is good for getting money,' he wrote to a boyhood friend in England, Rachel Smithers, 'if a person is industrious and enterprising. In every other respect the country is miserable. Exactly the contrary of what I expected it. The land is bad – rocky – houses wretched – roads impassable after the least rain. Fruit in quantity, but good for nothing. One apple or peach in England or France is worth a bushel of them here. The seasons are detestable. All burning or freezing. There is no spring or autumn. The weather is so very inconstant that you are never sure for an hour, a single hour at a time. Last night we made a fire to sit by and today it is scorching hot. The whole month of March was so hot that we could hardly bear our clothes, and these parts of the month of June there was a frost every night and so cold in the day time that we were obliged to wear great coats. The people are worthy of the country – a cheating, sly, roguish gang. Strangers make fortunes in spite of all this, particularly the English. The natives are by nature idle, and seek to live by cheating, while foreigners, being industrious, seek no other means than those dictated by integrity, and are sure to meet with encouragement even from the idle and roguish themselves; for however roguish a man may be, he always loves to deal with an honest man.'[2]

Cobbett's gloomy reflections closely followed the move to Philadelphia and a series of personal tragedies. His second child was stillborn, and then two months later his elder child, Toney, suddenly died. 'I hope you will never experience a calamity like this,' he told Rachel Smithers. 'All I have ever felt before was nothing – nothing,

nothing at all, to this – the dearest, sweetest, beautifullest little fellow that ever was seen – we adored him. Everybody admired – When we lived at Wilmington people came on purpose to see him for his beauty. He was just beginning to prattle, and to chace [sic] the flies about the floor with a fan – I am sure I shall never perfectly recover his loss – I feel my spirits altered – a settled sadness seems to have taken possession of my mind – For my poor Nancy I cannot paint to you her distress – for several days she would take no nourishment – we were even afraid for her – never was a child so adored.'[3]

In this depressed state of mind Cobbett toyed with the idea of leaving America and going to the West Indies to teach for a few months before returning to England. Since he had arrived in America his intentions had been uncertain. Originally, armed with a letter to the Secretary of State and future President Thomas Jefferson from the American Ambassador in Paris, he had hoped to get a job working for the American government, but Jefferson was unable to help (at that time the staff of the State Department amounted to seven people). Eventually, seeing the large number of French refugees, many of whom had fled from the recent slaves' uprising on Santo Domingo, he decided to set himself up as a teacher of English, taking lodgers into the house he had rented and approaching the job with his usual energy. He worked all day every day, as well as doing the housework to assist his wife. He began writing a textbook to help French people learn English. Published in 1795, *Le Maître Anglais, Grammaire régulière de la Langue Anglaise en deux Parties* was enormously successful, running eventually, according to its author, to no fewer than sixty editions.

It was one of Cobbett's French pupils who was the indirect cause of his becoming a political pamphleteer. In 1794 Dr Joseph Priestley, the British chemist and nonconformist theologian, had emigrated to America, landing in New York where he received a rapturous reception from various republican coteries.

One of my scholars [Cobbett recounted], who was a person that we call in England a Coffee-House politician, chose, for once, to read his newspaper by way of lesson; and, it happened to be the very paper which contained the addresses presented to Dr. Priestley at New York together with his replies. My scholar, who was a sort of Republican, or at best but half a monarchist, appeared delighted with the invective against England, to which he was very much disposed to add. Those Englishmen who have been abroad, particularly if they have had the time to make a comparison between the country they are in and that which they have left, well know how difficult it is, upon occasions such as I have been describing, to refrain from expressing their indignation and resentment: and there is not, I trust, much reason to suppose, that I should, in this respect, experience less difficulty than another. The dispute was as warm as might be expected between a Frenchman and an Englishman not remarkable for *sangfroid*: and, the result was, a declared resolution on my part, to write and publish a pamphlet in defence of my country, which pamphlet he pledged himself to answer: his pledge was forfeited: it is known that mine was not. Thus it was that, whether for good or otherwise, I entered in the career of political writing: and, without adverting to the circumstances which others have entered in it, I think it will not be believed that the pen was ever taken up from a motive more pure and laudable.

American politicians, previously united in the fight for independence, were already dividing into two camps – the federalists, those who followed President George Washington, who were fundamentally pro-British, or at least in favour of neutrality; and the republicans (or the Democrats, as they were later to be called), who rallied round Thomas Jefferson in his championship of all things French. Public opinion in Philadelphia was so strongly in favour of the latter that when Cobbett's pamphlet was first published it carried neither the name of the author nor even that of the publisher, Thomas Bradford, who was frightened that the angry mob might break his windows. He need not have worried. 'The Observations on the Emigration of Joseph Priestley' was an immediate success, and there were eventually five Philadelphia editions as well as several in England. The fourth edition was credited to 'Peter Porcupine', Cobbett's chosen pseudonym.

It opened with words that could serve as a text for the thousands and thousands Cobbett would write in a lifetime of journalism: 'No man has a right to pry into his neighbour's private concerns and the opinions of every man are his private concerns . . . but when he makes those opinions public . . . when he once comes forward as a candidate for public admiration, esteem or compassion, his opinions, his principles, his motives, every action of his life, public or private, become the fair subject of public discussion.' 'The Observations on the Emigration of Joseph Priestley' is an extraordinarily assured performance for someone coming new to political pamphleteering. Dr Priestley (1733–1804) was a considerable figure, a distinguished scientist who had written voluminously on religious matters, whilst at the same time making pioneering experiments with oxygen, sulphuric acid and various gases. Yet the unknown Hampshire farmer's son held him in no respect whatsoever. For a start, Cobbett had little interest in science, and regarded Priestley's experiments as merely the hobby of an eccentric. As for religion, Cobbett, a faithful defender of the Church of England despite his generally low opinion of the clergy, nourished throughout his life the strongest possible contempt for all varieties of nonconformism – Methodism, Quakerism or, as in Priestley's case, Unitarianism, a system of belief that denied the Trinity and the divinity of Christ (Priestley addressed his prayers to 'the Great Parent of the Universe').

Central to Cobbett's argument was a denial of Priestley's claim to be seeking asylum in America from the allegedly repressive and tyrannical authorities in Britain. Priestley had been an enthusiast for the French Revolution, unwavering in the face of the Jacobin excesses that had horrified public opinion in his native country. Middle-class

Dissenters who had welcomed the Revolution's campaign for religious tolerance and equality had formed debating clubs and societies throughout England to propagate French ideas and send messages of support to the revolutionaries. In Priestley's home town of Birmingham, as in many other cities, a dinner had been organised to commemorate the second anniversary of the storming of the Bastille, an event that sparked off a major riot lasting for four days. During the disturbance Priestley's house and library were burnt to the ground, to the gratification of many, including King George III. Priestley fled to London and three years later emigrated to America to join his sons, already resident there.

In Cobbett's eyes Priestley's hypocrisy lay in seeking 'asylum' from a supposedly tyrannical system which he claimed had denied him protection or redress. In fact, following the Birmingham riot, eleven of its ringleaders were indicted, of whom four were found guilty and two executed. In the meantime Priestley sued the Birmingham city council and was awarded damages of £2502.18s. to compensate for the loss of his property:

> If he had been the very best subject in England in place of one of the very worst, what could the law have done more for him? Nothing certainly can be stronger proof of the independence of the courts of justice, and of the impartial execution of the laws of England than the circumstances and result of this case. A man who had for many years been the avowed and open enemy of the government and constitution, had his property destroyed by a mob, who declared themselves the friends of both, and who rose on him because he was not. This mob were pursued by the government whose cause they thought they were defending: some of them suffered death, and the inhabitants of the place where they assembled were obliged to indemnify the man whose property they had destroyed. It would be curious to know what sort of protection this *reverend* Doctor, this 'friend of humanity'

wanted. Would nothing satisfy him but the blood of the whole mob? Did he wish to see the town of Birmingham, like that of Lyons, razed and all its industries and inhabitants butchered; because some of them had been carried to commit unlawful excesses from their detestation of his wicked projects? BIRMINGHAM HAS COMBATTED AGAINST PRIESTLEY, BIRMINGHAM IS NO MORE.

Such an extract is enough to show Cobbett's clear, strong invective – his meaning immediately clear, his mastery of the language absolute. *En passant* he could not avoid indicting Priestley, not only for his political and religious failings, but for writing bad English: 'His style is uncouth and superlatively diffuse. Always involved in minutiae, every sentence is a string of parentheses in finding the end of which, the reader is lucky if he does not lose the proposition that they were meant to illustrate. In short, the whole of his phraseology is entirely disgusting; to which may be added, that, even in point of grammar, he is very often incorrect.'

Cobbett's energies however were in the main directed, not just in the Priestley pamphlet but in all his American writings, to attacking the Democrat party, and particularly, during his first years, to supporting the treaty with Britain that Washington, along with his Chief Justice John Jay, was desperately trying to get the Senate to ratify. The British government, now at war with revolutionary France, was naturally keen to stop America allying itself with the enemy. But such were the strong pro-French feelings among the Democrat politicians and the Philadelphians that it was proving a difficult task. A hysterical enthusiasm for France and the French Revolution was then the dominant political passion in the United States, and especially in Philadelphia. France had assisted America with troops and money during the War of Independence, and many Americans felt that their own revolution had inspired the French. None of the excesses of the French Jacobins could dampen the enthusiasm. Street names which included the words 'King', 'Queen' or 'Prince' were changed, democratic societies were formed, and men cut their hair in the 'Brutus crop'.

Cobbett noted how some Americans even adopted the French habit of referring to one another as 'Citizen' and wore tricolour cockades. 'The delirium seized even the women and children. I have heard more than one young woman, under the age of twenty, declare that they would willingly have dipped their hands in the blood of the Queen of France.'

As the birthplace of American independence, Philadelphia was one of the main centres of revolutionary pro-French frenzy. Following the execution in January 1793 of Louis XVI (formerly the ally of America), a celebratory dinner was held in the city at which a pig was decapitated and the head carried round for all the diners to mutilate with their knives. When France declared war on England the following month the French Ambassador to the United States, Edmond Genet, sent to win over America to the French cause, was given an ecstatic welcome by the Philadelphians. He had been preceded by the French frigate *Ambuscade* which sailed up the Delaware and anchored off the Market Street wharf flying a flag with the legend 'Enemies of equality, reform or tremble!'. When Genet himself arrived two weeks later the citizens went wild with excitement. John Adams recalled: 'Ten thousand men were in the streets of Philadelphia day after day, threatening to drag Washington out of his house and effect a revolution in the government, or compel it to declare in favour of the French, and against England.' At a dinner given at Oeller's Hotel toasts were drunk to 'Liberty' and 'Equality', a special ode recited and the Marseillaise sung – with everyone joining in the chorus ('I leave the reader to guess,' wrote Cobbett, 'at the harmony of this chorus, bellowed forth from the drunken lungs of about a hundred fellows of a dozen different nations').

The bulk of Cobbett's early journalism was concerned with combating such hysteria. In gruesome and gory detail he catalogued all

the excesses of the Jacobins in France, poured scorn on their supporters such as Thomas Paine and, generally speaking, commended
those Americans, like Washington, who advocated neutrality in the
dispute between France and England. In 'A Bone to Gnaw for the
Democrats' (1795), published under his pseudonym 'Peter Porcupine',
he savaged those American republicans who were currently predicting
an English revolution. The following year he published a much longer
pamphlet with a much longer, if self-explanatory, title: 'The Bloody
Buoy, Thrown Out as a Warning to the Political Pilots of America:
or a Faithful Relation of a Multitude of Acts of Horrid Barbarity, Such
as the Eye Never Witnessed, the Tongue Never Expressed, or the
Imagination Conceived, Until the Commencement of the French Revolution, to Which is Added an Instructive Essay, Tracing These Dreadful Effects to Their Real Causes'. Although they went against the
general mood, these pamphlets enjoyed an immediate success. Three
editions of 'A Bone to Gnaw' were published in less than three
months, and Cobbett's other pamphlets were constantly reprinted in
both England and America.

In the meantime, Cobbett had become a father again, and this
time the child was destined to live. A daughter, Anne, was born on
11 July 1795, at a time of great heat in the city. His wife Nancy, who
was having trouble breastfeeding, was also unable to sleep because of
the incessant barking of the Philadelphia dogs:

> I was, about nine in the evening sitting by the bed. 'I do
> think' said she 'that I could go to sleep now if it were not *for
> the dogs.*' Downstairs I went, and out I sallied, in my shirt
> and trousers, and without shoes and stockings; and going to
> a heap of stones lying beside the road, set to work upon the
> dogs, going backward and forward, and keeping them at two
> or three hundred yards distance from the house. I walked
> thus the whole night, bare-footed, lest the noise of my shoes
> might possibly reach her ears; and I remember that the bricks
> of the causeway were, even in the night, so hot as to be

27

disagreeable to my feet. My exertions produced the desired effect; a sleep of several hours was the consequence, and, at eight o'clock in the morning, off I went to a day's business, which was to end at six in the evening.[4]

Cobbett went to enormous pains to help his wife with the baby: 'I no more thought of spending a moment *away from her*, unless business compelled me, than I thought of quitting the country and going to sea.' Apart from the dogs, Nancy was alarmed by the frequent and violent thunderstorms in Philadelphia. Cobbett used to run home as soon as he suspected a storm was on the way. 'The Frenchmen who were my scholars, used to laugh at me exceedingly on this account; and sometimes when I was making an appointment with them, they would say, with a smile and a bow, "*Sauve la Tonnerre toujours, Monsieur Cobbett.*"'[5]

Such devotion to his wife's needs was all the more commendable in someone who was, as always, intensely active. Cobbett was now doing so well from his journalism and teaching that he decided to set up on his own as a publisher and bookseller. In May 1796 he moved with wife and baby into a house-cum-shop at 25 North Second Street, opposite Christ Church and near the terminus for the coaches to Baltimore and New York. He was taking a considerable risk. For the first time he was emerging in public from the cloak of anonymity, and setting up shop in the centre of town. 'Till I took this house,' he wrote later, 'I had remained almost entirely unknown as a writer. A few persons did, indeed, know that I was the person, who had assumed the name of Peter Porcupine: but the fact was by no means a matter of notoriety. The moment, however, that I had taken a lease on a large house, the transaction became a topic of public conversation, and the eyes of the Democrats and the French, who still lorded it over the city, and who owed me a mutual grudge, were fixed upon me. I thought my situation somewhat perilous. Such tracts as I had published, no man had dared to utter, in the United States, since the rebellion. I knew that those truths had mortally offended the leading men amongst the Democrats, who could, at any time, muster a mob quite sufficient to destroy my house, and to murder me . . . In short, there were, in Philadelphia, about ten thousand persons, all of whom would have rejoiced to see me murdered: and there might, probably, be two thousand, who would have been very sorry for it: but not above fifty of whom would have stirred an inch to save me.'

As the bookshop's opening day approached Cobbett's friends, from among the fifty, urged him to be cautious, to do nothing to provoke retaliation. He, however, like Nelson, decided that the bravest course was also the safest. His shop had large windows, and on the Sunday prior to opening he filled them with all the prints he possessed of '*Kings, Queens, Princes and Nobles*. I had all the English ministry; several of the bishops and judges; the most famous admirals: and in short, every picture that I thought likely to excite rage in the enemies of Great Britain. Never since the beginning of the rebellion, had any one dared to hoist at his window the portrait of George the Third.'

On Monday morning Cobbett took down his shutters and opened the shop. Although a large crowd collected, nothing happened. The only threat of violence came in the form of an anonymous letter to his landlord John Oldden, a Quaker merchant of Chesnut (sic) Street:

> Sir, a certain William Cobbett alias Peter Porcupine, I am informed is your tenant. This daring *scoundrell* [sic] not satisfied with having repeatedly traduced the people of this country; in his detestable productions, he has now the astonishing effrontery to expose those very publications at his window for sale . . . When the time of retribution arrives it may not be convenient to discriminate between the innocent and the guilty. Your property may suffer. As a friend therefore I advise you to save your property by either compelling Mr Porcupine to leave your house or at all events oblige him to cease exposing his abominable proclivities or any of his courtley [sic] prints at his window for sale. In this way only

you may avoid danger to your house and perhaps save the rotten *carcase* of your tenant for the present.

Cobbett used the letter as the pretext for another fiery pamphlet, 'The Scarecrow' (1796). But although he affected great indignation he actually enjoyed engaging in controversy with his opponents. There was to be more than enough of this now that he had come out into the open and revealed the true identity of Peter Porcupine. Several pamphlets resulted: Cobbett was accused of being a deserter, a British government spy and a criminal who had fled to America to escape the gallows. They said he had been whipped when he was in Paris – hence his hatred of the French.

Cobbett was astute enough to realise that all such attacks were not just good for business but a tribute to the success of his campaign. He also knew that he was a better writer than any of his critics. In reply to them he quoted a letter to his father: '"Dear Father, when you used to get me off to work in the morning, dressed in my blue smock-frock and woollen spatterdashes, with my bag of bread and cheese and bottle of small beer slung over my shoulder on the little crook that my old god-father Boxall gave me, little did you imagine that I should one day become so great a man as to have my picture stuck in the windows and have four whole books published about me in the course of one week" – Thus begins a letter which I wrote to my father yesterday morning and which, if it reaches him, will make the old man drink an extraordinary pot of ale to my health. Heaven bless him. I think I see him now by his old-fashioned fire-side reading the letter to his neighbours' – an unlikely scenario, in view of the fact that George Cobbett had been dead for four years. It would have been most unlike Cobbett to deceive his readers about this, and the assumption must be that, having been out of the country since early 1792 he had not been in touch with his family. This in turn suggests that, contrary to the impression he liked to give, Cobbett had never been close to either his father or his three brothers.

In 1796, as part of his continuing campaign to answer his critics, Cobbett published his short autobiography *The Life and Adventures of Peter Porcupine*, in which he gave the Americans a vivid and appealing account of his boyhood in Farnham, his escape from home and his army career. It is one of his best pieces of writing, and served its purpose in showing that he was not just a hack pamphleteer but a writer with a genuinely independent spirit. The following year, 1797, he launched a daily newspaper, *Porcupine's Gazette*, and closed down his monthly periodical the *Political Censor*. The paper was an immediate success, Cobbett claming in the first issue that he already had a thousand subscribers. By November three thousand copies were being printed. The paper flourished for the simple reason that, as the sales figures suggest, the American public, even though they might disagree with Cobbett's views, enjoyed his writing – the robust straightforward style, the knockabout, the jokes and the nicknames.

As a journalist Cobbett was at his best when he could focus his animosity on a particular individual rather than a set of principles or ideas. This is not to say that he was uninterested in ideas, only that he needed someone, like Dr Priestley, to personify the particular variety of political hypocrisy he was attacking at any time. Labelled with appropriate nicknames, these favoured targets (mentioned at every opportunity) lent a powerful spice to his political journalism, making it compulsive reading even for his enemies. Many of the victims of his most savage attacks were not necessarily his political opponents, but had aroused his indignation by being humourless, puritanical in their attitude to morality or, above all, vain. Priestley was one such. William Wilberforce would later be another. A third was Noah Webster (1758–1843) of *Webster's Dictionary* fame, a lexicographer, a grammarian, the author of a spelling book for American schools and the man responsible for the differences between American and English spelling ('color' for 'colour', etc.). Webster came from a family of strict Puritans and was highly industrious in any number of fields – though Jefferson called him 'a mere pedagogue of very limited understanding'. Cobbett was even ruder, despite the fact that Webster supported the federalists, and missed no opportunity to call him names:

> despicable creature . . . viper . . . mean shuffling fellow . . . were this man indeed distinguished as being descended from a famous race, for great learning and talents, for important public services, for possessing much weight in the opinions of the people, even his vanity would be inexcusable but the fellow is distinguished, amongst the few who know him, for the very contrary of all this. He comes of obscure parents, he has just learning enough to make him a fool, his public services have all been confined to silly, idle *projects*, every one of which has completely failed, and as to his weight as a politician, it is that of a feather, which is overbalanced by a straw, and puffed away by the gentlest breath. All his measures are exploded, his predictions have proved false, not a single senti-ment of his has become fashionable, nor has the Federal Government ever adopted a single measure which he has been in the habit of recommending.[6]

Webster later saw a chance of revenge following the passing of a Sedition Act by Washington in 1798 which made it illegal 'to write, print, utter or publish any false, scandalous and malicious writing or writings against the Government of the United States'. Although the Act was intended to be used against French writers – by this time the USA had broken off relations with France and was preparing for war – Webster decided it could equally well be used against people like Cobbett. Affecting, like many of his type, not to have personally seen the attacks, he wrote to the Secretary of State Timothy Pickering: 'The violence and resentment of the English knows no bounds. They are intolerably insolent and strive, by all possible means to lessen the circulation of my papers.' (He need not have bothered, as by that stage proceedings were already under way.)

A more formidable opponent than Webster was Thomas McKean (1734–1817), a lawyer of Scottish descent who involved himself in politics, became one of the most ardent advocates of separation prior to the war with Britain, and was a signatory of the Declaration of Independence in 1776. The following year McKean became the Chief Justice of Pennsylvania (a post he occupied for twenty years), and he was elected President of Congress in 1781. Though a keen Democrat and francophile, McKean was deeply conservative in matters of law, besides being, in the words of his contemporary Thomas Rodney, a man 'of great vanity, extremely fond of power and entirely governed by passions, ever pursuing the object present with warm, enthusiastic zeal without much reflection or forecast'.[7] A recent biographer describes him as 'almost pathological in his insistence upon deference in his political and judicial capacities'. Among other insults, Cobbett called him 'a little upstart tyrant', or 'Mrs McKean's husband' (the suggestion being that he was under the thumb of his dominating wife).

Already needled by these jibes, McKean was only too happy to act when his prospective son-in-law Don Carlos Martinez de Yrujo, the Spanish Ambassador, complained of certain disobliging comments which Cobbett made about himself and the Spanish King Charles IV, who had appointed him. On 18 August 1796 Cobbett was arrested and charged with criminal libel (the first of a long series of such setbacks). In a lengthy indictment McKean expressed his distaste not just for Cobbett but for all forms of satire against public figures (such as himself): 'where libels are printed against persons employed in a public capacity they receive an aggravation, as they tend to scandalize the government by reflecting those who are entrusted with the administration of public affairs'. Political journalism had got quite out of hand, in McKean's view:

> Everyone who has in him the sentiments of either a Christian
> or a gentleman cannot but be highly offended at the envenomed
> scurrility that has raged in pamphlets and newspapers . . . in

so much that libelling has become a kind of national crime, and distinguishes us not only from all the states around us, but from the whole civilized world . . .

Impressed with the duties of my station, I have used some endeavours for checking these evils, by binding over the editor and printer of one of them, licentious and virulent beyond all former example, to his good behaviour; but he still perseveres in his nefarious publications; he has ransacked our language for terms of reproach and insult, and for the basest accusations against every ruler and distinguished character in France and Spain, with which we chance to have any intercourse, which it is scarce in nature to forgive . . .

McKean created something of a precedent by appearing as both judge and witness at the trial, but despite this the jury sided with Cobbett by a majority of one. Not content with the verdict, McKean now made efforts to have Cobbett deported from the United States as an undesirable alien. When these failed he compiled a selection of Cobbett's writings, including various alleged libels on public figures. Following a trial Cobbett was bound over for $4000 to be of good behaviour, at which point a more prudent man might have left McKean alone. Cobbett however was determined not to be silenced. He was especially eager to prove that despite the First Amendment the American press was no more free than the British. In a pamphlet, 'The Democratic Judge' (1798), he railed against the iniquity of the proceedings, pointing out (*inter alia*) that his comments about the King of Spain and his Ambassador were mild stuff compared to some of the scurrilous comments on George III and his allies which McKean had allowed freely to circulate. In the English edition (copies of which no doubt reached America) Cobbett tore into McKean in what must be one of the most defamatory attacks ever launched against a public figure:

His private character is infamous. He beats his wife and she beats him. He ordered a wig to be imported for him by Mr.

Kid, refused to pay for it, the dispute was referred to the court of *Nisi Prius*; where (merely for want of the *original invoice* which Kid had lost) the Judge came off victorious! He is a notorious drunkard. The whole bar, one lawyer excepted, signed a memorial, stating, that so great a drunkard was he, that *after dinner, person and property were not safe in Pennsylvania*. He has been horsewhipped in the City Tavern, and kicked in the street for his insolence to particular persons; and yet this degraded wretch is *Chief Justice* of the State!

McKean, a proud, vain man, was not the sort of person to forget such an attack. In 1797, following the second of two outbreaks of yellow fever in Philadelphia, a further opportunity for prosecution arose as a result of Cobbett's libels of another of the city's most distinguished citizens, Dr Benjamin Rush. Rush (1745–1813) was, like McKean, a signatory of the Declaration of Independence, a close friend of Noah Webster and a fanatical republican. He had begun his career as a lawyer but changed to medicine, studying at Edinburgh University and St Thomas's Hospital, London (where he met Dr Johnson, Oliver Goldsmith and Joshua Reynolds). Returning to Philadelphia, he began to practise medicine and had already made a name for himself when the War of Independence broke out. Rush was appointed Surgeon General to the armies, but quarrelled with George Washington and returned to his medical practice. Though a pioneer in many medical and veterinary fields (he has been credited with the possibly dubious distinction of being the founder of American psychiatry), his approach to more conventional medical matters was misguided, to put it mildly. Following the lead of the famous Edinburgh physician John Brown, Rush came to believe that nearly all ailments, even the common cold, sore throat or headache, were caused by 'a state of excessive excitability of a spasm in the blood vessels', and hence in most cases called for the one treatment of 'depletion' through bleeding and purging. 'This conception was so simple that it came to hold for his speculative mind all the fascination of an ultimate panacea.'[8]

The test of Rush's theory came in 1793 when the first of the epidemics of yellow fever struck Philadelphia, resulting in the death of several thousand citizens. Basing his remarks on Rush's own account (published in 1794), Cobbett later described the doctor's technique, prior to his discovery of bleeding.

> At the first breaking out of the Yellow Fever, he made use of *'gentle purges'*; these he laid aside, and had recourse to *'a gentle vomit of ipecacuanha'*; next he *'gave bark* in all its usual forms, *of infusion, powder and tincture, and joined wine, brandy and aromatics with it'*; this was followed by *'the application of blisters to the limbs, neck and head'*; these torments were succeeded by *'an attempt to rouse the system by wrapping the whole body in blankets dipped in warm vinegar'*; he next *'rubbed the right side with mercurial ointment, with a view of exciting the action of the vessels through the medium of the liver'*; after this he again returned to bark, which he gave *'in large quantities and in one case ordered it to be injected into the bowels once in four hours'*; and, at last, having found that wrapping his patient in *blankets dipped* in warm vinegar did no good, he *directed buckets full of cold water to be thrown frequently upon them*!!!
>
> Surprising as it may seem his patients *died*!

Rush was not a bad man, in fact he was a very conscientious and industrious practitioner. But he was excessively vain, quick-tempered and lacking in humour (he must have been painfully aware that the high death rate disproved his claim that the yellow fever was no more dangerous than measles or influenza). The attack coming from an Englishman, one moreover with no knowledge at all of medicine, was doubly insulting to a man of his self-importance. He later wrote of receiving torrents of abuse from 'one Cobbett, an English alien who then resided in Philadelphia',[9] and in October 1797 he issued a writ for libel. But if he was hoping thereby to silence his antagonist, he was unsuccessful. 'The Doctor,' Cobbett wrote, 'finds his little reputation as a physician, in as dangerous a way as ever a poor yellow fever man was in, half an hour after he was called to his aid. We wanted no hints from Dr Rush. We know very well what we ought to do; and, if God grants us life we shall do it completely.'

Cobbett accordingly redoubled his attacks on the doctor. Among other misdeeds, Rush, he claimed (7 October 1797), had 'appointed two illiterate negro men and sent them into the alleys and bye places of the city, with orders to bleed and give his sweating purges, to all they should find sick, without regard to age, sex or constitution; and bloody and dirty work they have among the poor miserable creatures that fell in their way ... I know several that he terrified into chilly fits, some into relapses and some into convulsions, by stopping them in the street and declaring they had the fever – You've got it! You've got it! was his usual salutation upon seeing anyone with a pale countenance.'

Rush's action against Cobbett for libel was set down for trial in December 1797. Realising that he had little chance of successfully defending the suit in Philadelphia, Cobbett had made an application to Chief Justice McKean to have the case transferred to the Federal Court – which, he claimed, as an alien, he was entitled to do by the American Constitution:

> It was towards the evening of the last day of the session when Mr Thomas [Cobbett's lawyer], albeit unused to the modest mode, stole up gently from his seat, and in a faint and trembling voice, told the Bashaw [Pasha] McKean that he had a petition to present in behalf of William Cobbett. For some time he did not make himself heard. There was a great talking all round the bar; Levi, the lawyer was reading a long formal paper to Judges, and the judges were laughing over the chit-chat of the day. Amidst the noisy mirth that surrounded him, there stood poor Thomas, with his papers in his hand, like a culprit at school just as the boys are breaking up. By and by, one of those pauses, which frequently occur in even the most

numerous and vociferous assemblies, encouraged him to make a fresh attempt. 'I present' says he 'may it please your honours, a petition in behalf of William Cobbett.' The moment the sound of the word Cobbett struck the ear of McKean he turned towards the bar, and having learnt the subject of the petition, began to storm like a madman. A dead silence ensued. The little scrubby lawyers (with whom the courts of Pennsylvania are continually crowded) crouched from fear, just like a brood of poultry, when the kite is preparing to pounce in amongst them; whilst hapless Thomas, who stood up piping like a straggled chicken, seemed already to feel the talons of the judicial bird of prey. He proceeded, however, to read the petition, which being very short was got through with very little interruption, when he came to the words, 'subject of his Britannic Majesty,' McKean did, indeed grin most horribly, and I could very distinctly hear, 'Insolent scoundrel!' – 'damned aristocrat' – 'damned Englishman!' etc etc from the mouths of the sovereign people. But neither their execration, nor the savage looks that accompanied them, prevented me from fulfilling my purpose. I went up to the clerk of the court, took the book in my hand, and holding it up, that it might be visible to all parts of the hall, I swore, in a voice that everyone might hear, that I preserved my allegiance to my King; after which I put on my hat, and walked out of the Court followed by the admiration of the few and by the curses of the many.

McKean, predictably, threw out the petition, and after many delays the case finally came in on 13 December 1799. By this time, anticipating certain defeat, Cobbett had left Philadelphia and was living in New York. The move was only partly dictated by prudence. The political mood had changed, the pro-French frenzy had subsided – Napoleon had taken charge in France – and as a result the circulation of *Porcupine's Gazette*, which had relied so much on attacking the Jacobins, had declined. Cobbett's intention, however, was to resume publication of the paper in New York, where he would be out of McKean's jurisdiction. 'Yesterday,' he wrote to his friend Edward Thornton at the British Embassy (18 November 1799), 'all my goods sailed for New York, so that they are no longer, I hope, within the grasp of the sovereign people of Pennsylvania. I have some few things left at my house in 2nd Street, which will there be sold by auction, under the direction of one of my friends: in the meantime I am preparing to follow the rest, and I propose to set out from here about this day week.' Cobbett left town on 9 December, and four days later McKean brought on the Rush libel action before three of his old colleagues. The president was Justice Edward Shippen, a candidate for McKean's former position of Chief Justice. At the end of the case, which lasted only two days, the jury awarded Rush damages of $5000, and four days later Justice Shippen was rewarded with the job.

It was a shattering blow for Cobbett, who claimed that the damages amounted to more than the total of all those ever awarded by the Philadelphia court in libel actions. One of his lawyers, Edward Tilghman, advised him to flee the country immediately, but, very typically, Cobbett was determined to stand his ground. He wrote to Edward Thornton (25 December 1799):

> 'No,' said I to Tilghman, in answer to his advice for immediate flight. 'No, Sir, the miscreants may, probably, rob me of all but my honour, but that, in these degenerate times, I cannot spare. To flee from a *writ* (however falsely and illegally obtained) is what I will never do; for though, generally speaking, to *leave the United States* at this time, would be little more disgraceful than it was for Lot to run from Sodom under a shower of fire and brimstone; yet with a writ at my heels, I will never go.'

Nancy Cobbett was in full agreement:

> Though she feels as much as myself on these occasions, nothing *humbles* her; nothing sinks her spirits but personal danger to me or our children. The moment she heard Tilghman's advice,

she rejected it . . . she nobly advised me to stay, sell off my
stock, pay the money, and go home with the trifle that may
remain. It is the misfortune of most wives to be cunning on
these occasions. 'Ah, did I not tell you so!' – Never did I hear
a reproach of this kind from my wife. When times are smooth
she will contradict and blame me often enough in all conscience; but when difficulties come on me, when danger
approaches us, then all I say and do, and all I have said and
done is *right*.[10]

Cobbett had his revenge on Rush by publishing a new paper, running
to five numbers in all, called the *Rush-Light*, which for the power of
its invective outclassed anything he had so far done. Dubbing Rush
variously 'the noted bleeding physician of Philadelphia . . . the Philadelphia phlebotomist . . . the Pennsylvania Hippocrates', he subjected
the doctor, his character and his career to savage ridicule, seizing on
all his more preposterous theories – his belief that Negroes were black
because of leprosy and would turn white once the disease had been
eradicated – or the fact that in the grounds of the Pennsylvania Hospital Rush had erected a kind of gallows 'with a rope suspended from
it . . . for the purpose of curing insanity by swinging'. He went on to
demonstrate the absurdity of Rush's claim that the yellow fever of
1793 constituted no more of a threat than measles or the common
cold simply by producing the daily mortality figures following Rush's
pronouncement:

> Thus, you see, that though the Fever was, on the 12th Sep-
> tember, reduced to a level with a common cold; though the
> lancet was continually unsheathed; though Rush and his sub-
> alterns were ready at every call, the deaths did actually
> increase; and, incredible as it may seem, this increase grew
> with that of the very practice which saved more than ninety-
> nine patients out of a hundred! Astonishing obstinacy! Per-
> verse Philadelphians! Notwithstanding there was a man in
> your city who could have healed you at a touch, you continued

to die! Notwithstanding the precious purges were advertised at every corner, and were brought to your doors and bedsides by Old Women and Negroes; notwithstanding life was offered on terms the most reasonable and accommodating, still you persisted in dying! Nor did barely dying content you. It was not enough for you to reject the means of prolonging your existence, but you must begin to drop off the faster from the moment that those means were presented to you: and this, for no earthly purpose I can see, but the malicious one of injuring the reputation of the 'Saving Angel' whom 'a kind providence' had sent to your assistance![11]

Cobbett also pointed out with glee that on the very same day that the jury had found against him in the Rush libel action, the President, George Washington, had died after being copiously bled in accordance with Rush's theories. 'On that day,' he wrote, 'the victory of RUSH and of DEATH was complete.'

Cobbett's barbs were directed not only at McKean, Rush and the judge (Shippen), but at the jury, all of whose names and addresses he listed, and all the lawyers, including his own, Robert G. Harper, who he maintained had let him down while secretly supporting the other side. In common with almost every other libel lawyer through the ages, Rush's counsel Joseph Hopkinson (the author of the patriotic poem 'Hail Columbia') had emphasised the great personal distress caused not only to his client but to his whole family:

Hopkinson, towards the close of a dozen pages of lies, nonsense, and bombast, gave the tender-hearted Jury a most piteous picture of the distress produced in Rush's family by my publications against the '*immaculate* father.' He throws the wife into hysterics, makes a deep wound in the heart, and tears, with remorseless rage, all the '*fine fibres* and *delicate sympathies* of *conjugal love.*' From the mother, whom I have never mentioned in my life till now, he comes to the children, 'of *nice feelings* and *generous sensibility.*' The daughters, he, of course, sets to weeping: 'but manlier passions swell, agitate and inflame the breasts of HIS SONS. They burn, they burst with indignation; rage, revenge, drive them headlong to desperate deeds, accumulating woe on woe.

The *Rush-Light* had a huge sale as well as being printed in England, and may well have caused Dr Rush to regret having sued Cobbett in the first place. Certainly it would seem to have upset him more than the original libel (Cobbett, he complained, had 'vented his rage in a number of publications of the same complexion with those he had published in his newspaper, but with many additional falsehoods. They were purchased, lent and read with great avidity by most of the citizens of Philadelphia, and my children were insulted with them at school, and in the public streets'). Shortly afterwards he began writing a long, self-justifying memoir, *Travels Through Life*, in which he set out to correct the damage done to his reputation by Cobbett.

By this time Cobbett, threatened with renewed legal prosecution by McKean and realising that his journalistic scope was limited by his being effectively barred from Philadelphia, decided to return to England, where he knew he had acquired a host of readers, not to mention influential admirers in government circles. 'The court of Philadelphia will sit again on the 2nd of June next,' he wrote to Thornton (25 April 1800), 'when the cause of old McKean versus Peter Porcupine will be brought on . . . In order, therefore, to save 2000 dollars, I propose sailing by the June packet, and am making my preparations accordingly . . . By the assistance of my friend Morgan, I shall be able to carry home about 10,000 dollars which . . . will leave me wherewith to open a shop somewhere in the West End of the town. I have revolved various projects in my mind; but this always returns upon me as the most eligible, most congenial to my disposition, and as giving the greatest scope to that sort of talent and industry which I possess . . . A stranger in the great city of London, and not only a stranger to the *people*, but to the mode of doing business, I shall feel very awkward for a time; but this will wear away.'

The Cobbetts set sail from Halifax on 11 June 1800 on the *Lady Arabella*. They took with them a young Frenchman, Edward Demonmaison, who was working as Cobbett's secretary. It was not a pleasant voyage. Captain Porteus Cobbett described as 'the greatest blackguard I ever met with', while two army officers travelling on the boat 'smoked Mrs Cobbett to death . . . talked in the most vulgar strain, and even sang morsels of bawdry in her presence'. The ship had narrowly escaped being captured by a French privateer, and on arrival in Falmouth the 'gentry' went into the custom house and attempted to embarrass Cobbett by reporting that he was accompanied by a foreigner (Demonmaison) – 'when, to their utter astonishment, the collector asked if it was that Mr Cobbett who had gone under the name of Porcupine and upon receiving the affirmative, ordered the Capt. to send on board to tell me, that he should be happy to oblige me in any way he could, and that the rules concerning foreigners should be dispensed with concerning my clerk, or any person for whom I would pass my word'.[12]

3

ENGLAND REVISITED

WITH ONLY a short interval in 1792, Cobbett had been away from England for sixteen years, and on his return he was struck by how everything – 'the trees, the hedges, even the paths and woods' – seemed so small in comparison with New Brunswick and America. After a month in London he revisited Farnham. His parents had died, and his two brothers (the third had joined the East India Company) were in financial difficulties. 'They are obliged to work very hard,' he wrote to Thornton, 'and their children are not kept constantly at school – I have given them a lift on and am devising means for making a provision for some of their sons – Never till now did I know the *value* of money.'

As the coach neared his old home Cobbett was overcome with mixed emotions and memories. 'My heart fluttered with impatience mixed with a sort of fear to see all the scenes of my childhood, for I had learned before, the death of my father and mother . . . But now came rushing into my mind, all at once, my pretty little garden, my little blue smock-frock, my little nailed shoes, my pretty pigeons that I used to feed out of my hands, the last kind words and tears of my gentle and tender hearted and affectionate mother! I hastened back into the room! If I had looked a moment later I would have dropped. When I came to reflect, what a change! What scenes I had gone through! How altered my state . . . I felt proud.'

Cobbett had every reason to feel proud. As his reception at

Falmouth indicated, he had returned to England a famous man. His anti-Jacobin pamphlets, all of them published in London, had been widely read and appreciated, especially by those politicians opposed to the French Revolution and now keen on prosecuting the war against Napoleon. William Windham, who was to become Cobbett's close friend and patron, said in the House of Commons that he merited for his services in America 'a statue of gold'.* Instead Cobbett commissioned a portrait by J.R. Smith, and this was engraved by the most fashionable engraver of the day, Francesco Bartolozzi, and put on sale in the London print shops. It shows the thirty-seven-year-old journalist looking supremely energetic and confident, ready to take on all comers from Napoleon downwards.

But the country that Cobbett had returned to was weary of the war. After nine years little had been done to restrain the march of the French across Europe, whilst at the same time the expense of the war had placed enormous tax burdens on the people (it was during this first period of hostilities that income tax was first introduced by the Prime Minister William Pitt). The pressures on the government to reach an agreement became too great, and in 1802 the Peace of Amiens was signed by the new Prime Minister Henry Addington (Pitt was awaiting developments at Walmer Castle in Kent). Persuading themselves that Napoleon had restored order to France and that the threat of Jacobinism was no more, the British people rejoiced. But a small group of politicians, implacably opposed to Napoleon, courted Cobbett. He had already been entertained only a few days after his arrival from America at a dinner given by William Windham and attended by Pitt and the future Foreign Secretary and Prime Minister George Canning. One can imagine Cobbett's intense feeling of pride at finding himself dining with the Prime Minister when only a few years previously he had fled the country, a wanted man facing possible

* The same thing was said by Napoleon of Thomas Paine.

trial at a court martial. Cobbett was more than willing to assist the anti-peace campaign, but he remained adamant that he would never in any circumstances become a tool of the government.

This decision, immensely important in determining the course his career was to take, was not dictated entirely by principle, but by prudence and even commercial considerations. From his experiences in America Cobbett knew not only that he could attract a large readership for his paper even amongst those who disagreed profoundly with his politics, but also that his popularity was due as much to his writing skill as to the fact that his readers valued his independence in a society where the bulk of journalism was written by paid hacks. In England at this time the press comprised a number of small four-page papers with circulations of only two or three thousand, all heavily dependent on advertising and government subsidy (either in the form of advertisements or direct payments). It was only later, with the progress of *The Times*, that something resembling a modern news-paper emerged, commercially and editorially independent of the government. At the beginning of the century, when Cobbett returned to England, the links between politicians and the press were closer and more corrupt than they have ever been, before or since. The spread of radical opinions in the wake of the French Revolution had encouraged the view in conservative circles that the press was in some way responsible, and that steps must be taken to curb its powers either by taxation or by making papers and individual journalists and pamphleteers dependent on the government for their continued existence. The result was that almost all writers, not merely journalists, ended up in the pay of the state. As Cobbett wrote later:

> The cause of the people has been betrayed by hundreds of men, who were able to serve the people, but whom a love of ease and of the indulgence of empty vanity have seduced into the service of the bribing usurpers, who have spared no means to corrupt men of literary talent from the authors of folios to

the authors of baby-books and ballads, *Caricature-makers, song-makers* all have been bribed by one means or another. Gillray and Dibdin were both pensioned. Southey, William Gifford all are placed or pensioned. *Playwriters, Historians.* None have escaped. Bloomfield, the Farmer's Boy author, was taken in *tow* and pensioned for fear that he should write for the people.[1]

And the rewards could be very considerable. Cobbett noted later that one journalist, John Reeves, a clever lawyer of whom he was very fond, left £200,000 when he died – 'without hardly a soul knowing that there ever was such a man'. For Cobbett, with his huge following, nothing was too much. The government offered him the editorship of either of its two papers, the *Sun* and the *True Briton*, along with the office and the printing press and the leasehold of a house, the whole package worth several thousand pounds. He refused. 'From that moment,' he wrote, 'all belonging to the Government looked on me with great suspicion.'

An exception was William Windham. Born in 1750, Windham was an unlikely politician, a rich Norfolk landowner from Felbrigg near Cromer, where his family had lived since the Middle Ages. Educated at Eton and University College Oxford, he was not only a classical scholar, but also an amateur mathematician who had been deeply influenced by his friendships with Edmund Burke and Dr Johnson. It was Johnson who, when Windham was debating whether to accept a political appointment in Ireland, famously urged him to go ahead, saying that he would 'make a very pretty rascal'. Windham later visited Johnson on his deathbed and agreed to become the guardian of his black servant Francis Barber. At the same time Johnson secured his promise that he would devote one day a week to a consideration of his failings. 'He proceeded to observe,' Windham wrote, 'that I was entering upon a life that would lead me deeply into all the business of the world: that he did not condemn civil employment but that it was a state of great danger; and that he had therefore one piece of advice earnestly to impress upon me – that I would set apart every seventh day to the care of my soul: that one day, the seventh, should be employed in repenting what was amiss in the six preceding and justifying my virtue for the six to come: that such a portion of time was surely little enough for the meditation of eternity.'

In addition to their political opinions, Cobbett and Windham shared a love of 'manly sports', Windham being an enthusiastic boxer who had excelled at games as a schoolboy at Eton, where he was known as 'fighter Windham'. A portrait by Reynolds shows an earnest, pale-faced man whose expression gives little away. According to Hazlitt he was an outstanding speaker, though 'a silent man in company'. Windham described himself as 'a scholar among politicians and a politician among scholars'. Aside from his love of boxing, what appealed to Cobbett was his obvious integrity in an age when most contemporary politicians had been compromised by corruption of one form or another. 'My friendship with Mr Windham,' he wrote in 1807, 'is founded in my knowledge that he is an upright and honourable man: that in all the many opportunities that he has had, he has never added to his fortune (though very moderate) at public expense; that according to my conviction, no man can charge him with ever having been concerned in a job* and that whether his opinions be right or wrong he always openly and strongly avows them.'

In other ways Windham was more typical of his class. His attitude to the press, in particular, was shared by many (including even Cobbett in his early years, it has to be said), which helps to explain the hostility shown to so many journalists in the years to come. Newspapers, Windham once said, 'circulated poison every twenty four hours and spread their venom down to the extremity of the kingdom. They were to be found everywhere in common ale-houses

* 'Job: A low mean lucrative busy affair' (Johnson).

and similar places frequented chiefly by the most ignorant and unre-flecting section of the community.'[2] Before any good could be done by the discussion of political subjects in newspapers, he said, the capacity of the people ought to be enlarged. However, as Windham was opposed to popular education, it was by no means clear how this desirable aim of his was to be achieved.

For Windham, and for Cobbett too in his early career, the French Revolution hung over their lives like a black cloud. At the back of their minds was the fear that what had happened in France – the Terror, the guillotine, the execution of the King and countless aristo-crats – might happen in England. With such a different social system there was little likelihood that this would occur, but the fear that it might turned men like Windham, who could otherwise have favoured political reform and who in his younger days had been a republican, into reactionaries. To others less scrupulous, the cry of Jacobinism remained a valuable propaganda weapon to be used indiscriminately against all who advocated reform or who campaigned against political corruption. Throughout his later career, Cobbett was branded as a Jacobin by his opponents, though even when he became a radical anyone less like Marat or Robespierre would be hard to imagine. Except for a very brief period following the aborted court martial, he had never in any sense been a republican, and as for aristocrats, if they behaved like gentlemen, managed their estates well and cared for their labourers, then they generally had his approval. William Windham was a man of principle, a countryman, a sportsman and a Christian, and Cobbett respected him, and even when they later fell out, refrained from ever attacking him in print.

To Windham Cobbett owed his start in British journalism. He had originally launched a daily newspaper, the *Porcupine*, in October 1800, a continuation of his American paper, entirely financed with about £450 of his own money and produced from offices in South-ampton Street. Cobbett was determined to take a more principled

approach to journalism than his rivals. 'Not a single *quack* advertise-
ment will on my account be admitted into the *Porcupine*,' he announced. 'Our newspapers have been too long disgraced by this
species of falsehood, filth and obscenity. I am told that, by adhering
to this resolution, I shall lose five hundred a year.' His main editorial
purpose was to support those few politicians like Windham who
opposed the negotiations, then in hand, to make peace with Napoleon.
It was not a policy likely to appeal to the public, which at all levels
favoured an end to the hostilities. When the Preliminaries of Peace
were declared on 10 October 1801 there were extraordinary scenes in
London. From his house in Pall Mall, Cobbett wrote to Windham in
Norwich:

> With that sort of dread which seizes on a man when he has
> heard or thinks he has heard a supernatural voice predicting
> his approaching end, I sit down to inform you, that the guns
> are now firing for the Peace and that half an hour ago a
> very numerous crowd *drew the Aide-de-Camp of Bonaparte in
> triumph through Pall Mall!* The vile miscreants had, it seems,
> watched his motions very narrowly and perceiving him get
> into a carriage in Bond Street with Otto* they took out the
> horses, dragged him down that street, along by your house,
> down to White-hall, and through the Park, and then to Otto's
> again, shouting and rejoicing every time he had occasion to
> get out or into the carriage . . . This is the first time an
> English mob ever became the cattle of a *Frenchman* . . . This
> indication of the temper and sentiments of the lower orders
> is a most awful consideration. You must remember Sir, that
> previous to the revolutions in Switzerland and elsewhere, we
> always heard of some *French messenger of peace* being *received
> with caresses* by the people: the next post or two brought
> us an account of partial discontents, tumults, insurrections,
> murders and revolutions always closed the history. God pre-

---

* Louis Otto, French agent in Britain.

serve us from the like, but I am afraid our abominations are to be punished in this way.[3]

Meanwhile the mob went on the rampage and attacked Cobbett's house as well as the bookshop he had opened in St James's. 'It happened precisely as I had expected,' he wrote later: 'about eight o'clock in the evening my dwelling house was attacked by an innumerable mob, all my windows were broken, and when this was done the villains were preparing to break into my shop. The attack continued at intervals, till past one o'clock. During the whole of this time, not a constable nor peace officer of any description made his appearance; nor was the smallest interruption given to the proceedings of this ignorant and brutal mob, who were thus celebrating the Peace. The Porcupine office experienced a similar fate.'

The same scenes were repeated a few months later when the Peace of Amiens was finally ratified. Even though on this occasion the Bow Street magistrate intervened with the help of a posse of Horse Guards to try to protect him, Cobbett's windows were again broken and his house damaged in various ways. Shortly afterwards he was forced to sell the *Porcupine*, and it was merged in the *True Briton*, a government propaganda paper.

It was at this point that Windham and a group of friends including Dr French Laurence, Regius Professor of Civil Law at Oxford and the MP for Peterborough, stepped in to help Cobbett relaunch himself. Windham was a rich man with an annual income of £6000, so it can be assumed that he provided the bulk of the £650 (about £23,000 in today's money). It would seem to have been a gift rather than an investment, and one which Cobbett only accepted on his own terms – 'Upon the *express* and written *conditions* that I was never to be looked upon as under any sort of obligation to any of the parties.'

Any possibility of a clash between the editor and his patron would have seemed, in 1802, a very remote one. Windham had already made public his enormous admiration for Cobbett. Cobbett in his turn showered praises on his patron. 'I shall not I am sure merit the suspicion of being a flatterer,' he wrote to Windham in May 1802, 'when I say that it is my firm persuasion that you, and you alone, can save our country. This persuasion is founded, not only upon my knowledge of your disposition and abilities, but upon the universal confidence in your integrity and patriotism, which at this time more than ever exists. I see and hear of men of all parties and principles, and I find the confidence of the nation to be possessed by you in a greater degree than by any other person.'[4]

The Peace of Amiens had been signed only a few weeks earlier, on 27 March 1802. For a short time there was a feeling not only of relief but of euphoria – not dissimilar to the mood following the Munich agreement of 1938. Napoleon, who had until then been an object of hatred, was turned into a tourist attraction. Crowds of British visitors flocked to Paris to see the First Consul in the flesh, shortly before he was to declare himself Emperor. In the House of Commons Windham, almost a lone voice, led the opposition, while Cobbett kept up the attack in his paper. The Emperor was apparently in the habit of lying in his bath and having Cobbett and other critics read aloud to him by an interpreter. When a particularly offensive passage was read out he would bang the bath with the guide rope, shouting out, '*Il en a menti*.'[5] Napoleon, via the French Minister in London, M. Otto, ordered the British government to prosecute Cobbett (among others): 'The perfidious and malevolent publications of these men are in open contradiction to the principles of peace.'[6] In order to appease him the government did actually bring libel proceedings against a French émigré writer, Jean Gabriel Peltier, who was prosecuted by the Attorney General (later Prime Minister) Spencer Perceval and found guilty in February 1803 of libel by the judge, Lord Ellenborough (the first of his appearances in this narrative). Cobbett wrote to Windham, 'Lord Ellenborough and the Attorney-General both told the Jury, that *if they did not find him guilty*, we would have war with France!!!'[7]

But the mood of euphoria following the signing of the peace did not last long. Napoleon showed quite soon that he was not only arrogant and sensitive to criticism in the British press, but cavalier in the extreme when it came to observing the terms of the 1802 treaty. The alarm was raised when he invaded Switzerland, and in the face of mounting concern the British government led by Addington finally refused to evacuate Malta on the grounds that Napoleon had failed to carry out his pledges with regard to Italy. In May 1803 war was resumed, and a year later Pitt ('who was to Addington as London was to Paddington') returned to take charge. The threat of a French invasion now took hold of the country, as Napoleon assembled a fleet of barges and gunboats on the French coast. Patriotic citizens rallied to the flag and joined the local militias. Broadsheets and songs were printed in their thousands, beacons were prepared to warn of invasion, and Martello towers were erected along the eastern coast. The government issued its own propaganda pamphlet, 'Important Considerations for the People of this Kingdom', which was distributed to the entire clergy with instructions 'that you will be pleased to cause part of them to be deposited in the pews and part to be distributed in the aisles amongst the poor'. In stirring terms the anonymous author rallied his countrymen against the peril of the French: 'For some time past, they have had little opportunity to plunder; peace, for a while, suspended their devastations, and now, like gaunt and hungry wolves, they are looking towards the richer pastures of Britain; already we hear their threatening howl, and if, like sheep, we stand bleating for mercy, neither our innocence nor our timidity will save us from being torn to pieces and devoured.' There was general speculation at the time as to the authorship of 'Important Considerations', and various candidates were suggested, including Lord Hawkesbury (later the Prime Minister Lord Liverpool). It was not until 1809, when Cobbett came under attack from government ministers, that he revealed that he himself had written the pamphlet, offered it to the then Prime Minister

Addington and refused to take any money when it was printed and distributed all over the country.

Many of his later readers might have been surprised to learn of Cobbett assisting the government in this way. But the Cobbett of this period, the four or five years following his return from America, was a different character from what he became later or what he had been before. The change of title of his paper from *Porcupine* to *Cobbett's Political Register* said it all. In his Porcupine role in Philadelphia he had been a thorn in the flesh of the political establishment, famous for his barbs, his knockabout abuse and his nicknames. The title *Cobbett's Political Register* was indicative of a more serious and responsible role. Cobbett was now the friend of statesmen like Windham, the man who dined with Pitt and Canning, the man who boasted that royalty and dukes were among the subscribers to his paper. He now saw himself as a major player, and the *Political Register* of this period is much concerned with the traditional political matters – who's in, who's out, the advisability of this or that different policy.

Despite the resumption of the war, the resignation of Addington and the return of Pitt, Cobbett's friend Windham remained out of the government and in opposition. Pitt had wanted to include the great Liberal Charles James Fox (now disillusioned about Napoleon – 'a young man who was a good deal intoxicated with his success') in his cabinet, but the mad King George III, who hated Fox for having opposed the war in the first place, refused to allow this. Windham, along with Pitt's former Foreign Secretary William Grenville and others, refused to take office unless Fox was included in the cabinet, with the result that in the short period before his death in January 1806, Pitt was confronted by three separate opposition parties, led respectively by Addington, Windham (the so-called New Opposition) and Fox, leader of the Old Opposition – those, that is, who had been against the war in its early stages (1793–1802). It was not the ideal situation for a country at war.

In his *Political Register* Cobbett (with Windham's support) attacked Pitt almost as savagely as he had previously attacked Addington. His charge was that Pitt had reneged on his pledge to pursue the war against France – a course, Pitt claimed, that could be pursued without any increase in taxes. Cobbett no doubt saw himself as someone at the centre of the political stage, a view reciprocated by, among others, Charles James Fox, one of the few outstanding politicians of this period. 'Cobbett is certainly an extraordinary man,' Fox wrote to Windham in November 1804, 'and if any good is ever to be done, may be powerfully instrumental in bringing it about.'[8]

In keeping with the image of himself as the friend and confidant of statesmen, Cobbett purchased a spacious country mansion at Botley near Southampton in 1805. Unfortunately it was later demolished, but a contemporary print shows a three-storeyed house with an ornamental turret and more than enough accommodation for his family and a small army of servants. Despite the success of the *Political Register* Cobbett could scarcely afford to live in such style. But throughout his life he was careless with money, almost always living beyond his means and relying on loans from wealthy supporters. His daughter Anne writes that his wife had little faith in Cobbett's 'business wisdom', particularly as it applied to the ambitious farming and tree-planting schemes he embarked on whenever he had the opportunity, as he now did at Botley.

'Botley is the most delightful village in the world,' Cobbett wrote to his publisher John Wright (August 1805). 'It has everything, in a village, that I love, and none of the things I hate. It is in a valley; the soil is rich, thickset with wood: the farms are small, the cottages neat; it has neither workhouse nor barber nor attorney nor justice of the peace, and, though last not least, it has no volunteers. There is no justice within SIX miles of us and the barber comes once a week to shave and cut hair! "Would I were poetical" I would write a poem in praise of Botley.'

Cobbett was supremely confident in his future. By the end of 1805 the circulation of the *Register* had reached four thousand – a very high figure for these times. In the meantime he had launched a new publication, *Cobbett's Parliamentary Debates* (the original of today's Hansard, named after the printer Cobbett eventually sold the business to). Carried away by his popularity, he felt sure enough of his prospects to expand. Shortly after buying his Botley house he bought a neighbouring farm for his brother and began negotiating the purchase of a farm for himself. Eventually he was to take on an estate of over eighty acres, on which he farmed and planted thousands of trees. 'I have planted 20,000 oaks, elms and ashes besides about 3000 fir trees of various sorts,' he wrote to his brother-in-law Ian Frederick Reid serving in Wellington's army in the Peninsula. 'How everybody laughed,' his daughter Anne remembered, 'at his planting such little bits of twigs at Botley.' But although Cobbett took great aesthetic pleasure in trees, he regarded them always as a commercial venture, convincing himself that they were a valuable investment for his children and ignoring his wife's insistence that he would be better off growing crops 'instead of burying the money on the land with trees which he would never see come to perfection'.

It is here at Botley that we get for the first time a lengthy description of Cobbett and his family from an independent observer, and it is almost with a feeling of relief that the biographer finds it confirming Cobbett's own view of himself and his achievements. Mary Russell Mitford was a girl of about eighteen when she visited Botley with her father Dr George Mitford, man-about-town and ruddy-faced old rogue who had changed his name from Midford to make himself sound more grand. Mitford, who combined radical opinions with social snobbery, was a compulsive gambler who quickly squandered his rich wife's fortune as well as the £20,000 his daughter won on the Irish lottery at the age of four. Still, as with Little Nell and her grandfather in *The Old Curiosity Shop*, she remained devoted to her father until his death at the age of eighty, despite being plagued by money worries even after the great success of her book *Our Village* (1832) describing life in Three Mile Cross near Reading, where she lived in later years with her dissolute parent.

Dr Mitford was, for a time, a close friend of Cobbett. He mixed with a number of politicians in London, but more importantly he shared with Cobbett a love of hare-coursing and like him kept a kennel full of greyhounds. Mary remembered:

He [Cobbett] had at that time [about 1806] a large house at Botley, with a lawn and gardens sweeping down to the Burlesdon River which divided his territories from the beautiful grounds of the old friend, where we had been originally staying, the great squire of the place. His own house – large, high, massive, red, and square and perched on a considerable eminence – always struck me as being not unlike its proprietor ... I never saw hospitality more genuine, more simple or more thoroughly successful in the great end of hospitality, the putting of everybody at ease. There was not the slightest attempt at finery or display or gentility. They called it a farm-house and, everything was in accordance with the largest idea of a great English yeoman of the old time. Everything was excellent, everything abundant, all served with the greatest nicety by trim waiting-damsels: and everything went on with such quiet regularity, that of the large circle of guests not one could find himself in the way. I need not say a word more in praise of the good wife ... to whom this admirable order was mainly due. She was a sweet motherly woman; realising our notions of one of Scott's most charming characters, Ailie Dinmont, in her simplicity, her kindness, and her devotion to her husband and her children.

At this time William Cobbett was at the height of his political reputation; but of politics we heard little, and should, I think, have heard nothing, but for an occasional red-hot patriot who would introduce the subject, which our host would fain put aside and get rid of as soon as possible.

There was something of Dandie Dinmont about him, with his unfailing good humour and good spirits – his heartiness, his love of field sports, and his liking for a foray. He was a tall, stout man, fair, and sunburnt, with a bright smile and an air compounded of the soldier and the farmer, to which his habit of wearing an eternal red waistcoat contributed not a little. He was I think the most athletic and vigorous person that I have ever known. Nothing could tire him. At home in the morning he would begin by mowing his own lawn, beating his gardener Robinson, the best mower, except himself, in the parish, at that fatiguing work.

Cobbett was also a keen devotee of rural sports. Besides hare-coursing, for which he kept a huge army of dogs – thirty or forty pedigree grey-hounds, pointers, setters and spaniels – hunting was another passion. 'A score or two of gentlemen,' he wrote, 'riding full speed down a hill nearly as steep as the roof of a house, where one false step must inevitably send horse and rider to certain death, is an object to be seen nowhere but in England.' Boxing and wrestling helped to preserve the strength and spirit of the working man, Cobbett being convinced during this period that an evil alliance of government ministers and Methodists was trying to eliminate such sports in order to make the 'lower orders' weak and compliant. Boxing matches attracted big crowds: 'They tend to make the people bold, they tend in short, to keep alive even amongst the lowest of the people, some idea of independence.'

Another Cobbett favourite was the now forgotten 'sport' of single-stick. Two combatants, each with a wooden cudgel, each with an arm tied behind his back, would attempt to break their opponent's head by drawing an inch of blood from his skull. He explained in a letter to William Windham: 'The blows that they exchange in order to throw one another off their guard are such as require the utmost degree of patient endurance. The arms, shoulders and ribs are beaten black and blue and the contest between the men frequently lasts for more than an hour.'

Cobbett, who encouraged his young sons to engage in this so-called game, invited Windham to attend a grand single-stick competition which he organised in Botley in October 1805, and which attracted crowds of about five thousand people from all over the country. A first prize of fifteen guineas and a gold-laced hat was offered, and the event was such a success that it was repeated the following year, when even more people came, and the prize was increased to twenty guineas and the hat. 'The whole village was full,' Cobbett wrote. 'Stages in the form of amphitheatres were erected against the houses and seats let to the amount of thirty or fifty pounds. Every gentleman round the country was there.'

The conventional view of Cobbett is of a man who was a Tory in his youth and who became a radical in later life, but, as usual, it is not as simple as that. Cobbett's early American journalism was informed not so much by his political inclinations as by the simple patriotism of a man who disliked to see his country run down by foreigners. Nor was he ever in sympathy with the advocates of violent revolution or, for that matter, those whose politics were based on abstract theorising rather than, as in his own case, a practical examination of the situation. There was no 'road to Damascus' experience in Cobbett's life to explain his conversion to radicalism. Instead a gradual sequence of events, culminating in his imprisonment in 1810, fundamentally altered his view of politics and the social scene. It was a repetition, on a grander scale and over a longer period, of his army experiences. In both cases he had become involved with institutions of which initially he entertained good opinions and high hopes. But the more he found out – as always with Cobbett, from his personal study and investigation – the more disillusioned he became. And in both cases it was the discovery of corruption, generally accepted as a way of life, that most roused his indignation.

But other important issues played their part in the process. In 1802, the year of the founding of the *Political Register*, Cobbett was beginning to realise that his knowledge of economics was minimal. 'I knew nothing of this matter in 1802,' he wrote. 'I did not know what had made the Bank of England. I did not know what the slang terms of consols meant. I did not know what Dividend, omnium scrip, or any of the rest of it imported.' Most of us are quite happy to go through life with only a shaky grasp of economics, but Cobbett was not like that. He had to find out for himself. He read Adam Smith – 'I could make neither top nor tail of the thing.' He read the Acts of Parliament setting up the Bank of England, which he says gave him some sort of insight 'with regard to the accursed thing called the National Debt'. But it was not until he read Thomas Paine's pamphlet 'Decline and Fall of the English System of Finance' (1796) that the scales fell from his eyes.

Leaving economics aside for the moment, Cobbett's discovery of Paine as a purveyor of truth did perhaps have something of the road to Damascus about it, in that until this date he had persecuted Paine, just as St Paul had persecuted the followers of Jesus. Paine's involvement with the rebels in the American War of Independence and later with the French Revolutionaries – in both cases against the British interest – and above all his denial of the divinity of Christ in his book *The Age of Reason* had turned him, in the eyes of the establishment, into a Guy Fawkes figure, responsible for all the unrest and the Jacobinism, all the subversive ideas that seemed to threaten the peace and tranquillity of good Englishmen.

During his *Porcupine* years in America Cobbett had joined in the hate campaign as wholeheartedly as anyone. His pamphlet 'The Life of Thomas Paine' (1796) is as vituperative as anything he ever wrote: 'The scoundrel of a staymaker . . . the hoary blasphemer . . . he has done all the mischief he can in the world and . . . whenever or wherever he breathes his last, he will excite neither sorrow nor compassion.' Cobbett again abused him in his paper the *Political Censor*, calling him an 'atrocious infamous miscreant' and many things besides.

(George Washington approved, though making 'allowances for the asperity of an Englishman for some of his strong and coarse expressions'.[9]) Yet it was now this very same blasphemer and miscreant who had managed to open Cobbett's eyes to the nature of the economic system. Had he been wrong about Paine? And was it possible that all those politicians and writers who had portrayed Paine as the devil incarnate were equally mistaken?

In 1796 Paine had written a famous letter to Washington, whose victory over the British he had helped so much to secure, attacking the President for failing to come to his aid when he was in prison in Paris facing execution. The letter is an eloquent testimony to the general ingratitude of politicians, once they achieved power, to those who have helped them along the way. Cobbett himself was beginning to experience the same reaction. He might have thought, after the assistance he had given the government by writing, for free, 'Important Considerations' at the time invasion threatened, that he and his *Political Register* would be helped in return. On the contrary, in 1804 he found himself once again facing a libel charge.

As usual, England's difficulty was Ireland's opportunity. In 1803 the Irish republicans, on this occasion led by Robert Emmet, mounted a rebellion, killing the Lord Chief Justice and several English soldiers. In the *Political Register* Cobbett attacked the Addington government for its lack of foresight, stating that Ireland was 'in a state of total neglect and abandonment'.[10] The article was followed by three anonymous letters from Ireland signed 'Juverna'. With a stylish and satirical pen 'Juverna' accused the English authorities, and in particular the Lord Lieutenant, Lord Hardwicke, of failing to do anything to prevent the uprising although they had advance information that it was going to take place. Hardwicke, it was claimed, had even returned to his official residence in Phoenix Park in order not to be in any personal danger, and had subsequently done everything possible to blame the military commander, General Fox, for what had happened. Obviously well informed, 'Juverna' peppered his account of the incident with a number of satirical asides on the British politicians involved, suggesting, for example, that Hardwicke was typical of 'that tribe who have been sent over to us to be trained up here into politicians as they train the surgeons' apprentices in the hospitals by setting them at first to bleed the pauper patients'. He was, the author continued, 'in rank an earl, in manners a gentleman, in morals a good father and a good husband . . . celebrated for understanding the modern method of fattening sheep as well as any man in Cambridgeshire'.

The offence of criminal (or seditious) libel with which Cobbett was now charged had been a convenient weapon in the hands of successive governments since the sixteenth century, when according to a modern commentator 'the Star Chamber regarded with the deepest suspicion the printed word in general, and anything which looked like criticism of the established institutions of Church and State in particular'.[11] John Wilkes, the great champion of press freedom, had been prosecuted for criminal libel, and throughout the first decades of the nineteenth century the charge was regularly used to silence persistent critics of the government, when necessary by putting them in prison.

In Cobbett's trial the thrust of the attack by the prosecuting attorney Spencer Perceval (later the Prime Minister) was to humiliate Cobbett in the eyes of the court by emphasising his lowly social origins. 'Who is Mr Cobbett?' Perceval asked contemptuously. 'Is he a man of family in this country? Is he a man writing purely from motives of patriotism? *Quis homo hic est? Quo patre natus?*' (Who is this man? Who was his father?) The Latin tags would have been chosen deliberately by the lawyer in the knowledge that Cobbett would not understand them. Such an attitude, in an age when the government consisted almost entirely of members of the aristocracy educated in the classics at the best public schools, would not have struck the jury as unjust. But it was typical of the snobbery that

Cobbett was to face throughout his career. Snobbery aside, Perceval went on to suggest (with the judge's obvious approval) that it was not permitted, by law, to ridicule the government and its ministers in the way 'Juverna' and the *Political Register* had done. An indication of the lengths to which the law officers were prepared to go in arguing this case is the way Perceval even introduced the fact that Cobbett's paper had referred to the Prime Minister as 'the Doctor'. In fact Addington was generally known to all his colleagues by this nickname, the origin of which was that his father had been a doctor:

> I do not mean to say that the describing such a man as Mr Addington, by the epithet of Doctor Addington, is degrading to him, nor that I would advise that such an epithet should become the subject of a prosecution in a Court of Justice: but, surely no one who has the least liberality of feeling, or the least sense of decency, could think it becoming to taunt such a gentleman as Mr Addington: a gentleman who, the more he is known, the more his character will be admired. For my part, I feel no sympathy with those who think there is any wit in such titles. Mr Addington is the son of a man who most ably and skilfully practised in a liberal profession, who by his talents became justly eminent in that profession, and whose son raised himself, by his great abilities, to one of the highest offices in this country. I again say, that for any publication calling Mr Addington 'Doctor Addington', or for any flippancy of that nature, standing by itself, I should think it beneath the dignity of the Right honourable gentleman to make it the subject of a prosecution; but I also say, that when you see an epithet of this nature introduced, it does show the spirits with which the libel was published and that it was a systematic attack upon the whole government of Ireland, by bringing into contempt and ridicule the persons placed by his Majesty at the head of the Government.[12]

'The bestowing of nicknames is a practice to which Englishmen are peculiarly addicted,' Cobbett's counsel William Adam answered, but

Head of Lord Ellenborough by George Cruickshank

he made little or no attempt to justify 'Juverna's' account of the Dublin rebellion, instead devoting his speech to extolling his client as a great English patriot. Summing up, the judge, Lord Ellenborough, did nothing to disguise his bias. His final words to the jury were an ominous warning not only to Cobbett but to others who might be so foolhardy as to attack the government: 'It has been observed [by Cobbett's counsel] that it is the right of the British subject to exhibit the folly or imbecility of members of the Government. But gentlemen, we must confine ourselves within limits. If, in so doing, individual feelings are violated, there the line of interdiction begins, and the offence becomes the subject of penal visitation.' Taking their cue from the learned judge, the jury brought in a verdict of guilty following deliberations which lasted for only ten minutes.

Cobbett had secured a number of prominent individuals, including

Windham, to appear as character witnesses, and it was perhaps thanks to them that he escaped a prison sentence on this occasion (the *Register* was fined £500). It may also have been the case that he was leniently treated in comparison with other libellers for divulging to the court the identity of 'Juverna' – Robert Johnson, a judge of the Irish Common Pleas. Cobbett handed over some of the manuscripts of the letters to the Attorney General, and later appeared as a Crown witness when Johnson himself was put on trial in November 1805. At first sight Cobbett's betrayal of his contributor seems despicable. But, as his biographer E.I. Carlyle points out, it is significant that the incident was never referred to afterwards by his political enemies, and given the fact that they seized on anything, however trivial, to discredit Cobbett, the likelihood is that Johnson himself agreed to be identified as the author. After being found guilty he was allowed to resign with a pension of £1200 a year.

The 'Juverna' trial and the threat of possible imprisonment will have unnerved Cobbett and shown him that he could not expect any favours from the establishment (what he called 'The Thing'). But in the meantime, as the threat of invasion by Napoleon receded, he was beginning to become interested in matters beyond the political controversies of the day, the sort of issues he discussed with Windham in their regular exchange of letters.

Having been out of the country for most of his adult life, Cobbett had little or no first-hand knowledge of British politics or social institutions. In the ten years he had spent in America he had retained in his memory a picture of England as he remembered it from his boyhood, a picture of rural prosperity, cottage gardens, contented villagers – an idyllic scene. In 1804, however, he went house-hunting with his wife Anne in Hampshire (prior to their settling in Botley), and saw for himself how conditions had changed:

> When I revisited the English labourer's dwelling and that too,
> after having recently witnessed the happiness of labourers in

America; when I saw that the clock was gone; when I saw those whom I had known the most neat, cheerful and happy beings on earth, and these my countrymen too, had become the most wretched and forlorn of human beings, I looked seriously and inquired patiently into the matter and this inquiry into the causes of the effect which had made so deep an impression on my mind, led to that series of exertions, which have *occupied my whole life, since that time*, to better the lot of the labourers.[13]

What had caused the decline? Cobbett instanced two major factors: firstly, the continuing series of enclosures, whereby the common lands which traditionally provided labourers with a source of food and fuel to supplement their earnings had been taken over or 'privatised' by the rich farmers and landowners in the interest of 'greater efficiency'. Secondly, the newly introduced Poor Laws, known as the Speenhamland System, intended when they were launched in 1795 to help the poorest labourers by making up their pay from the rates, but which had the effect of branding them as paupers, so robbing them of all self-respect.

'The labourers are humbled, debased and enslaved,' Cobbett wrote. 'Until of late years, there was, amongst the poor, a horror of becoming chargeable to the parish. This feeling, which was almost universal, was the parent of industry, of care, of economy, of frugality and of *early* habits of labour amongst children . . . That men should possess *spirit*, that there should be any independence of mind, that there should be frankness among persons so situated, is impossible. Accordingly, whoever has had experience in such matters, must have observed, with deep regret, that instead of priding himself upon his little possessions, instead of decking out his children to the best advantage, instead of laying up in store the trifling surplus produce of the harvest month, the labourer now, in but too many instances, takes care to spend all as fast as he gets it, makes himself as poor as he can and uses all the art that he is master of to cause it to be believed that he is still more miserable than he really is. What an example for the children! And what must the rising generation be!'[14]

The reason Cobbett became a champion of the farm labourers, who at this time, prior to the Industrial Revolution, made up the largest single section of the British workforce, was his own personal involvement with them at Botley and in the surrounding countryside. As always with Cobbett, he started from what he saw with his own eyes – in this case, workers living in an impoverished and demoralised state, in marked contrast to what he remembered from his own boyhood.

When he himself began to farm and employ labourers at Botley, Cobbett refused to have anything to do with the Speenhamland System. 'I have made it a rule,' he wrote, 'that I will have the labour of no man who receives *parish relief*. I give him, out of *my own pocket*, let his family be what it may, enough to keep them well, without any regard to what wages other people give: for I will employ *no pauper*.'

The result, he claimed, was a contented little community: 'It is quite delightful to see this village of Botley, when compared to the others that I know. They seem here to be quite a different race of people.' This was no empty boast, because it was confirmed by the many witnesses like Miss Mitford who visited Cobbett at Botley. He encouraged, he said, with his workers 'freedom in conversation, the unrestrained familiarity . . . without at all lessening the weight of my authority'.

And the same principle, he said, applied with his children. By 1805 when Cobbett bought the Botley home he had four children – Anne born in America in 1795, William in 1798, John in 1800 and James in 1803. They were followed by two girls, Eleanor and Susan (born 1805 and 1807), and finally by Richard (born 1814). In spite of his workload as a journalist Cobbett took an enormous interest in the welfare and education of his children. His ideas were surprisingly liberal. Remembering, perhaps, his own harsh treatment at the hands of his father, he urged parents to make their children's lives '*as pleasant as you possibly can*':

> I have always admired the sentiment of ROUSSEAU upon this subject. 'The boy dies, perhaps, at the age of ten or twelve. Of what *use*, then, all the restraints, all the privations, all the pain that you have inflicted upon him? He falls, and leaves your mind to brood over the possibility of you having abridged a life so dear to you.' I do not recollect the very words; but the passage made a deep impression upon my mind, just at the time, too, when I was about to become a father . . . I was resolved to forgo all the means of making money, all the means of making a living in any thing like fashion, all the means of obtaining fame or distinction, to give up everything, to become a common labourer, rather than make my children lead a life of restraint and rebuke.[15]

Cobbett moved to Botley with the welfare of his children in mind. He wanted them, first of all, to be healthy and to be able to play out of doors:

> Children, and especially boys, will have some out-of-doors pursuits: and it was my duty to lead them to choose such pursuits as combined future utility with present innocence. Each has his flower-bed, little garden, plantation of trees, rabbits, dogs, asses, horses, pheasants and hares; hoes, spades, whips, guns; always some object of lively interest, and as much *earnestness* and *bustle* about the various objects as if our living had solely depended upon them.

Cobbett did not believe in forcing 'book-learning' on his children at an early age. There were no rules or regulations:

> I accomplished my purpose indirectly. The first thing of all was *health* which was secured by the deeply-interesting and never-ending *sports of the field* and *pleasures of the garden*. Luckily these two things were treated in *books* and *pictures* of endless variety: so that on *wet days*, in *long evenings*, these

came into play. A large, strong table in the middle of the room, their mother sitting at her work, used to be surrounded with them, the baby, if big enough, set up in a high chair. Here were ink-stands, pens, pencils, india rubber, and paper, all in abundance, and everyone scrabbled about as he or she pleased. There were prints of animals of all sorts; books treating of them – others treating of gardening, of flowers, of husbandry, of hunting, coursing, shooting, fishing, planting, and, in short, of everything with regard to which *we had something to do*. One would be trying to imitate a bit of my writing, another *drawing* the pictures of some of our dogs or horses, a third poring over *Bewick's Quadrupeds*, and picking out what he said about them; but our book of never-failing resource was the French MAISON RUSTIQUE or FARM-HOUSE ... Here are all the *four-legged animals* from the horse down to the mouse, *portraits* and all; all the *birds, reptiles, insects* ... and there was I, in my leisure moments to join this inquisitive group, to read the *French,* and tell them what it meaned in *English*, when the picture did not sufficiently explain itself. I have never been without a copy of this book for forty years, except during the time that I was fleeing from the dungeons of CASTLEREAGH and SIDMOUTH in 1817, and, when I got to Long Island, the *first book I bought* was another MAISON RUSTIQUE.[16]

Cobbett was busily writing at this time, but he never let it interfere with his children's pursuits: 'My occupation to be sure was chiefly carried on at home,' he remembered. 'Many score of papers have I written amidst the noise of children and in my whole life never bade them be still. When they grew up to be big enough to gallop about the house I have written the whole day amidst noise that would made [sic] some authors half mad. That which you are pleased with, however noisy, does not disturb you.'

The children were teased by friends about not going to school, and his wife Nancy was especially anxious about it, but Cobbett resisted all the pressure. 'Bless me, so tall and not learned anything yet,' a friend would say of one of his sons. 'Oh yes he has,' Cobbett replied. 'He has learned to ride, and hunt and shoot and fish and look after cattle and sheep and to work in the garden and to feed his dogs and to go from village to village in the dark.'

Cobbett's methods bore results. His children were soon able to help him with his work, copying and taking dictation. The boys learned French and three of them later became lawyers and published books, as did his eldest daughter Anne.

4

A Convert to Reform

IN JANUARY 1806 the Prime Minister William Pitt died and George III invited Lord Grenville to form a new coalition government. This was the short-lived 'Ministry of All the Talents', so called because it included members of the New and Old Opposition, like Cobbett's friend and patron Windham and also Charles James Fox, to whom the King was now partially reconciled.

Cobbett was delighted by the new situation. The old enemy Pitt was gone, and at last there was an opportunity for the new ministers to introduce reform. The general assumption was that Cobbett, as Windham's friend and protégé, would now be given some political office or sinecure. 'Everyone thought,' he wrote, 'that my turn to get rich was come. I was importuned by many persons to take care of myself as they called it.' He could benefit not just himself but also his relatives. He could obtain, with Windham's help, promotion for his father-in-law and brother-in-law, both of whom were serving in Wellington's army.

But Cobbett continually stressed that he had no wish to obtain favours of this kind, as anyone else in his position would have done. All he wanted was to be an adviser, to have his opinion listened to and respected not only by Windham, but by his fellow ministers like Fox. Two particular things demanded action, in his view. He was especially incensed about the activities of Francis Freeling, the Secretary of the Post Office, who had control over newspaper distribution through the post and whom he had accused of working a number of fiddles. Cobbett wanted him sacked. He also complained vehemently about the dismissal of a clerk in the Barrack Master General's office who had exposed corruption – a story that must have affected him particularly, as it echoed his own experience in 1792 when he himself had tried to eradicate corruption in the army, only to be forced to flee the country.

As Minister for War, Windham ought to have been sympathetic to Cobbett's various proposals, which included a long and detailed plan for the reform of the army. The trouble was that he was now part of a system so riddled with corruption of every kind that even had he felt the urge, any reforming measures would have been difficult if not impossible for him to put into effect. Though never a 'pretty rascal' in Dr Johnson's phrase, Windham was surrounded by pretty rascals on every side, the War Ministry being the most notorious for corruption and nepotism. Quite apart from that, as the tone of the *Political Register* became more radical, more *Porcupine*-like, Windham had for some time been embarrassed by his association with Cobbett. Such was the way of things, with the close association of politicians and the press, and most journalists in the pay of one party or another, that the public would have assumed that Cobbett's articles were written to Windham's dictation. It was certainly the case that, even at this stage, people still referred to the *Political Register* as 'Windham's Gazette'. In February 1806 Windham had taken the issue up with Cobbett: 'You can do more, too, than you have done to show that your opinions are your own.' For his part, Cobbett resented the suggestion that anyone should feel ashamed or embarrassed at being wrongly assumed to have written his articles. He wrote to Windham: 'Wright states that you appeared extremely vexed at the prevalence or supposed prevalence of an opinion that "all the most *violent* parts of the *Register* were either written or suggested by you . . ." I must confess that I am vain enough to think that, having so long been obliged to listen to the cant of the most despicable of our opponents, he has mistaken *strength* for *violence*: and I must further confess myself proud enough to hope that, from having my writings imputed to him, no man's character has ever suffered an injury.'[1]

Sooner or later a break between the two men was inevitable. It came on 28 February 1806, only two weeks after the formation of the new ministry. Windham wrote in his diary: 'Came away in carriage with Fox: got out at end of Downing St and went to office, thence to Cobbett. Probably the last interview we shall have.' The Ministry of All the Talents collapsed, and for the remaining three years before his death in 1810 Windham did not hold office again. On 19 February 1809, in his final reference to Cobbett, he wrote: 'Nearly the whole time from breakfast till Mr Legge's coming down, employed in reading Cobbett. More thoroughly wicked and mischievous than almost anything that has appeared yet.' He may have reflected ruefully that of all his achievements, the most significant had been the financing in 1802 of *Cobbett's Political Register*, which came in the end to represent almost everything he most strongly disapproved of.

By now it was beginning to dawn on Cobbett, as it has dawned on others before and since, that there was no real difference between the parties at Westminster. The Whigs and the Tories were led by two groups of aristocrats – Windham was one of the few commoners – merely competing for power. There was therefore no point in expecting that a change in the ministry would lead to radical reform. The war, it was true, had formerly divided politicians, but now the old consensus had been restored. By 1809 Cobbett was able to describe quite clearly what the situation was like:

> It must have struck every man, who has been in the habit of contemplating political motives and actions, that the interest and the importance, which discussions in the House of Commons formerly owed to consideration of *Party*, now exist but in a comparatively trifling degree ... Parties were formerly

distinguished by some great and well known principles of foreign or domestic policy. Now there are no such distinguishing marks ... There are still persons wishing for a change of ministry because there are always persons who wish to obtain possession of power and emolument, but beyond that circle there are ... absolutely none at all who sincerely believe that such a change would be attended with any substantial national benefit.[2]

Following the collapse of the Ministry of All the Talents the Whigs virtually gave up hope of forming a government, and for the next twenty-five years there was a succession of Tory ministries under a series of reactionary prime ministers, all adamantly opposed to reform of any kind. The Duke of Portland (1807–09) was followed by the lawyer Spencer Perceval (1809–12), who in turn was followed by the long-serving Lord Liverpool (1812–27), described by Disraeli as an 'arch-mediocrity' and referred to by Cobbett as 'Lord Picknose'.* So opposed to any form of change was Liverpool that a Frenchman remarked that if he had been present at the Creation he would have said, '*Conservons-nous le chaos.*'

These men and their influential lieutenants Addington, who became Lord Sidmouth and Home Secretary, and the notorious Lord Castlereagh saw the purpose of government as merely to preserve the existing order. They took reassurance from Dr Johnson's couplet (frequently quoted against them by Cobbett – though he was ignorant of its authorship):

> How small, of all that human hearts endure
> That part which laws or kings can cause or cure.

Ignoring the lessons of the French Revolution and convincing themselves that there was little any government could do to eradicate

---

* 'I know a Prime Minister who picks his nose and regales himself with the contents. I solemnly declare this to be true. I have witnessed the worse than beastly act scores of times' (*A Year's Residence in the United States of America*, para 290).

the inequalities and injustices in society, they were united in their determination, at all costs, to uphold the status quo, including the power of the aristocracy and its ally the Church of England, which helped to maintain a tradition of acceptance amongst the 'lower orders'. Cobbett on the other hand proclaimed: 'It is the chief business of a government to take care that one part of the people do not cause the other part to lead miserable lives.' Such a view, in the eyes of Lord Liverpool, was not only deluded but dangerous. Above all, any ideas about parliamentary reform smacked of Jacobinism and had to be resolutely suppressed.

Yet there was nothing new, let alone revolutionary, about a campaign for parliamentary reform. It went back to the last decades of the eighteenth century, when it had been embraced by any number of politicians, notably Lord Grey, and even including Pitt himself. But with the spread of revolutionary ideas to England, reaction against the French Terror and the subsequent anti-Jacobin war, the country became overtaken, in Wordsworth's words, by 'a panic dread of change'. Following a spate of repressive measures the campaign for reform fizzled out, and the cause was kept alive only by a group of colourful individuals, all known to one another, who enjoyed loose and often temporary alliances. They had no formal organisation, though there was a wide measure of agreement as to what needed to be done.

As things stood, the majority of parliamentary seats were in the gift of wealthy landowners and members of the peerage. Others were openly put up for sale. Sitting in Parliament had little to do with benefiting the community or advocating particular policies. It was sought after for social reasons. 'The moment a man became such [i.e. an MP],' Cobbett's one-time friend the diarist Thomas Creevey wrote, 'he became at once a public man and had a position in society which nothing else could give him.' Apart from the social advantage, being an MP was an easy means of financial gain. Members loyal to the government of the day could expect to be rewarded with sinecures or pensions (not, as we understand them, paid on retirement, but during the working life of those favoured), and their families could look forward to similar benefits. The reformers campaigned for an end to this corruption, the introduction of parliamentary constituencies based on population, and the extension of the franchise.

With Fox dead and Windham estranged from him, Cobbett now found himself more and more in the company of these reformers, 'the dangerous, discontented half noble, half mischievous advocates for reform and innovation', as Francis Jeffrey, editor of the *Edinburgh Review*, described them.[3] Although government ministers and their tame journalists were doing everything possible to discredit the reformers by calling them 'Jacobins' and 'Levellers', they were all eminently respectable and in no way revolutionary. The most considerable figure among them (apart from Cobbett himself) was Sir Francis Burdett (1770–1844), a wealthy, somewhat haughty baronet married to Sophia, daughter of the banker Thomas Coutts. Thanks to his rich father-in-law Burdett had been able to buy a seat in Parliament for £4000 in 1796. A tall, slender figure and an excellent speaker, he immediately and single-handedly began to agitate for reform, proposing constituencies based on population, the right to vote being extended to freeholders, and all subject to direct taxation.[4]

The senior and most radical member of the group, Major John Cartwright, was born in 1740 and became known as 'the father of reform'. Brother of the inventor Edmund, Cartwright campaigned for universal male suffrage and annual Parliaments, and had been a radical since before the French Revolution. From his home in Boston, Lincolnshire, the Major issued appeals and pamphlets and toured the country, tirelessly organising his 'Hampden Clubs' in towns and villages where men and women could meet to discuss the case for annual Parliaments and equal electoral districts. In 1806 Cartwright wrote a fan letter to Cobbett:

Sir, It was only lately I became a reader of your Weekly Register. Your energy, your indignant warmth against peculation, your abhorrence of political treachery, and your independent spirit command my esteem. As a token of it, I beg to present you with a few essays written to serve our injured country, which has for too long lain a bleeding prey to devouring factions, and which cannot be preserved, unless that public spirit and courage that were once the characteristics of England, can be revived.

Cobbett, who admired Cartwright, perhaps because he was an army man and a farmer (we find Cobbett selling him two cows in May 1808), printed a number of his pieces in the *Register*. 'The Major is the very best writer that I know,' he told Wright, 'though he has scarcely a drop of blood in his veins. Oh, that my mind, at his age, may be like his.'[5]

In fact Cartwright was a rather ponderous writer, and it is a sign of Cobbett's great affection for him that he seems to have been prepared to overlook the fact. He admired his industry, noting 'That he answered with the punctuality of a counting-house, a hundred letters in a week, by way of episode to his other labours.' The Major's only recreation was an occasional game of backgammon. Later it was Cartwright, 'the old Major', who converted Cobbett to the idea of a universal male suffrage as a necessary reform.

The exception to these generally rich upper- or middle-class reformers was Francis Place, who like Cobbett was a self-educated man of phenomenal industry. He earned his living as a tailor – 'the radical breeches-maker of Charing Cross', Cobbett called him. Place was a faithful follower of Burdett, even when the latter became an orthodox Whig, and both men were friends with Major Cartwright, who often dined with Place, 'eating some raisins he brought in his pocket and drinking weak gin and water'.[6] Place was a tireless organiser behind the scenes and campaigner, especially for workers' rights. But his character was not likely to appeal to the churchgoer and father

Cobbett, Place being an atheist and an advocate of contraception and follower of the Reverend Thomas Malthus, who believed that the poor had only themselves to blame for their condition. It was inevitable that they would later fall out, just as it was inevitable that Cobbett fell out with Burdett and also with the radical Henry 'Orator' Hunt, their quarrels being marked by what the historians J.L. and Barbara Hammond call 'that peculiar bitterness which often makes the controversies of vital reformers the most truculent controversies of all'.[7]

A more endearing though less influential reformer than Place, William Bosville (1745–1813) was always known as 'Colonel' Bosville, though in his brief military career he only ever reached the rank of lieutenant. He was enormously rich, and equally generous with his money. (He had helped Tom Paine, gave Cobbett £1000 when he was in Newgate in 1810, and once offered Place £400 to enable him to buy a house. Place refused, not wishing to be indebted to the Colonel, but later in life he deeply regretted his decision.[8]) Bosville gave a dinner party every weekend at his house in Welbeck Street. There was a slate in the hall on which any of his friends who wanted to dine could write their names. The maximum was twelve. Even on the day of his death the slate was hung up as usual. Bosville can be seen in many of Gillray's election cartoons, dressed in an old-fashioned single-breasted coat with straggly powdered hair and a pronounced stoop.[9]

Cobbett's support was welcomed by all reformers because, through the *Register*, he exercised enormous influence and at the same time provided them with an outlet for their own opinions. He in turn was flattered by the attention of the reformers and their support of the *Register*. All the same, the idea of becoming an MP appealed to him, as it was to do throughout his career. As an MP Burdett, like Windham, enjoyed respect in the papers and was covered by parliamentary privilege, so that he ran no risk of libel prosecution for what he said in the House.

But there were practical difficulties. Parliament met in London, and Cobbett was ensconced at Botley, with an estate and farm to manage, a large workforce, trees to plant, animals and crops to care for. He liked to supervise everything down to the tiniest detail himself, and he enjoyed the country life, hunting, hare-coursing and shooting. He was spending most of his time now at Botley, sending his copy up to London and leaving the running of the *Register* to his faithful factotum John Wright. And then there were the children, who were growing up. His eldest son William, he told Wright, 'copies a page of the History of England every day, reads my part of the Register every week. He frequently rides to Winchester by himself, puts his horse up at the inn, and when he has done his business, goes off home again. He is not yet ten years old, what a base thing it would be to put such a boy to have outlandish words flogged into him by an old dotard in a big white wig.'

Sir Francis Burdett, who had no wish to have a rival reformer in Parliament, persuaded Cobbett to remain a journalist, and in view of everything he was, for the time being, prepared to accept Burdett's advice. He wrote to John Wright: 'I am of the opinion (and I should like to hear what the Major [i.e. Cartwright] says of the matter) that I am the most weight as a *spectator* and *comment maker*. This way my words and opinions pass for a good deal; but I am not clear that whatever good I could do as an *agitator* would not be more than counterbalanced by the loss of weight in the other character. I know it is the opinion of Sir Francis that to put me in Parliament would be to lessen my weight. In fact we cannot *act* and *write* with so much advantage . . .'[10]

But in 1806 something happened to make Cobbett change his mind. In that year Cavendish Bradshaw, the Member of Parliament for Honiton in Devon, accepted a sinecure* as Teller of the Exchequer of Ireland, but announced at the same time that he would stand for

---

* 'Sinecure: An office that has revenue without employment' (Johnson).

re-election. Enraged by the idea that Bradshaw would 'draw into his own pocket some thousands a year' out of the public purse – and this too, at a time when 'the load of indispensable taxes [was] impoverishing his honest and industrious constituents to the earth', Cobbett appealed, through the *Register*, for someone to step forward and oppose him at the election. When no offers were forthcoming he announced that he intended to stand himself, informing the voters firstly that if elected he would never accept 'a farthing of public money', and secondly that he would not part with a farthing of his own money as an inducement to gain an elector's vote:

> The candidates who have resorted to such means have always been amongst the most wicked of men; men who, having, by a life of adultery or of gambling, or of profligacy of some other sort, ruined both their character and their futures, have staked their last thousand upon an election, with the hope of thereby obtaining security from a jail . . .[11]

At this point the wealthy Colonel Bosville, who had never before met Cobbett, offered his coach and four to drive him and his friends down to Devon. 'The offer was accepted,' Cobbett's sons wrote later, 'and thus the affair became one of pleasure.' On arrival in Honiton Cobbett was met by a young Admiral, Thomas, Lord Cochrane, who had read of his appeal in the *Register* and decided to offer himself as a candidate. Cobbett duly withdrew from the contest in favour of Cochrane. Admirals are traditionally weatherbeaten old sea dogs, but Cochrane was only thirty at the time, already with a string of daring exploits to his name fighting against the French, exploits which later inspired a host of famous sea stories ranging from those of Captain Marryat, who served under him, to C.S. Forester and Patrick O'Brian. Cochrane was not only a brilliant sailor: he was, like his father, an inventor, many of whose nautical devices were adopted in his lifetime. A tall, impulsive, daredevil figure, he was a man of great personal charm, a natural leader with a streak of recklessness that appealed to Cobbett, especially since the Admiral campaigned against corruption in the War Office and the armed services. Miss Mitford, who met him later when he was staying with Cobbett at Botley and watched him playing with the children under the trees, said Cochrane was 'as unlike the common notion of a warrior as could be – a gentle, quiet, mild young man'.

Cochrane, who was later to join the reformers in between his nautical adventures, adopted Cobbett's pledge of refusing to pay any bribes. Predictably he lost to Bradshaw by 259 votes to 124 (that being the extent of the franchise in this fair-sized market town). Cochrane then did an extraordinary, but for him quite typical, thing. He sent the town crier through Honiton with the good news that anyone who had voted for him would receive a ten-guinea reward. When a general election was held only four months later the voters of Honiton assumed that the same amount would be on offer, but when they came forward having voted for Cochrane and expecting their ten guineas, the victorious Admiral told them, 'Not one farthing.'

It was during the Honiton campaign that Cobbett first engaged in public speaking, something he was to continue to do until his death. He made two long speeches and succeeded in shouting down all the hecklers. More importantly, he gained a first-hand impression of the way in which bribery and corruption were practised quite openly amongst the very small number of people entitled to vote. This inspired a typically purple passage in the next issue of the *Register*, contrasting, as so often with Cobbett, the beauty of the countryside with the infamy of politicians:

> In quitting this scene; in looking back from all of the many hills that surround the fertile and beautiful valley in which Honiton lies, with its houses spreading down the side of an inferior eminence crowned by its ancient and venerable church; in surveying the fields, the crops, the cattle, all the

blessings that nature can bestow, all the sources of plenty and all the means of comfort and of happiness, it was impossible to divest oneself of a feeling of horror at reflecting upon the deeds which the visiting sun was about to witness, upon this one of his most favoured spots. And, is there, said I to myself: can there be a statesman, who can say that he has done his duty; who can quiet the calls of his conscience; who can calmly lay his head down upon his pillow; who can close his eyes without a dread as to where or how he shall awake; is there a statesman in England who can do these things, until he has formed a solemn resolution to endeavour to correct this shocking abuse; to remove this terrible curse from the land committed to his care?[12]

The Honiton experience left Cobbett not just with a taste for political activity, but with a conviction that only the election of an independent Member of integrity could effect a lasting change in the political system. The difficulty was that the majority of parliamentary seats were in the personal gift of the aristocracy, or could only be acquired with large sums of money, to be paid either to the proprietor or the voters, or both. Some 'rotten boroughs' like the notorious Old Sarum, the prehistoric hill-fort outside Salisbury, had no voters at all; others (like Honiton) a handful of a few hundred. In only a few were there sufficient numbers to make some form of democratic contest possible. One such was the constituency of Westminster, with over twelve thousand ratepayer-voters, mostly small tradesmen, 'journeymen' and craftsmen; and it was this seat that now became the focus of Cobbett's attention.

The two Westminster seats had been held for some years, by mutual arrangement of the parties, by one Whig and one Tory – the Whig being, since 1780, Charles James Fox. When Fox died in September 1806 a by-election ensued at which, thanks to some clever political manoeuvring, Lord Percy, son of the Duke of Northumberland, was elected unopposed. But a general election followed soon afterwards, and with Cobbett's support in the *Register* and £1000 provided by Burdett, James Paull, the son of a tailor and a one-time friend of Windham, who introduced him to Cobbett, stood as an independent. Paull was a hot-tempered man who had already lost one arm in a duel in India.

Although the official candidates were victorious, Paull won 4481 votes out of the total of 14,717, which inspired the reformers to try again when yet another election was held only a few months later. Unfortunately, in the interim Paull quarrelled with Burdett, resulting in another duel in which both men were badly injured. Cobbett then dropped Paull (who not long after committed suicide) and gave his support to Burdett and also to Cochrane. Thanks to the organisational skills of Francis Place the aristocratic reformers were returned with large majorities. Their victory was celebrated with a triumphant procession through Westminster, with bands and buglers and the electors marching four abreast. Burdett rode in a carriage drawn by four grey horses, followed by Cobbett side by side with Colonel Bosville in his famous coach and four. 'When we arrived at Covent Garden, we found all the low buildings in the middle of the square so loaded with people that the chimney tops were hidden from view: hundreds were sitting or standing upon the roofs and ridges of the houses round the square and upon a moderate computation, there could not be less than one hundred thousand persons who here saw the procession at one and the same time.'[13]

There followed a celebratory dinner at the Crown and Anchor in the Strand attended by two thousand people, each of whom paid twelve shillings. Cobbett noted that while about half a million people had taken part in the event, not a single act of violence was committed – contrary to the fears of the government and the commander in chief, the Duke of York, who had put troops on alert to deal with any trouble.

Following the return of a Tory government in 1807 Cobbett, who no longer had any supporters in the administration, was especially aware of the risks he was now running. With the 'Juverna' case fresh in his memory, he resolved to take more care when attacking ministers. He wrote to John Wright on 10 April 1807: 'I am deeply impressed with the necessity of caution; but if they are resolved to plague, plague they may ... Villains, they profess liberty –; they get their hired scoundrels to write me and truth out of countenance: and the moment they feel the weight of my lash, they talk of the *law*.' He wrote to Wright that after the election 'I shall set about writing sober essays of exposure. Quote from original documents, state the bare facts, and lament, as I most sincerely do, the inevitable consequences.' Cobbett was anticipating trouble, in particular from Spencer Perceval, who was promoted to Chancellor of the Exchequer in 1807. Perceval was a narrow-minded, pious, respectable lawyer – in Cobbett's words 'a hard, keen, sour looking man ... with no knowledge of the great interest of the nation, foreign or domestic'. He had been Cobbett's prosecutor in the 'Juverna' libel action, and Cobbett was wary of him: 'I see the fangs of law open to grasp me,' he told Wright on 10 May 1807, 'and I feel the necessity of leaving no hold for them ... upon the score of coarseness or violence.' And again, in another letter: 'I am deeply impressed with the necessity of caution.'[14]

But caution and restraint were not qualities that came easily to a man whose normal state was one of righteous indignation. Before long the italics, the capital letters and the exclamation marks would once again break out into print. Especially was this true when he dealt with any scandal relating to the British army, Cobbett retaining from his own military days a fierce loyalty to serving soldiers. 'I like soldiers,' he wrote later, 'as a class in life, better than any other description of men. Their conversation is more pleasing to me; they have generally seen more than other men; they have less of vulgar prejudice about them; to which may be added, that, having felt hardships themselves, they know how to feel for others.'[15]

In 1809 a major scandal was exposed by Colonel Wardle, the Member for Okehampton, concerning the Duke of York, George III's son and the commander in chief of the army (remembered today only for his army of ten thousand men, which he marched up to the top of the hill and down again). Wardle accused the Duke's two successive mistresses, Mrs Clarke and Mrs Carey, of selling commissions in the army. In a six-week-long inquiry the House of Commons tried to establish, without success, to what extent the Duke knew what Mrs Clarke – 'a damned mercenary bitch', according to Cobbett – had been up to, and in the end voted by 278 to 196 that there were no grounds to charge the Duke with corruption, though he resigned as commander in chief on the day of the vote.

The affair excited a huge amount of public interest, and Cobbett devoted whole issues of the *Register* to reporting verbatim the evidence given to the inquiry. He himself was less interested in attacking the Duke of York than in defending the British soldiers who were fighting a war against Napoleon in Spain and Portugal under the command of officers some of whom, he claimed, could simply have bought their commissions by paying £200 or so to Mrs Clarke:

> The chief evil here is that unworthy and base persons of a different description; that the vile and corrupt vermin who hang about the metropolis, step over the heads of veterans, who have passed their lives in toil and dangers; that boys become entrusted with commands, which ought never to be in any hands but those of men of experience; that the comfort, the happiness, the *backs* and the *lives*, of our brave soldiers are committed to the power . . . of men, whose promotion to that power has been obtained by means such as those which have now been brought to light. To be a good military officer requires not only bravery, but *wisdom, experience* and integrity; a good understanding and a just mind. And, can these be expected in men, who have gained their posts by bribes given to a kept mistress?[16]

85

In spite of his resolution to be cautious, Cobbett could not control his feelings when dealing with the behaviour of Spencer Perceval. Perceval aroused his contempt when cross-examining one of the witnesses against Mrs Clarke, Mary Taylor, whom he tried to discredit by forcing her to admit that she was illegitimate and that her mother had been imprisoned for debt. As a result of her being forced to give evidence, Cobbett claimed, Taylor's business running a boarding school in Cheyne Row, Chelsea, with her sister had been ruined and she had lost all her pupils.

In his defence of Colonel Wardle against suggestions from ministers like First Lord of the Admiralty Charles Yorke and Canning that he was just a libeller, Cobbett wrote some of his finest passages on the question of press freedom.

There are two positions, one from Mr Yorke and the other from Mr Canning to which I am disposed to pay particular attention – The first of these gentlemen said, that libels had, of late, been more abundant *against persons in authority* than at any period in this country . . . and the latter said, that, in publications *rank* ought to be regarded like *sex*, and that to assail persons of exalted rank was an act of baseness and cowardice, equal to that of assaulting a defenceless woman . . . There was much said about the 'blessings of a free press' but, if it is to be regarded as an act of baseness to assail men of rank, I should be glad to know in what these 'blessings' consist. The 'freedom of the press' means, the freedom of examining and exposing the actions of *public* men; men who are entrusted with the nation's affairs; and these are necessarily men of high rank . . . In short, it is farcical to talk about freedom of the press, unless by it we mean the *Right*, the acknowledged *legal right*, of freely expressing our opinions, be they what they may, *respecting the character and conduct of men in power*; and of stating any thing, no matter what, if we can prove the *truth* of this statement . . .

It is in the character and conduct of *men in power* that

the public are interested. These are *the very matters*, upon which they want, and ought to receive information. The babble of the day is of no public utility. The particulars of who walks or rides out with the King: of where and when the Duke of York salutes his royal parents; of the breakfasts and dances of Frogmore; of Generals Cartwright and Fitzroy's going to chapel and hearing a sermon; of the cabinet and other grand dinners; these may amuse some few gossiping people; but of what use are they to the nation?[17]

The Duke of York affair seriously rattled the administration. It was not only the sale of commissions that had surfaced; there had been considerable discussion of other forms of corruption, all involving ministers and Parliament. As a heading in the *Register*, Cobbett now regularly listed all the sinecures and perks accruing to ministers: for example the Speaker, Charles Abbot, had in addition to his salary of £6000 p.a. and his house 'a sinecure place of Keeper of the Signet in Ireland worth £15,000 which place he has for life'. Spencer Perceval had a salary of £2600 as Chancellor of the Exchequer, a further £4525 as Chancellor of the Duchy of Lancaster, £4525 as Surveyor of Meltings and Clerk of the Irons in the Mint, as well as standing to gain £12,562 on the death of his brother Lord Arden 'in reversion of sinecure offices'.[18]

It was not surprising that such exposures, not confined to *Cobbett's Register*, should predispose the Tory government to a 'crackdown' on the press. There was talk of a resurgence of Jacobinism and a 'conspiracy' to undermine the Crown and Parliament. Between 1807 and 1810 there were forty-two prosecutions threatened – though none was actually brought to trial, partly for fear that juries might not convict. But the mere filing of information against a journalist was usually sufficient to intimidate him, as well as incurring a considerable bill of costs.[19]

As an independent and widely read commentator owing nothing to political sponsors, Cobbett represented by far the greatest threat to the administration. Not only was he free to say whatever he liked, but his provocative style made the *Register* required reading even for his opponents. As it was well put by the diplomat Lord Dalling and Bulwer after Cobbett's death: 'Whatever a man's opinions, he sought the Register on the day of its appearance and read it with amusement, partly, perhaps, if De la Rochefoucauld is right, because whatever his party he was sure to see his friends abused.'[20]

It is unclear whether or not the ministry took a deliberate decision to 'get' Cobbett. What is undeniable is that by 1809 they were doing everything possible to smear him. Throughout his later career Cobbett was being forcibly reminded of his earlier opinions when as Peter Porcupine he had attacked Tom Paine, the Jacobins and the reformers. Thus, in 1809 the government issued a pamphlet, 'Elements of Reform by William Cobbett', which looked as if it had been published by Cobbett himself but was in fact a compilation intended to discredit him. Replying in the *Register*, Cobbett made no bones about the fact that he had changed his opinions on many matters:

> The doctrine of *consistency* as now in vogue is the most absurd that ever was breached. It teaches, that, if you once think well of any person or thing, you must always think well of that person or thing whatever changes may take place either in them, or in the state of your information respecting them. Where is the man who has not changed his opinion of men as well as of things?[21]

A number of papers, all of them subsidised by the ministry in one form or another, were busy meanwhile attacking Cobbett. Not that this was especially new. As long ago as 1803 he had claimed that the Addington government had subsidised two papers, the *Pilot* and the *Royal Standard*, to attack the *Register*.

An anonymous pamphlet, 'Thoughts on Libels by a Patriotick Loyalist', repeated the charge that a group of writers led by Cobbett was intent not just on discrediting the Duke of York:

The libellers do not aim at the Duke *alone*. 'Destroy' say they 'the son of our King, the Commander in Chief *first* and how soon shall we strike you with panick my good first Lord of the Admiralty! *Then* Chancellors of the Exchequer, Secretaries of State, for the Home and Foreign Department, Lords of the Treasury, Archbishops and Bishops, Judges of the law – all – all vanish at the motion of our quills.

Cobbett was the leader of this conspiracy, Cobbett – 'Apostate, spy, incendiary, Ruffian, Traitor, Prevaricator, liar'. Cobbett, the author reminded his readers, was the suspected author of 'The Soldier's Friend', a seditious pamphlet published in 1792, 'exciting our troops to mutiny, a man who nevertheless managed to obtain a discharge and certificate of good behaviour from his commanding officer – though was this surprising when we learn that this officer was none other than the *arch-traitor*, Lord Edward Fitzgerald who afterwards lost his life in resisting those who came to apprehend him for *high-treason*'. This 'Satan' Cobbett was the man who was now responsible for 'the hebdominal poison vomited forth in a *Weekly Register*'.

A still more virulent campaign was conducted by the *Satirist*, launched in 1807. The owner was an obscure figure, George Manners, who was almost certainly in receipt of government funds. The *Satirist* accused Cobbett of having been a British government spy when he was in America, as well as having deserted from the army. Manners also revived the story of the long-forgotten court martial of 1792, when Cobbett charged three officers with corruption but fled to France when it looked as if he himself would be prosecuted, and accused Cobbett of maltreating one of his young farmworkers at Botley, Jesse Burgess.

Both these stories subsequently formed the basis of further substantial attacks. An anonymous pamphlet, 'Proceedings of a General Court Martial Held at the House of Guards etc.', was published in 1809. Thousands of copies (according to Cobbett) were printed and widely distributed, especially in his home county of Hampshire – even given away free. 'The robbers,' he wrote, 'as they have come down from London in the carriages, have brought with them whole bales which they have tossed out to all whom they met or overtook upon the road. A few days ago, a landau full of *he* and *she* peculators passed through Alton, tossing out these pamphlets as they went. The thing has been put into all the inns, and other public places, particularly in Winchester, where it would certainly be put into the churches.'

Whether, in spite of those efforts, the pamphlet had a great deal of effect is doubtful. As Cobbett pointed out in his lengthy denunciation in the *Political Register*, it was a poor effort, consisting mostly of the exchange of letters between Cobbett and the Secretary at War Sir George Yonge prior to the court case. But, as Cobbett revealed, the letters were carefully edited, and the most important, such as the letter to Pitt requesting that the hearing be held in London rather than Portsmouth, or the one in which he set out his reasons for not appearing (on the grounds that his chief witness, Corporal Bestland, was still in the army) were omitted altogether.

A possibly more effective piece of anti-Cobbett propaganda was the set of eight Gillray prints published at this time, on 29 September 1809. James Gillray was by far and away the most gifted satirical artist of the day, though sadly he compromised his talent by hiring himself out to various politicians, in the process becoming a mere hack taking instructions from his masters. The most prominent of these was the Foreign Secretary, George Canning, and it was Canning whom Cobbett accused in a letter to John Wright of being behind Gillray's prints – 'Ministers and their partizans have been employed for more than six months publishing libels, of me . . . there were caricatures prepared under the eye of Canning etc.'[22]

Basing his attack on Cobbett's own memoir (*The Life and Adventures of Peter Porcupine*) and the information in the court-martial pamphlet, with Cobbett's own rebuttal in his *Political Register*, Gillray (probably with Canning's help) traced his career from farmer's boy chasing pigs in the yard of the Jolly Farmer, to soldier following the colours, and finally to the court martial, where through the door of the courtroom filled with red-coated soldiers and spectators Cobbett can be seen making his escape in a little boat. 'Call away and be damned I'm off,' he cries in answer to the summons, 'Call William Cobbett into court to make good his charges.'

Like the anonymous pamphleteers, Gillray did everything possible to portray Cobbett as a Jacobin, linking him not just with the reformers but with his old commanding officer, the 'arch-traitor' Lord Edward Fitzgerald. Artistically the series of prints is a brilliant *tour de force*, but it says little for Gillray's character that he was prepared to make this elaborate attack on a journalist whom he knew quite well, at a time when he was living under threat of a prison sentence.

Cobbett had been anticipating a possible prosecution well before the Duke of York hearings or even the advent of a Tory government. In April 1807 he was confiding to Wright that he was worried on that score. The government, and Spencer Perceval in particular, were meanwhile looking for an excuse to bring a prosecution. On 7 May 1809 we find Perceval calling on the Speaker, a fellow barrister, Charles Abbot, and bringing along the latest issue of the *Register*. Abbot wrote in his diary:

> He thought Cobbett had at last committed himself in his paper upon the House of Commons vote, for rejecting Lord Folkestone's motion for a committee to inquire into the sales of all the places in the State etc but, when he showed me the paper, it did not so strike me that the libel was more violent than what all the opposition papers contained every day; or was such as could usefully be proceeded upon.[23]

A much better opportunity arose two months later, following an army 'mutiny' at Ely in Cambridgeshire. There is some confusion about what actually happened. According to the *Courier*, whose report

Cobbett relied upon and quoted in full, the soldiers surrounded their officers over 'a stoppage of their knapsacks', demanding their arrears (i.e. provisions). *The Times* stated that the soldiers had come from some distance, had received no pay for several days, as a result of which many of them were half-starved, and that they had put their officers under arrest. In his A *Year's Residence in the United States of America* (1818) Cobbett tells a third version, saying the young men had been press-ganged into service with no knowledge of military discipline, 'had been promised a *guinea each* before they marched [and] had refused to march *because the guinea had not been wholly paid them*'.[24]

Whatever precisely happened, the incident would not seem to deserve the description of 'mutiny'. But the so-called ringleaders, according to the *Courier*, were court martialled and sentenced to five hundred lashes each. It was the nature and severity of the punishment that especially enraged Cobbett. During his army days he had witnessed several times this barbaric form of discipline:

> At the flogging of a man I have frequently seen seven or eight men fall slap upon the ground, unable to endure the sight, and to hear the cries without swooning away. We used to lift them back a little way, take off their stocks and unbutton their shirt collars and they came to after a little while. These were as stout, hardy and bold men as anywhere to be found.
>
> The whip-cord may be large or small. Ours used to be as thick as the very thickest twine made use of to tie up stout and heavy parcels. The knots were about the size, as nearly as I can recollect, of a dwarf-marrow-fat pea; and the length of the cosh was about fifteen or sixteen inches . . . The drummers used to do the flogging; they were always stripped for the work, and each, by turns, laid on his twenty five lashes, and then another came.[25]

The issue of army flogging had only recently been raised in Parliament by Sir Francis Burdett, who proposed a motion to ban it. Cobbett,

forgetting all his resolutions to be cautious, exploded in an outburst
of indignation over the Ely affair:

> *Five hundred lashes* each! Aye, that is right! Flog them: flog
> them: flog them! They deserve it, and a great deal more. They
> deserve a flogging at every meal-time. 'Lash them daily, lash
> them duly'. What, shall the rascals dare to *mutiny*, and that,
> too, when the German Legion is so near at hand! Lash them,
> lash them, lash them! They *deserve* it. O, yes. They want a
> double-tailed cat. Base dogs! What, mutiny for the sake of the
> *price of a knapsack*! Lash them! Flog them! Base rascals!
> Mutiny for the price of a goat's skin; and, then, upon the
> appearance of the *German soldiers*, they take a flogging as
> quietly as so many trunks of trees! – I do not know what sort
> of place Ely is; but I really should like to know how the
> inhabitants looked one another in the face, while this scene
> was exhibiting in their town, I should like to have been able
> to see their faces, and to hear their observations to each other,
> at the time – This occurrence at home will, one would hope,
> teach *the loyal* a little caution in speaking of the means, which
> Napoleon employs (or, rather, which they say he employs) in
> order to get together and discipline his conscripts. There is
> scarcely any one of these loyal persons, who has not, at various
> times, cited the *hand-cuffings* and other means of *force*, said
> to be used in drawing out the young men of France; there is
> scarcely one of the loyal, who has not cited these means as
> proof, a complete proof, that the people of France *hate Napo-
> leon and his Government, assist with reluctance in his wars,
> and would fain see another revolution.* I hope, I say, that
> the loyal will, hereafter be more cautious in drawing such
> conclusions, now that they see, that our 'gallant defenders'
> not only require physical restraint, in certain cases, but even
> a little blood drawn from their backs, and that too, with the
> aid and assistance of *German* troops.

Cobbett never forgot being served with the Attorney General's writ.
'I was leaning over a gate,' he wrote shortly before his death in 1835,

'and looking at the turnips in a field, when the paper was put into my hands. I saw at once the hell-born *intention*, and I saw the consequences. The beautiful field disappeared, and, in my imagination I saw the *walls of a prison*. My blood boiled and cramming the paper into my pocket, I made *an oath* which I have kept with a little more fidelity than Tories keep their pledges.'

His state of mind over the next six months oscillated between depression and elation, between an urge to defy the government and submission to its controls. In the issue following the offensive outburst he printed what looked like a curious kind of retraction:

> Those . . . who, at Ely, and elsewhere, have quelled the spirit of mutiny amongst the local militia, are certainly entitled to the thanks of the country. No one can be pleased to see his countrymen flogged; but when, as in this case, they have *voluntarily* entered, and that, too, for the sake of a bounty – I say, as I said before, 'flog them' if they do not abide by their bargain, and strictly obey their officers.

Throughout the months that followed it was Cobbett's concern for his family that most strongly predisposed him, at times, to succumb to the government's threats and reach some form of settlement with it, either by toning down the *Register* or possibly closing it altogether. In contrast to free spirits like Paine or Hazlitt, Cobbett was unusual among the ranks of great rebels in being a devoted family man. Despite his ferocious activity he remained resolutely committed to his wife and children. His views on a father's duties would find favour with modern feminists:

> The man who is to gain a living by his labour, must be drawn away from home, or at least, from the cradle-side in order to perform that labour; but this will not, if he be made of good stuff, prevent him from the duty due to his children. There is nothing more amiable, nothing more delightful to behold,

than a *young* man especially, taking part in the work of nursing the children.[26]

Cobbett disapproved strongly of nannies, or of parents who left their children in the care of servants, and insisted that he himself had remained true to this principle. 'What! Can I plead *example*, then in support of this rigid precept? Did we, who have bred up a family of children, and have had servants during the greater part of the time, *never* leave a young child to the care of servants? Never, no, not for *one single hour*. Were we then tied constantly to the house with them? No; for we sometimes took them out, but one or the other of us was always with them.' If he and Nancy were invited out they asked if they could bring their children, and if this was not possible then one of them stayed at home. There were no babysitters in the Cobbett home – and as for babies: '"I can't bear that squalling!" I have heard men say, and to which I answer, that "I can't bear such men!" It never disturbed me and my occupation was one of the most liable to disturbance by noise. Many a score of papers have I written amidst the noise of children and in my whole life never bade them be still.'[27]

To a man with such a strong bond with his children, the thought of a two-year prison sentence must have seemed a truly terrible prospect. But as time went on and nothing happened, Cobbett began to reassure himself that perhaps he would escape this fate. His writing was as provocative as ever, as when in October 1809 he denounced the Royal Jubilee of George III in two successive issues of the *Register*. In the first he explained why he would not be contributing to a local Jubilee appeal in Hampshire to buy bread, meat and beer for poor parishioners. Apart from the condescension involved, what was there to celebrate, he asked. In the fifty years of George III's reign the nation had seen an increase in the national debt from £90 million to £700 million, and had suffered disastrous defeats in America and more recently in Holland and Spain. Returning to the theme the following month, he congratulated his friend Colonel Bosville on refusing to illuminate his house on Jubilee night and having his window smashed by the mob, just as Cobbett's had been when the Peace of Amiens was proclaimed in 1802. Cobbett mocked the general sycophancy of the press and deplored the fact that 'the song of God Save the King, that clumsy and stupid flattery without one poetic thought or elegant expression' had been sung in many churches.

That same month, November, he wrote to his paper-supplier John Swann in Oxfordshire: 'You have I suppose heard of the dead-set the Attorney General is making upon us. My opinion is that it will come to nothing at all. But, if it does, we must beat them. If there be either spirit or honesty left in England.'[28] The Attorney General, Mr Vicary Gibbs (nicknamed 'Vinegar' Gibbs on account of his acerbic character), was well known for initiating libel proceedings and then leaving them hanging over the heads of journalists as a means of gagging them. But during this period ministers had more important issues to distract them. In August 1809 the Prime Minister, the Duke of Portland, had a stroke and died a month later, being replaced by Cobbett's old adversary Spencer Perceval. The Foreign Secretary, Canning, and the Chancellor, Castlereagh, fought a duel with pistols on Putney Heath, leaving Canning wounded in the thigh, and Lord Chatham, Pitt's brother, led an expedition to capture the island of Walcheren off the coast of Holland and to sail up the River Scheldt to destroy French ships and armaments in Flushing and Antwerp. It was a disaster: the French had ample warning of the attack, malaria broke out among the troops, and thousands of lives were lost. The subsequent debate in the House of Commons and the extraordinary events that followed were to seal Cobbett's fate.

The history of the months of February to May 1810 was succinctly described in the *Register* of 19 May. It began with what Cobbett calls 'the death-dealing, the unspeakably disgraceful expedition to Walcheren'. The House of Commons then decided to have an inquiry into the planning and prosecution of the expedition. But as the inquiry was about to begin Charles Yorke moved a standing order to exclude the reporters from the press gallery – 'by which means the evidence is retarded in its way to the people and the knowledge of the speeches and questions of the several members is wholly kept from them'. John Gale Jones, Secretary of the British Forum Society (a radical debating club), then said in print that Yorke's conduct was 'an outrage on public feeling', and other things besides:

> Mr Yorke complains of this to the House. The House puts Mr Gale Jones in Newgate for having used the words. In a day or two after this, Mr Yorke receives from the minister, a sinecure place for life of £2,700 a year to be raised upon the people. Sir Francis Burdett publishes an argument [in the *Political Register*] to show that the House has wrongfully imprisoned Mr Gale Jones and is in breach of the Magna Carta. The House orders Sir Francis to be imprisoned in the Tower.

At this point, on 6 April, all hell broke loose, to the consternation of Spencer Perceval and his ministers. A huge mob took to the streets. Burdett barricaded himself in his house at 78 Piccadilly, and anyone trying to walk through Piccadilly without crying 'Burdett for ever' was showered with mud. Perceval had no alternative but to call out troops to try to restore order, while Cobbett's friend the dashing Admiral Cochrane called on Burdett with a cask of gunpowder 'so that he might blow the invaders to the devil'.[29] For three days chaos reigned, but eventually, on Monday, 9 April, Burdett, whose followers had been persuaded by Francis Place not to resist, allowed the troops to enter his house, where they found him reading Magna Carta to his son. He was arrested and taken to the Tower of London by a circuitous northern route.

Cobbett had once again put himself in the firing line not only by printing Burdett's speech in the *Register* but also, as was alleged, helping him to write it in the first place. Spencer Perceval, in discussion with his friend the Speaker Charles Abbot, had wanted to summon Cobbett to the bar of the House along with Burdett, though he was persuaded not to. Instead, with Burdett now safely in the Tower of London, he decided to put the libel proceedings, already launched, into action. In May Cobbett learned that he would face a trial the following month.

Fox's Libel Act of 1792 had restored the jury to libel actions. But the authorities attempted to redress the balance by the institution of the 'special jury', consisting of men drawn from a list of those thought to be reliable. Sometimes known as 'guinea men', they were paid a guinea per case and were kept on the list so long as they reached the right verdicts.[30] Even so, by 1810 there had been a number of recent acquittals in criminal libel actions. James Perry, editor of the *Morning Chronicle*, was acquitted early that year of libelling George III, to general rejoicing in journalistic circles. From the first rumours of the prosecution Cobbett had determined, like Perry, to take the risky path of conducting his own defence. He was advised to do this by friends like Francis Place and Admiral Cochrane on the grounds that no barrister would want to go out of his way to offend the Attorney General Gibbs or the Chief Justice Ellenborough. It proved to be a mistake. Like many litigants-in-person, Cobbett discovered that much of what he wanted to say was held to be inadmissible. As the law stood, there could be no defence on the grounds of the truth of what was said. But he tried to show that his comments on the army floggings at Ely were tame stuff compared with some of the speeches by MPs in the recent Walcheren debate attacking the army's treatment of soldiers. Ellenborough intervened: 'Mr Cobbett, I must prevent this: I cannot allow speeches stated to have been spoken in Parliament on other matters to be read to the jury.'

In his letters to John Wright prior to the trial Cobbett frequently mentions how he is going to bring up all the government's own smears and libels against him over the previous months, to show the political nature of the prosecution. His friend Francis Place, 'the breeches-maker of Charing Cross', urged him to produce as evidence the complimentary letters he had received from ministers and MPs about the *Register* (with the same aim, Cobbett himself had recently revealed his authorship of the 'Important Considerations' circulated throughout the country by the government when Napoleon threatened to invade). 'You must put in the letters,' Place said. 'You must then ask the jury whether a person so addressed must be considered as a source of sedition.' But when the day came, Cobbett made no mention of the letters (though to be fair to him, these too might well have been deemed inadmissible). He also made the mistake of admitting that the article in question had been written in a hurry.

Many people, including friends like the Mitfords, had come to court to witness what they hoped would be a display of verbal fireworks from Cobbett. But they were disappointed. Everything suggests that, nervous perhaps in the unfamiliar courtroom atmosphere and worried about the future, he failed to rise to the occasion. This was certainly the view of Place, who wrote scornfully: 'He was not at all master of himself and in some parts where he meant to produce great effect he produced laughter. So ludicrous was he in one part that the jury, the Judge and the audience all laughed at him. I was thoroughly ashamed of him and ashamed of myself for being seen with him.'[31] This view was echoed by a young barrister, John Campbell, who sat behind Cobbett and recorded that his speech was 'the poorest that I ever heard'.[32] (Later, in 1845, when Lord Chancellor, Campbell changed the criminal libel law to allow a defendant to plead the truth of what he had written – a change that came too late for Cobbett.)

Summing up, Ellenborough had no scruples about leaving the verdict to the jury. Cobbett's plain intention, he said, was to incite the troops to further mutiny, to hold the government and constitution up to contempt. 'I do pronounce this,' he said finally, 'to be a most infamous and seditious libel.' The jury did not even bother to retire.

After five minutes' deliberation they returned a verdict of guilty. The case had lasted from nine in the morning till 12.30 at night.

There followed a crucial turning point in Cobbett's life. He had been found guilty but had yet to be sentenced. It was possible now for him to reach some kind of agreement with the government and so escape imprisonment. He went down to Botley to be with Nancy, who was pregnant again, and his children. All, especially Nancy and his eldest daughter Anne, were in a tearful state, alarmed at the thought of losing him. Not only that: 'I had just begun farming projects and also planting trees with the hope of seeing them grow up as my children grew.' These things meant as much to Cobbett as his journalism and the cause of reform. Why not now turn his back on all that and enjoy the life of a country gentleman, looking after his family, his farm labourers and his beloved trees? Cobbett decided to surrender. He sat down and wrote a long article for what was to be the final edition of the *Political Register*:

> ... I cannot after what has taken place think it proper to continue any longer this publication and therefore with the present Number ... I put an end to it for ever ...
>
> It must be manifest that if the work was continued, *it could not be what it has been.*
>
> I know that there will, nevertheless be enough persons to say that *I have deserted the cause*: but, I shall ask, whose cause? It is I presume meant to be the cause of the *Public* or the *People*, or the *Country* give it what name you please. Well, if putting a stop to this work be any injury to the country, let it be recollected that it is *the country* itself who have condemned me ... The Jury, without a minute's hesitation said GUILTY. Now therefore, it is exceedingly impudent, or, at least, exceedingly stupid to accuse me of *deserting* the cause of *the public*, that public itself having, by its representatives, the Jury, condemned me, and in effect put an end to my writing.
>
> ... it is barely possible that some may accuse me of deserting the cause of *the Press*. This however, can hardly be.

Two or three of the newspapers called upon the Attorney General to prosecute me: one expressed its *hope*, about three months ago, the Attorney General would not forget me and that the prosecution *was not dropped* . . . and in no one publication in the Kingdom has there appeared, so far as I have seen, a single word in my defence, or even in the way of apology for me . . . To that profession, I, this day, cease to *belong* . . . And to these declarations I will add that I NEVER WILL AGAIN, UPON ANY ACCOUNT, INDITE, PUBLISH, WRITE OR CONTRIBUTE TOWARDS, ANY NEWSPAPER, OR OTHER PUBLICATION OF THAT NATURE SO LONG AS I LIVE.

Cobbett must have been aware of the weakness of his arguments, just as, later, he must have wished that his farewell to his readers (though it was never printed) had not survived. John Wright, who kept it, and who released it after he quarrelled with Cobbett, urged him not to commit himself until he could be sure that the government, if indeed it had offered a deal, would keep its word and guarantee his freedom in exchange. There was nothing to suggest that it would. Cobbett's lawyer friend John Reeves, who acted as his intermediary, promised to pass on the statement to Charles Yorke – he assured Cobbett that 'no doubt they will take such a sacrifice into consideration'. But there was never any indication that Cobbett would be let off the hook. And in the meantime Nancy and Anne had dried their eyes. A spirit of defiance replaced the earlier gloom at Botley. On 28 June Cobbett wrote to Wright: 'No. I will not sacrifice *fortune* without securing freedom in return. This I am resolved on. It would be both *baseness* and folly . . . from the bottom of my soul I would *rather* be called up than put down the *Register*.'

He presented himself for judgement on 5 July, and after four days in the King's Bench prison in Southwark was ordered to be arraigned once again on the ninth. Sir Vicary Gibbs, the Attorney General, addressed the court in typically high-flown and insincere tones:

The present libel [he said] went to subvert society itself and whatever might be thought of the atrocity of others which had preceded it, the present was one of a much darker and blacker hue. The court were therefore called on to inflict such punishment as should, at least, make men pause before they embarked on libels similar to that published by the Defendant Mr. Cobbett. The army, against whom this libel was directed, called on the court for justice against its traducer. The Government called on them for confirmation of its legal powers; for what Government could possibly exist if it were not protected against such attacks as these. The country, which looked with horror on the mischievous treachery of the libel now under consideration, called on them for protection against the numerous evils which the propagation of such publications were calculated to engender, going, as they did to the total subversion of social order, and to the existence of the country as a nation.[33]

The judges Ellenborough, Grose, LeBlanc and Bailey then sentenced Cobbett to two years' imprisonment and a fine of £1000. In the years to come he never allowed the four men to forget their role, and reeled off their names at every possible juncture. He also, as was his custom, printed the names and addresses of the twelve jurymen who had found him guilty: 'As to the future,' he wrote, 'I can reasonably promise myself days of happiness, while continued dread must haunt their guilty minds; while every stir and every sound must make them quake for fear. *Their* day is yet to come.'

5

BEHIND BARS

NEWGATE PRISON, which was to be Cobbett's home for the next two years, was a grim, forbidding fortress standing along-side the Old Bailey in the shadow of St Paul's Cathedral. 'This gloomy depository of the guilt and misery of London', Dickens called it, recalling how as a boy he used to gaze 'with mingled feelings of awe and respect . . . at its rough heavy walls and low massive doors'. Later, as a man, he visited the prison, describing in gruesome detail the exercise yard, the bare, dirty chapel with its special 'condemned pew' for prisoners awaiting execution, and the condemned cell itself. Hangings were regular occurrences, and during his time there Cobbett was much distressed by what his daughter Anne called 'the frequent executions for forgery and other things under his windows. Blinds were drawn down but we heard what was going on. It was very sad, and so often occurred then.'

With no experience of prison life, Cobbett was appalled by his first impressions:

> That part of the prison, to which I was committed, consisted of a yard and divers rooms. The rooms were numerous, the yard about 35 feet by 25 feet. Each room contained, or was intended to contain two, three or more beds. The windows were barred with iron. The walls that surrounded the yard were the sides of houses and of course there could be little sun or air. But the *companions*! What companions had I? Men

guilty of the most odious and contemptible crimes. Swindling, fraud, embezzlement and even those crimes which are too horrid to name but which have been committed by so many within the last two or three years. Here was I sentenced to live for two years amongst felons and men guilty of unnatural crimes and to pay a thousand pounds to the King; aye, to the King at the end of that time.[1]

In point of fact Cobbett had things a good deal better than he described. As a rich prisoner he was soon able to get a room to himself, while a friend, Peter Walker, brought in a bed, chairs, table and bedding. Colonel Bosville gave him £1000, and thanks to the Sheriff Sir Matthew Wood, himself a keen reformer, Cobbett was eventually given the use of the top floor in the house of Mr Newman, the gaoler, consisting of a sitting room and two bedrooms. The rent was twelve guineas a week, with another eight guineas for fees. This meant that his wife Nancy and the children (taking it in turns) could be with him whenever they wished.

The pregnant Nancy, who had accompanied Cobbett to Newgate and seen his dejection when the time came for her to leave, had originally taken lodgings in Skinner Street, near Smithfield – 'so that there she was amidst the rattle of coaches and butchers carts and the noise of cattle, dogs and bawling men: instead of being in a quiet and commodious country house with neighbours and servants and everything about her'. Her baby girl, christened Mary, lived for only three weeks and was buried in St Sepulchre's. Cobbett never forgot this chain of events. If he was indignant about his own treatment, he was filled with fury (and remained so to some extent for the rest of his life) over the distress caused to his family. 'The blow was to be sure a terrible one and O God! how it was felt by those poor children.' He recalled many years later the scene at his home when the family first learned of his imprisonment, and the anger still smoulders on the page:

When the news arrived at Botley, the three boys, one eleven, another nine and the other seven years old were hoeing cabbages in the garden which had been the source of so much delight. When the account of the savage sentence was brought to them, the youngest child could not for some time, be made to understand what a jail was; and when he did, he all in a tremor exclaimed 'Now, I'm sure, William, that papa is not in a place *like that!*' The other, in order to disguise the tears and smother his sobs, fell to work with the hoe, and chopped about like a blind person. This account when it reached me, affected me more, filled me with deeper resentment than any other circumstance . . .[2]

Now, from prison, he wrote to his wife:

My pretty Nancy, you must take the Judge's sentence as you find it in the newspapers and read it to the boys and point out *what it is*. Tell them what to think of it and tell them how good the final consequence will be to us. Put good spirit into them. Make them see my enemies in their true colours and God knows you need do no more. Explain to them *who* and *what* those enemies are, and *why* they are my enemies.[3]

Once he had settled into his Newgate routine Cobbett found that his children were now old enough to be able to help him. The two eldest boys, John and James, aged eleven and nine respectively, could be entrusted with jobs on the farm and with transmitting Cobbett's instructions to his labourers ('They were very little fellows for this,' his daughter Anne commented). 'What a blessing it is to have such healthy and clever and sober and sensible and industrious and dutiful and affectionate children,' he wrote. 'The miserable, malignant, poisonous wretches who hate me have no such children. Their race is rotten in carcase and limbs as well as in heart. They are eaten up with infection from the top of their senseless heads to the bottom of their lazy feet.'

The most helpful of his children, and the closest to him for many years, was his eldest daughter Anne, fifteen at the time of his imprisonment. She was quick-witted and sharp, devoted to her father (whom she called 'the Governor'). 'Very plain but very clever and very charming', according to Mary Russell Mitford, Anne was the only one of his children to inherit something of Cobbett's humour, and the notes she left of the family history are invariably revealing. Even by this stage she was acting as a nanny to the small children as well as her father's amanuensis, taking dictation from him (one assumes that she must have mastered some form of shorthand). As Cobbett composed so quickly and fluently this can have been no easy task. 'He *felt* as he wrote,' she recalled. 'Would look pale with earnestness in the subject, folding his hands which would seem to get thinner and thinner, colder and colder and his voice would falter.'

Thanks to Sheriff Wood Cobbett was soon able to receive delegations from all over England, and a string of visitors including Admiral Cochrane, Major Cartwright and the distinguished judge and mathematician Francis Maseres, who 'always came in his wig and gown to show his abhorrence at the sentence'. Lord Folkestone, another of his aristocratic reformer friends, sent him hares from his estate at Coleshill, near Faringdon in Oxfordshire. Thomas Creevey, the diarist and MP, was another who responded to Cobbett's invitation. 'I give beef stakes [sic] and porter,' Cobbett told him on 24 September 1810. 'I may vary my food to mutton chops, but never vary the drink.'[4] No wonder that the radical Henry 'Orator' Hunt, who himself did two spells in prison, wrote scornfully in his memoirs that Cobbett's imprisonment was 'not much more than living two years in London in lodgings'.

An American visitor to England, Louis Simond, formed a similar impression when he visited Newgate in September 1811 and watched condemned men playing fives against the courtyard wall:

> I enquired for Mr Cobbett expecting to see him among the gentlemen – *Oh! no*, said my turnkey, *he is too great for that*

– Where is he then? Why he is in the governor's house, – I'll show you, – *plenty of money, and that is everything you know.* Then walking farther on the leads, he shewed me a grated door, through which I could see a carpeted room – Mr Cobbett's room. He has the key of the grated door and there-fore, free access to this leaden roof, which is extensive, high, and airy, with a most beautiful view of St. Paul's and over a great part of the city. His family is with him, and he continues to pour out his torrent of abuse as freely as ever, on everything and everybody in turn.[5]

Even so, to a very active man like Cobbett, used to physical work and exercise on his farm, the restrictions of life at Newgate were especially difficult to accept. Anne wrote:

Friends were afraid his health would suffer, the change being so great, but he soon set about pursuing a system of exercising himself. He used to get up at six o'clock, earlier in the height of summer, and go up on the roof of the prison where there were extensive leads, and with a pair of dumb bells go through various, and some violent exercises, military and others; go thro' the motions of digging, raking mowing etc etc with a dumb bell in each hand, come down in a state of perspiration, rest awhile, then wash and shave, with cold water, put on clean linen always and be ready for breakfast at eight o'clock. He was most concerned with his physical fitness and especi-ally with keeping his weight down.

Anne recorded how carefully he dieted. Breakfast was

tea and one penny roll, no meat even. He begun [sic] his imprisonment with *one whiting* and perhaps a little vegetable for his dinner, and nothing else whatever, pastry or cheese sweets he never did like or hold to be wholesome . . . At the end of about two months he begun to have one mutton chop for dinner, but no more. Those of his family who were with him were content to have but one chop also, because they were allowed to make up with pies and puddings. He said that if more than one chop apiece were put on the table before him he might be tempted to exceed bounds and he was so afraid of getting fat and heavy.[6]

The regime must have been effective, as Anne wrote to her uncle Fred on 12 January 1811: 'You never saw him look so well in all your life as he does at present.'[7]

But in the meantime Cobbett had multiple problems to face, what with keeping the *Register* going and also running his farm at long distance. 'I had a farm in hand,' he wrote in 1829.

It was necessary that I should be constantly informed of what was doing. I gave all the orders, whether as to purchase, sales, ploughing, sowing, breeding; in short, with regard to everything, and the things were endless in number and variety, and always full of interest. My eldest son and daughter could now write well and fast. One or the other of them was always at Botley; and I had with me (having hired the best part of the keeper's house) one or two besides either this brother or sister; the mother coming up to town about once in two or three months, leaving the house and children in the care of her sister. We had a HAMPER with a lock and two keys, which came up once a week, or oftener, bringing me fruit and all sorts of country fare . . . This HAMPER which was always, at both ends of the line, looked for with the most lively feelings, became our school. It brought me a Journal of Labours, proceedings and occurrences, written on paper of shape and size uniform, and so contrived, as to margins, to admit of binding. The journal used, when my son was the writer, to be interspersed with drawings of our dogs, colts or anything that he wanted me to have a correct idea of. The hamper brought me plants, bulbs, and the like, that I might see the size of them; and always every one sent his or her most beautiful flowers: the earlier violets, and primroses, and cowslips and blue-bells; the earliest twigs of trees; and in short, everything that they thought calculated to delight me.

When the hamper went back to Botley Cobbett gave the most detailed instructions to his men as to what was to be done on the farm – how much food should be given to the sheep; the exact dimensions of a new gate he wanted made and what wood was to be used. All such things were precisely set out along with general rules – 'Let the horses be well fed so they work.' So many and precise were the orders that the children found it all a strain. 'We carried on the farming during that [sic] two years in Newgate,' Anne wrote, 'and most troublesome and wearisome it was.'

It is clear from the above that Cobbett took a much more detailed day-to-day interest in the running of his farm than he did in running his newspaper. Ever since he sold his house in Duke Street and moved to Botley he had left the whole business of the *Political Register* to John Wright, sending his factotum copy by post or messenger and letting him handle all the administration and accounts. But he now discovered that Wright, like Windham and many of those in whom he trusted, had let him down. Once the news of his prison sentence was made public, Cobbett's creditors descended on him demanding payment, and he was forced for the first time to examine the state of his finances and try to raise some money. He found his affairs in a state of chaos and confusion. Encouraged by the early success of the *Register*, Cobbett had embarked upon a number of ambitious publishing ventures. *Cobbett's Parliamentary Debates*, 'the first attempt to provide a complete report of parliamentary proceedings',[8] was begun in 1803, along with *Cobbett's Parliamentary History in 36 Volumes (1066–1803)*, which was followed in 1809 by another massive compilation, *Cobbett's Complete Collection of State Trials*. These were all costly projects, and the evidence suggests that the books sold slowly and were never successful commercially. But, in his mood of supreme confidence during his early years back in England, Cobbett would seem to have been unaware of this. He left such matters to John Wright, who also helped to edit the volumes whilst he busied himself with farming and planting trees at Botley.

Newgate, Wednesday, January 23. 1811.

My dear Johnny,

You asked Papa the other day, whether he did not think that the Dogs better not be kept in the Stable. I told you a great while ago, that the Dogs should always sleep here at nights. ——— I hope you are all well. ——— As you are so very impatient about your Plans, I will draw them. ——— Why don't you write to me sometimes? I hope you will write to me about how many Birds you have shot.

This is a Plan of you and James shooting Rabbits. James is on his Jack ass, shooting, and you are galloping on the Don Fernando Septimoos.

This is a Plan of you and Jemmy, catching Magpies in the morning. You are up in the Tree, and James is tying the Birds, (Magpies) them up, at the bottom of the tree.

Uncle Tom is coming here next Saturday week; and Mama is going to ask him to get us a Terrier. ——— You and Nancy are coming up here, with Dean, in just 21 days; you will most likely come on the 15. of next month, it being the first day after shooting season.

God bless you.

Papa says you must be kept keep all the Plans   Wm Cobbett.   I send you.
(and bring them up with you.

Now, finding himself short of funds, he decided to sell his share of the book business to his partners (Wright and the publisher John Budd). But when he asked Wright to see the accounts in order to reach a fair price, Wright refused, later claiming that he did not possess them in the first place. Eventually they referred the dispute to an arbitrator, who ruled that Wright should pay Cobbett £6500. But he was unable to do this, and so began a ferocious quarrel between the two men which rumbled on, with accusations and counter-accusations, culminating, in 1820, in a full-scale libel action which Wright brought against Cobbett and which he won, being awarded £1000 in damages.

Having settled the ownership of the *Register* and gained sole control of his paper Cobbett devoted himself for a time to a study of economics which culminated in his book *Paper Against Gold and Glory Against Prosperity* (1815), most of which was reprinted from the *Political Register*. As usual when confronted by any subject he began with the conviction that he could perfectly well master all the facts – as he had done with grammar or gardening – and then explain them in simple terms and numbered paragraphs to his readers, and even to schoolchildren.

His researches into economics had already begun with his study of Paine's 'Decline and Fall of the English System of Finance', the origin of one of his obsessions – the paper money. Until 1797, when the Bank of England was threatened by a panic withdrawal of deposits following rumours of a French invasion, the British currency consisted of gold and silver coinage. After an approach to the government, which had been borrowing heavily since the start of the war in 1793, the Bank now began for the first time to issue notes instead of coins, with the promise to pay the value in gold on demand. Cobbett was to devote thousands and thousands of words to denouncing the new paper money, which he blamed for higher prices. Cobbett and Paine were both right in thinking that an increase in the amount of paper money – which, unlike gold, could be produced in unlimited quantities – would lead to inflation and a depreciation of the value of money. But behind the arguments of both men lay an instinctive, unscientific feeling, which was shared by many people at the time, that with the introduction of paper money a trick had been perpetrated by the government and the Bank. 'I can remember,' Cobbett wrote, 'when the farmers in my county hardly ever saw a bank note . . . people in those days used to carry little bags to put their money in, instead of the pasteboard or leather cases that they now carry.' There had to be something underhand behind the way in which those satisfying gold coins had now been replaced by mere pieces of paper. In spite of his gallant attempt to understand and explain economics, Cobbett, like Paine and many of their contemporaries who felt the same way about paper money, never acknowledged that whether money consisted of gold coins or pieces of paper made little difference. As Professor A.J. Ayer put it in his *Thomas Paine* (1988): 'There are grounds for suspecting that Paine thought of gold and silver as "real" money in a way that paper could never be, ignoring the fact that anything whatever of which there is a sufficient quantity available can serve as a means of exchange so long as those who employ it agree on its legitimacy.'

Behind all these developments lay the enormous cost of the Napoleonic War and the uncertainty that it created – though this was not a connection that Cobbett was too keen to stress, when he himself had so strenuously campaigned for the resumption of hostilities in the period following the Peace of Amiens. The war had already resulted in the introduction of income tax in 1793 and a huge increase in government borrowing. This in turn led to a huge increase in the national debt, originally created in 1694. Even by the start of what was called the Anti-Jacobin War in 1793 the debt already stood at £245 million. Those who lent money to the government had to be paid interest, which meant taxes for the rest. These 'fundholders', or 'tax-eaters' as he dubbed them, became for Cobbett a favourite Aunt

William Cobbett in
1800. Engraved by
Francesco Bartolozzi
after a painting by
J.R. Smith: 'A print by
Bartolozzi conveys a
correct outline of his
person' – Henry Fearon
(see page 144).

Below The house at
Farnham where
Cobbett was born in
March 1763.

Sergeant Major Cobbett gathering evidence against his officers with the help of Corporal Bestland. A portrait of the Irish revolutionary Lord Edward Fitzgerald is on the wall. No. 4 in Gillray's sequence 'The Life of William Cobbett' (see pages 90–1).

The court martial that never was. The three officers are in the dock, but Cobbett is seen (left) sailing away to France. No. 6 in the Gillray sequence.

Above Second Street,
Philadelphia, in about 1790:
'All the streets and houses
resemble each other'
(see page 19).

Right Dr Johnson's friend
William Windham
(1750–1810), Cobbett's early
patron who provided the
funds for the launch of the
Political Register in 1802.

The Westminster election of 1806, as seen by Gillray. James Paull addresses the crowd.
On his left are Cobbett, Burdett and Colonel Bosville. Cobbett's son James praised
Gillray's likeness of his father.

The court of Kings Bench sitting in Westminster Hall. Engraved by J. Black from a painting by Thomas Rowlandson and A.C. Pugin. Cobbett was sentenced here to two years' imprisonment in July 1810.

An execution at Newgate in 1809: 'One distressing thing was the frequent executions . . . under his windows' – Anne Cobbett.

Above Cobbett's daughter Anne (1795–1877). A silhouette made in Philadelphia in 1818: 'Very plain, but very clever and very charming' – Mary Russell Mitford.

Right Mary Russell Mitford (1787–1855), author of *Our Village*.

Above John Cartwright, 'the Major' (1740–1824).

Right Henry 'Orator' Hunt (1773–1835).

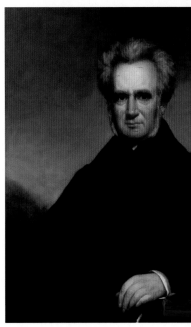

Admiral Lord Cochrane, Earl of
Dundonald (1775–1860).

Francis Place (1771–1854): 'the radical
breeches-maker of Charing Cross'.

Sally. They were *nouveaux-riches* or Jewish (or both), living off unearned income, relying on what the Tory MP Sir William Scott (the brother of Lord Chancellor Lord Eldon and later to become Lord Stowell) called, in a famous phrase, the 'elegant simplicity of the three per cents'.

Cobbett had little idea of the nature or purpose of banking, and disapproved of lending money at interest – it was one reason why he sympathised with the Catholic Church, which in its early days at least had condemned usury as sinful. He was to spend a lifetime calling on the government to reduce or cancel altogether the payment of interest: 'As to this National *Debt*, as it is called, it is just and proper never to pay another farthing of interest upon it, if the good of the whole nation, taking one part into another, require a cessation of such payment. The Fundholder is not to be thought of for a moment, if the prosperity and happiness of the Nation demand that the interest should no longer be paid. What a monstrous idea, that a Nation is to be bound to its ruin by individuals.'

The error Cobbett made was to conclude that the ever-increasing national debt would sooner or later become so great that it would bring about a collapse of the economic system, whereas so long as it was serviced, there was no reason why it should not continue to grow, as it has done to this day. But Cobbett clung to his belief that people had only to wait a little while and, thanks to the national debt, 'The Thing' would disintegrate of its own accord.

Cobbett's imprisonment in Newgate coincided with the beginning of a period of industrial unrest in England that was to last for twenty or thirty years. It saw in 1811 the introduction of a new word – 'Luddites'. The traditional view of these wreckers of machinery, who acted in the name of a mythical figure called Ned Ludd, or King Ludd, is that they were rebelling against the Industrial Revolution which threatened their jobs. That is only partly true, because machine-breaking had been going on intermittently throughout the eighteenth century, and had become for factory workers in the days before organised trades unions the only means of asserting their power in the hope of improving pay and conditions. What was new was the frequency and ferocity of the attacks on machines, which involved not only workers but, conveniently for the authorities, a large purely criminal element. The word 'Luddism' was first used in December 1811 in Nottingham, centre of the hosiery and lace industry and the scene of the first outbreaks of violence, which spread to the wool and cotton industries of Yorkshire and Lancashire. Lacking any sophisticated knowledge of economics beyond the *'laisser-faire'* approach of Adam Smith, the government and its subsidised press had only one remedy for the riots – violent repression. All the old fears of Jacobinism revived, and persuading itself that widespread revolution was imminent, the Tory government led by Spencer Perceval introduced a number of panic measures. Early in 1812 an Act making machine-breaking a capital offence was passed, inspiring one of Lord Byron's very occasional speeches in the House of Lords. Magistrates were given new powers to search for arms, and there was a series of arrests and executions.

For all these repressive measures the government had the full support of the subsidised press, which called for the suspension of Habeas Corpus and the introduction of martial law. 'While these things were going on in parliament,' Cobbett reported, 'the venal press was not idle, especially the newspapers called The *Times* and The *Courier* . . . the former of these prints began to announce that it wished to see the rioters "put out of the protection of the law" alleging, as a reason that they were become *assassins* and *incendiaries*. But even assassins and incendiaries have hitherto had the *law* applied to their case. I do not know why the word assassin is now so much in use. It seems that there are people who think it more horrible in its sound than the word murder.'[9]

Cobbett, as it happened, was strongly opposed to machine-breaking, arguing that machinery could increase economic prosperity. But this did not stop the government from blaming him and his fellow reformers for the industrial unrest. The view became widespread that an organised conspiracy was afoot, and that Cobbett was playing a central role in fanning the flames. As he wrote to his friend and fellow reformer 'Orator' Hunt at a later stage, 'They sigh for a PLOT. Oh, how they sigh! They are working and slaving and fretting and stewing: they are sweating all over; they are absolutely pining and dying for a plot!'

In the middle of this crisis an extraordinary event occurred which only helped to make things worse. On 11 May 1812, as he entered the House of Commons, Spencer Perceval was shot dead by one John Bellingham, a man who for some years had been claiming compensation from the government for the fact that he had been imprisoned for debt when working in Russia. Such a person, who sees a government conspiracy behind his personal troubles and to whom every rebuff is only further evidence of the plot, is a familiar figure to any politician or journalist. Bellingham had no political affiliations, but his act of murder coming at a time of widespread alarm about a possible revolution inevitably caused something of a panic in Parliament. The Speaker blocked the door to the House of Commons whilst MPs hurriedly passed a motion calling on the Prince of Wales, who because of his father George III's incapacity was acting as Regent, to prosecute the murderer without delay. In the meantime a huge and hostile crowd had collected outside Westminster, Horse Guards were summoned and Bellingham was eventually conveyed to Newgate at one o'clock in the morning. Thus was Cobbett placed in the extraordinary situation of being imprisoned in the same gaol as Perceval's murderer – 'into which I had been put in consequence of a prosecution ordered by this very Perceval'.

Cobbett thoroughly disapproved of acts of political violence, but he was always impressed by, and ready to praise, the courage and dignity with which the revolutionaries of his day, like the Cato Street conspirators of 1819 (see pages 174–6), went to their death on the gallows:

> Nothing ever heard of in man can exceed the calmness with which BELLINGHAM met his fate. He committed the deed on the Monday and was tried on the Friday and was executed the next Monday morning at eight o'clock. He wrote to his wife on the Sunday night, a letter in which he spoke in the greatest calmness of her and his children: told her that he sent her his watch and his prayer-book, and prayed GOD to preserve her and her children. After writing this letter he went to sleep as if nothing extraordinary was expected in the morning . . .
>
> The crowd was assembled in the open space just under the window at which I stood. I saw the anxious looks; I saw the half-horrified countenances: I saw the mournful tears run down. What, then, were these tears shed, and these blessings bestowed by Englishmen upon a murderer! He was a *murderer*, to be sure; the act was unjustifiable . . . but the people did not rejoice because a murder had been committed; they did not shed tears for and bless BELLINGHAM because he had committed a murder; but because his act, clearly wicked as it was in itself, had ridded them of one whom they looked upon as the leader amongst those whom they thought totally bent on the destruction of their liberties.[10]

Cobbett was released from Newgate on 9 July 1812. His two years in prison had altered him, as they were bound to do. The iron had entered into his soul. Miss Mitford wrote that 'his temper was soured and his heart cankered by the imprisonment'. Although his political views had radically changed, he had always remained fiercely patriotic and proud of the fact that he had defended his country in America and that that country, in the person of Pitt, Windham and others, had honoured him for it. That the political establishment of which, until recently, he had fancied himself a part had rewarded him with imprisonment, that the likes of William Wilberforce had done nothing to

defend him, rankled. His daughter Anne recorded that, before Newgate, Cobbett was seldom cross or impatient with her. 'Papa's health
did not suffer in prison, but his temper did. He left it an altered man
in many respects. Miss Mitford says truly that he never talked politics
in society, never broached them at least. After Newgate he talked of
little else. He was so angry at being so ill-used.' Cobbett himself
acknowledged the change: 'Had it not been for the treatment I received
in 1810,' he wrote some years later, 'I might have become comparatively indolent. Easy circumstances, a love of country-life and an
attention turned to other objects might, possibly, have prevented the
birth of the *Cheap Register* [see page 124]. But the imprisonment, the
fine, the seven years recognizances to be of good behaviour and
especially the conduct of Perceval and Gibbs: these demanded *a life*
of exertion.' He wrote elsewhere that though he had previously been
in the habit of drinking wine, after Newgate he confined himself to
beer. 'My hatred of the Borough Villains,' he wrote, 'and my anxious
desire to assist in the infliction of vengeance on them has made me
more and more rigid as to sobriety and abstemiousness.'

One consequence of the government's treatment of him was to
encourage Cobbett to identify more and more not just with the
reformers like Burdett but with the common people – 'those who do
the work and fight the battles'. And he was to be made aware of the
enormous support he had immediately on leaving prison. On the day
of his release a celebration dinner was held at the Crown and Anchor
tavern in the Strand, attended by about six hundred people. Toasts
were drunk, including one to 'The people, the source of all power',
and speeches were made by Cobbett himself and the Chairman, Sir
Francis Burdett. The following day he set off for Botley with Anne,
who later described their progress in a letter to her soldier uncle
Lieutenant Frederick Reid:

> We got to Bagshot about ten o'clock on Friday evening, where
> we slept, and the next morning left it about six o'clock, and

breakfasted at Alton, the bells rang a merry peal as we entered the town and continued to ring about an hour. We proceeded from Alton to Alresford, and thence to Winchester, where we arrived about one. About five minutes after we got there, Mama came in a post-chaise with all the children. After staying there a little while, Mama returned home with her three daughters, leaving the three boys to come home with Papa after the dinner. Parson Baker refused the keys of the church so that the people could not ring the bells which they minded very much to do. However they sufficiently testified their respect to Papa, and their pleasure at his return, without the assistance of the church. For a party of young men accompanied by a band of music which they had hired themselves for the purpose met him about a mile out of Botley . . . where they insisted upon taking the horses out of the carriage, and with colours flying, and the band of music marching before him, they brought him into Botley . . . Mama had ordered four hogsheads of ale at each of the public houses.

After the celebrations were over Cobbett had to confront his personal finances. He had been paying heavily for his privileged accommodation in prison, he had had to pay the £1000 fine, and he was heavily indebted to Sir Francis Burdett, who had lent him about £2000. Faced with this situation, he decided to sell his Botley mansion and rent a small house nearby from a neighbour, General Sir James Kempt. After two years shut up in London he was keen to resume his country life, and was delighted to find that the new house came with 'the best gardens in the country . . . I never sat myself down in any spot in my whole life without causing fruit and flowers and trees (if there was time) and all the beauties of vegetation to rise up around me.' General Kempt's house had nearly three quarters of a mile of high walls, and Cobbett was soon planting peaches, nectarines, apricots, plums, cherries, peas and apples. He was especially proud of his success with the vine, as well as growing 'as great a weight of melons as was grown in any 20 gentlemen's gardens in the country'.[11]

In Anne's opinion, however, her father made a mistake in settling at Botley again. She thought he should never have gone back: 'It was an unfortunate choice of a place for him at the first. Surrounded by Nabobs from India, and there being no small gentry except Army or Navy people. And there were Dock Yards and Barrack Departments close by us and whole hosts of people depending upon Court favour. It was like getting into a hornets nest.'

It was almost inevitable that Cobbett would involve himself in the traditional English country pursuit of quarrelling with the vicar. The Reverend Richard Baker, vicar of Botley from 1793 to 1847, had started out on good terms with Cobbett, who was a regular churchgoer along with his family. But Baker annoyed Cobbett first by selling him a bale of straw that turned out to be rotten, and then by preaching political anti-reform sermons which so angered Cobbett that he told the vicar that he 'longed to horsewhip him in public for talking such nonsense'. Cobbett's revenge was more effective – to turn this obscure cleric through his writings into a national figure of fun, whom he regularly ridiculed alongside the likes of Canning or Wilberforce. In *Rural Rides* he tells the story of how the Botley villagers once played a cruel trick on their vicar by persuading him that he had been left a legacy in London. Baker was so impatient to get to the capital that he rode on horseback all the way, and found when he got there that he was besieged by 'a whole tribe of applicants, wet-nurses, dry-nurses, lawyers with deeds of conveyance for borrowed money, curates in want of churches, coffin-makers, travelling companions, ladies-maids, dealers in Yorkshire hams, Newcastle coal, and dried night-soil from Islington'. When he managed to escape and return to Botley he found the village plastered with handbills offering a £500 reward for information regarding the hoaxers. Cobbett was delighted that Baker held him responsible for the whole thing, though he swore he had had nothing to do with it.

Cobbett's financial situation was not helped by his decision, on leaving Newgate, to give up the proprietorship of the *Register* in order to safeguard his position in case of further libel actions. As things stood he had had to provide £5000 surety for his good behaviour for the seven years following his release from prison. He got round this by filling the *Register* with asterisks, leaving the reader to supply his own offensive words. As it was, much of the paper was devoted to the events of the final stages of the Napoleonic War.

Apart from military matters Cobbett resumed his interest at this juncture in the story of the Princess Regent, later Queen Caroline – a long-running drama, farcical in most aspects, but one which was to assume great importance in the history of English radicalism, and in which Cobbett was to play a major role. The dissolute Prince of Wales (later Regent and later still George IV) had married his first cousin Princess Caroline of Brunswick in 1795, mainly as a means of getting his father, who desperately wanted an heir by the direct line, to pay off his very considerable debts. A daughter, Charlotte, was born nine months later, by which time the Princess had discovered that George had already been married to a Catholic widow, Mrs Fitzherbert, and had a mistress, Lady Jersey. Immediately after the birth of his daughter the Prince turned his wife out of his home at Carlton House, keeping the child with him and trying to deny Caroline access to her. It was only thanks to the intervention of George III that she was allowed to have contact with her daughter.

In 1806, following rumours that she had given birth to an illegitimate child, the King ordered the setting up of the so-called 'delicate investigation' into the charge, and for several weeks members of the House of Lords sat in secret session listening to all kinds of evidence about the Princess's private life from many witnesses including her servants. They concluded that there was no truth in the story of the child, but censured the Princess for frivolous conduct. Their report however was not published, though a few copies circulated privately and rumours were plentiful. Because the Princess was excluded from court the accepted opinion was that she must be the guilty party (Cobbett himself admitted that to begin with this was his own personal view). But with very definite ideas about a man's duties to his wife, Cobbett now took up the Princess's cause, persuading himself that in addition to being the victim of injustice she was also a woman of uncommon beauty, intelligence and virtue (none of which was unfortunately the case). He became convinced that the reason the Prince had allowed the Tories under 'the little pale-faced lawyer' Perceval to remain in office was that Perceval, who in his legal capacity had advised the Princess during the 'delicate investigation' but later quarrelled with her, was using his knowledge of the report (or 'The Book', as it was called) in effect to blackmail the Prince. (Though Perceval's biographer Denis Gray dismisses the theory as 'absurd', it seems clear that the Prince would have been most anxious to prevent publication by all means possible, and that keeping Perceval happy was an obvious way of doing this.)

In 1810, when Cobbett began his prison sentence, it was finally accepted by all concerned that George III would never recover his sanity, and his son Prince George was appointed Prince Regent. The Prince, who had once been an arbiter of fashion, had become fat, debauched and greedy. The Princess, who had been living quietly at Blackheath in the interim, now revived her campaign, demanding that she should be given the title Princess Regent and be allowed to hold receptions on a par with her husband. But in exchanges with ministers and the Privy Council she had been rebuffed. Cobbett had procured a copy of The Book whilst in Newgate, and realised it could not only damage the Prince but advance the case of reform, as showing once again the corrupt practices of the establishment. The important thing was to see it published: 'We wanted the exposure,' he wrote later, 'in the first place, from a love of justice, from a desire to see this injured lady righted: and in the next place for the purpose of making the people see what deeds this government was capable of.'

There could be no question of publishing anything in the *Register*. Not only was he bound to be of good behaviour, Cobbett was well aware of the libel risks when writing of the Prince Regent. Only recently, in December 1812, the critic Leigh Hunt and his brother John had been successfully prosecuted for libelling the Prince, whom they described in their *Examiner*, *inter alia*, as 'a libertine over head and ears in disgrace, a despiser of domestic ties . . . a man who has just closed half a century without one single claim on the gratitude of his country or the respect of posterity'. Cobbett would have shared this view, but having only recently been released from prison, he was not going to run the risk again. (Even after publication of The Book, when giving his account of the story he was careful to put the blame for what happened on the Prince's 'advisers' rather than the Prince himself).

Like many journalists since, Cobbett realised that the best way of getting round the libel laws was to persuade a Member of Parliament to raise the issue under the cloak of parliamentary privilege. He found an ally in the uncle of his great friend Admiral Cochrane. Like his nephew, Andrew Cochrane Johnstone was an MP, and the black sheep of the family. On what he later described as the proudest day of his life, Cochrane Johnstone stated the facts of the case and called for a full inquiry by the House. Ten days later The Book was published.

The next thing was to organise a public demonstration in London in support of Princess Caroline. Cobbett approached Sir Francis Burdett as the ideal person to head a delegation to present an address to the Princess, but to his annoyance Burdett, who like many radicals was beginning to move to the right as he got older, refused to be involved. He particularly irritated Cobbett by remarking that the Princess would never receive her just deserts, that the only thing she could do was 'to endure patiently and then "like the anvil she would outlive the hostility of the hammer"'. Cobbett never forgot this image, and it is probably from that moment that his feelings began to cool towards the man he later called, when describing this incident, 'our slow-blooded and suddenly-become prudent baronet'.

Eventually Cobbett's friend Alderman Matthew Wood, the man who had secured him decent accommodation in Newgate, agreed to organise the petition, and a humble address from the Lord Mayor, Aldermen and Livery of the City of London was drawn up commending Caroline for her 'forbearance . . . frankness and magnanimity' and assuring her of the City's loyalty. A procession of a hundred carriages was formed and set out for Kensington Palace watched by cheering crowds. The Lord Mayor, described by Cobbett as 'a poor creature', refused to take the procession via the Prince Regent's home at Carlton House in the Mall, but on the way back the other carriages broke away to Carlton House, 'opposite which the people groaned, hissed and uttered expressions of disapprobation'.

Cobbett did not take part in this extraordinary demonstration, preferring to remain at Botley tending his vines. Nor did he stir himself when a few months later Napoleon surrendered and was imprisoned on Elba. 'Papa angry, tormented', Anne noted. He observed the nationwide celebrations with a jaundiced eye:

> balls, plays, masquerades, illuminations, processions from the solemn and gawdy buffoonery of the freemasons down to the little ragged children at the Lancashire schools . . . Oxen were roasted whole: and it was a miserable town that did not roast whole one or more sheep. These animals were led to the slaughter in the true heathen style; decorated with orange ribands in sign of the triumph of the Dutch; white ribands in sign of the triumph of the Bourbons; and the whole always surmounted by the triumphant British flag, while the tri-coloured flag reversed, was placed under it. Upwards of two hundred oxen were roasted whole and upwards of two thousand sheep. One boundless scene of extravagance and waste, and idleness and dissipation pervaded the whole Kingdom, the people appeared to be all raving drunk, all raving mad.[12]

Those who had opposed the war or advocated making peace with Napoleon were now mocked. 'In its fit of drunken joy the nation in general laughed at me,' Cobbett wrote. The victory over Napoleon, to be finally established at Waterloo on 18 June 1815, seemed to confirm the status quo and strengthen the government's position – 'while everlasting taunts were poured out upon reformers, who were now spoken of as a race become obsolete'. But this complacent mood did not last long. As always seems to happen, economic depression followed the end of war. Conditions were especially bad on the land, where prices plummeted and thousands of farmers, unable to keep up their mortgage payments, were ruined. In the industrial Midlands and north unemployment was rife. There was renewed sabotage by Luddites in the Midlands in spite of the executions and transportations that had followed the initial attacks on machinery. The notorious Corn Law of 1815, introduced to maintain the high price of corn and prevent cheap foreign imports, only increased the hardship of the labouring man. Rioting and rick-burning took place in many southern counties, followed by arrests and hangings.

Against this background of riot and unrest Cobbett took a momen-tous decision – to reduce the price of his *Register* to 2d and address it directly to the working people. As things stood, the paper cost one shilling and a halfpenny, and if the workers read it (or, many being illiterate, had it read to them) they had to combine their money to buy a copy between them. Most of the poorest readers listened to the *Register* being read to them in pubs, but landlords were becoming increasingly worried about their licences being withdrawn for allowing these readings on their premises.

It was Admiral Cochrane, now living only a few miles away from Cobbett at Hamble, who was responsible for the move. Cochrane had only recently completed a prison sentence after being found guilty by Cobbett's old adversary Lord Ellenborough of complicity in a stock-exchange fraud when a group of speculators, including his unscrupulous uncle Cochrane Johnstone, had contrived to make a killing on a false report of Napoleon's death. The case against Cochrane, almost certainly trumped up, had done nothing to temper his radical zeal. He now urged Cobbett to write a cheap popular appeal setting out the case for reform whilst deploring acts of violence and machine-breaking. The Admiral, Cobbett wrote,

> was of opinion that it was in *my power* to effect this desirable purpose by writing an essay on the subject. But, though I had a strong desire to do it, I was aware that the high price of the Register, though it had not prevented it from being *more* read than any other publication, still, it prevented it from being so generally read as would be necessary to put the people right upon this important subject. Hence came the observation from one of us (I forget which), that if, for this one time, for this particular purpose, the price could be by some means or other, reduced to *twopence*, then the desired effect could be produced at once. I said, before we parted, that this should be done.

The *Political Register* at this time consisted of a twelve-page newspaper of solid text – no illustrations – most of it comprised of a long leading article by Cobbett, often in the form of an open letter to a particular politician, to which might be added letters to the editor, news items reprinted from other papers, advertisements for Cobbett's books, etc. On 3 November 1816 Cobbett issued alongside this conventional *Register* a cheap edition on a single sheet consisting only of his leading article and costing a mere 2d, which thus avoided the newspaper tax. The first issue was called 'Address to the Journeymen and Labourers', and in it he spoke to the working people directly for the first time. It opened with a verbal fanfare:

> FRIENDS AND FELLOW COUNTRYMEN
> Whatever the pride of rank, of riches or of scholarship may have induced some men to believe, or to affect to believe, the real strengths and all the resources of a country, ever have

sprung and ever must spring from the *labour* of its people; and hence it is, that this nation which is so small in numbers and so poor in climate and soil compared with many others, has, for many ages, been the most powerful nation in the world: it is the most industrious, the most laborious and therefore the most powerful. Elegant dresses, superb furniture, stately buildings, fine roads and canals, fleet horses and carriages, numerous and stout ships, warehouses teeming with goods; all these, and many other objects that fall under our view, are so many marks of national wealth and resources. But all these spring from *labour*. Without the journeyman and the labourers none of them could exist; without the assistance of their hands, the country would be a wilderness hardly worth the notice of an invader.

As well as rehearsing, once again, the arguments in favour of reform of Parliament, Cobbett took a swipe at those economists, particularly the Reverend Thomas Malthus, who believed that the country's difficulties arose from surplus population among the lower classes, that 'they are themselves the cause of their own poverty', and that 'the means of redress are in their hands'. Malthus urged the poor not to get married when they were young, and to refrain from what he called 'irregular gratifications'. Cobbett's fierce denunciation of Malthus, which he kept up till his dying day, sprang from his natural aversion to parsons and his objection to all forms of birth control (particularly when urged on the lower orders by an economist). His political instinct, as so often, was right, because it was Malthus's theory about overpopulation which underpinned the disastrous economic policies, or lack of them, of successive governments. According to Malthus, the human population was growing at such a rate that there was not sufficient food to support it. The Home Secretary Lord Sidmouth himself said, 'Man cannot create abundance where providence has inflicted scarcity.'[13] The only ways to deal with the problem were either emigration or discouraging the 'lower orders' from breeding. In the meantime something could be done to ameliorate the situation by the promotion of a cheaper diet (a 'coarser food'), especially in the form of potatoes. In this way Malthus provided ministers with a convenient all-purpose excuse for doing nothing – there were just too many mouths for the country to feed.

Cobbett, who had agreed with Malthus in his youth, now adopted him as a favourite bugbear, on a par with William Wilberforce, whom he regularly accused of campaigning for Negro slaves whilst ignoring the sufferings of his fellow countrymen – what Dickens would call 'telescopic philanthropy'. 'It is a disgrace to the country,' Cobbett wrote in his 'Address to the Journeymen and Labourers', 'that men should be found in it capable of putting ideas so insolent on paper. So then, a young man, arm in arm with a rosy cheeked girl must be a spectacle of evil omen!'

The 'Address to the Journeymen and Labourers' was a phenomenal success. By the end of November 1816, 44,000 copies had been sold; 200,000 by the end of 1817. E.P. Thompson in his classic book *The Making of the English Working Class* (1963) states that no writing had attained such popular influence since Paine's *Rights of Man* (1791–92). A contemporary source, the working-class agitator Samuel Bamford, wrote in his *Passages in the Life of a Radical* (1840): 'At this time the writings of William Cobbett suddenly became of great authority: they were read on nearly every cottage hearth in the manufacturing districts of South Lancashire, in those of Leicester, Derby and Nottingham, also in many of the Scottish manufacturing towns. Their influence was speedily visible; he directed his readers to the true cause of their sufferings – misgovernment; and to its proper corrective Parliamentary Reform. Riots soon became scarce and from that time they never obtained their ancient vogue with the labourers of this country.'

Bamford was right. For all its colourful language the 'Address' was in no way a revolutionary tract like Paine's *Rights of Man*. On the contrary, it urged the workers to support the cause of reform by non-violent means – by attending meetings or sending petitions to Parliament: 'I exhort you to proceed in a peaceable and lawful manner, but at the same time, to proceed with zeal and resolution in the attainment of this object. If the *Skulkers* will not join you, if the "decent fireside" gentry still keep aloof, proceed by yourselves. Any man can draw up a petition, and any man can carry it up to London.'

Cobbett's original plan was that the cheap *Register* would be a one-off, but such was its extraordinary success that he decided to continue with what the *Courier* had referred to as 'Twopenny Trash' (a title he later adopted himself). Leaving his family at Botley, he took lodgings at 8 Catherine Street off the Strand to superintend the major operation of distributing so many thousands of copies. As an unstamped periodical, the 2d *Register* could not be sent through the post. Copies were despatched all over the country by coach and shopkeepers were invited to sell it on commission. 'I wish again to impress it upon the Friends of Reform,' Cobbett wrote,

> that if they think that their publications tend to advance the interest of the country, the most *effectual* way in which *they* can promote the circulation, is by their carrying a few of the Numbers to Booksellers or any *other persons* in the *towns* and *villages* and *pointing out to them the way to go to work to obtain a regular supply*. With every parcel which goes to the country in future there will be sent a *placard* to be put up at the windows of the retailer in order to let the public know that *Register*s are to be had at that house – If a man in any little town, or in a village sell 50 copies a week, why that sale gives him about *five pounds a year clear money*; and where is he to get his five pounds a year for doing really nothing but receiving and paying the money? If, in this way, many of the Provincial Papers are lowered in their sale, do not their publishers deserve it? They, for the far greater part, convey no instruction to the people. They are either '*blind guides*' or no guides at all. They are some of them tools of corruption

and some of them 'dumb dogs' that have not the courage to take the part either of right or wrong. They are neither one thing nor the other; they are quite vapid; and therefore will the public 'spew them out of their mouths'.

It was a sign of the short-sightedness of Sidmouth and his colleagues that they should have interpreted the 'Address to the Journeymen and Labourers' as a dangerous and subversive publication when it was the precise opposite – a plea to the workers to abandon violent methods (an aim in which, according to Cobbett, it had been successful). Faced once again with what they wrongly perceived to be a threat, ministers used exactly the same tactics that had been tried before and that had failed before. They started with an attempt to 'write him down', and when that did not succeed they resorted to law. Following the issue of the 2d *Register* in the autumn of 1816 *The Times* published a four-column attack on Cobbett, and this was later reprinted as a pamphlet and widely circulated. Another instance of 'writing down' consisted of a pamphlet called 'Anti-Cobbett', eight issues of which were issued in the course of 1817 and which were advertised and circulated at a cost to the government, so Cobbett estimated, of £20,000.

Once again, as in 1809, the burden of the attack lay in extensive quotations from Cobbett's *Porcupine* writings in America, in which he abused Paine and the reformers. These showed, said the anonymous writer, that 'he had always been a shifter and a shuffler. You could never hold him any more than you could an eel.' The message was coupled with the traditional attempts to portray the reformers like Cobbett as deliberately fomenting sedition, 'their aim being to advocate the course of Revolution under the specious name of Reform'. *The Times* revived the story of Cobbett's aborted attempt to avoid imprisonment in 1810 by closing down the *Register*.

Cobbett writes that he was informed that the 'Anti-Cobbett' pamphlets were the work of his old enemy George Canning, William

Gifford, the editor of the *Quarterly Review*, a sour little man who in 1821 would be credited with writing the savage review of Keats's *Endymion* which was supposed to hasten the poet's death, and Robert Southey, the Poet Laureate, a prolific writer who had been a radical in his youth but was by now an extreme reactionary. Whoever the authors were, they were certainly no match for Cobbett when it came to writing for the labourers and journeymen, and after only eight issues the 'Anti-Cobbett' fizzled out.

Apart from the 'writing down', strenuous efforts were made by the authorities to stop the cheap *Register* being sold to the public. The message was clearly stated in *The Times* of 3 January 1817: 'It is a great evil of the present day, that such is the poverty of the more humble classes of the community – so that if they do read, or know anything of public affairs, it must be in the cheaper forms: and hence they become the dupes, to a certain extent, of the basest and most profligate of men' (i.e. Cobbett). The 'Anti-Cobbett' pamphlets were nationally distributed and sold without any difficulties, but Cobbett's salesmen were frequently arrested and fined. A Warrington bookseller whose house was found to contain a number of papers including the *Political Register* was imprisoned in irons, while two men who were arrested under the Vagrancy Act in Shropshire for selling the *Register* were ordered to be 'well flogged at the whipping post' by the magistrate the Reverend Townsend Forester, vicar of Brosely-on-Severn.[14]

The advent of the 2d *Register* coincided with the emergence as a radical leader of Henry Hunt, known as 'Orator' Hunt for the power of his public speaking. He was a Wiltshire farmer who had been friendly with Cobbett for some years. Hunt, who once made almost identical boasts to Cobbett's about farming – 'there being no part that I have not performed with my own hands' – had corresponded with him about politics and agricultural matters such as root crops and mouse poison. 'Those who oppose you,' Cobbett wrote to him in 1812, 'little imagine how much more happy you would be upon your farm if your duty did not call you from it,' a sentiment as familiar to Cobbett as to his friend. While Cobbett was busily advocating reform in print, Hunt addressed crowds all over the country, including three huge outdoor meetings at Spa Fields in Clerkenwell, north London, during the last months of 1816. These alarmed the government as much as Cobbett's 'Twopenny Trash', and here too an attempt was made to blacken Hunt as a dangerous revolutionary; but on Cobbett's advice he was very careful to avoid any incitement to violence in his speeches, many passages of which echoed Cobbett's own. (Cobbett pooh-poohed the hysteria about Hunt, who he once said was 'as inoffensive as Pistol or Bardolph'.)

'We want no tumults, no riots,' Hunt, again echoing Cobbett, told another huge meeting in December in Bristol, a town infested by the government's troops and special constables. 'The partisans of corruption want a Plot – they would give any thing for a Plot – but we shall disappoint them. Let them surround us with their cavalry and artillery . . . we will oppose them with the artillery of truth, reason and justice.' In spite of Hunt's assurances, tumults and riots had however occurred in the wake of the Spa Fields meeting. On 2 December 1816 a large body of men broke away from the main crowd and began looting gunsmiths' shops, and there were several hours of rioting in the Minories and one (accidental) killing.

Reports of the riots threw the reform movement into confusion. Burdett, who, as his biographer reiterates, disapproved already of the 'vulgarity' of Cobbett and Hunt, deliberately absented himself from a mass meeting of Major Cartwright's Hampden Clubs convened at the Crown and Anchor on 22 January 1817 to gather together petitions from all over the country for presentation to Parliament. One of those attending was Samuel Bamford, a weaver from Middleton, Lancashire, who in his *Passages in the Life of a Radical* gives vivid snapshots of the main participants gathered in 'the large hall wonderfully grand for a tavern', Major Cartwright 'in his long brown surtout and plain brown wig seating himself placidly in the head seat' while Cobbett stood near his right hand:

> Had I met him anywhere save in that room and on that occasion, I should have taken him for a gentleman farming his own broad estate. He seemed to have that kind of self-possession and ease about him, together with a certain bantering jollity, which are so natural to fast-handed and well-housed lords of the soil. He was, I should suppose, not less than six feet in height; portly, with a fresh, clear and round cheek, and a small grey eye, twinkling with good-humoured archness. He was dressed in a blue coat, yellow swansdown waistcoat, drab kersey small-clothes, and top boots. His hair was grey, and his cravat and linen were fine and very white.

(Anne Cobbett later recorded: 'However dirty and shabby his outer garments might be, he was particular about linen.')

Then, on 28 January 1817, the day of the opening of Parliament, a mass petition for reform bearing as many as a million signatures was taken to Westminster by Admiral Cochrane along with a crowd of about twenty thousand people. The same day the government was given what it took to be timely proof of the 'plot' when the Prince Regent was attacked in his coach while returning from the state opening. It was reported that he had been shot at, but no one was arrested and no bullets were found. Cobbett later claimed that the attack was deliberately staged to create a panic – not wholly improbable, given the government's employment at this period of an army of spies and *agents provocateurs*.

The attack on the Regent was the cue for a patriotic backlash and some extraordinary scenes. Cobbett was witness to one such when he attended a meeting in Winchester in March with Orator Hunt and Admiral Cochrane, at which a loyal address to the Prince was proposed by a gathering of local grandees. The Admiral put forward an amendment to the address, to insert after the word 'constitution' the

words 'as established by Magna Carta the Bill of Rights and Habeas
Corpus for which our forefathers fought and bled'. When he began
to speak he found himself attacked by a group of Hampshire parsons.
Cobbett wrote:

> In them I saw a band of more complete blackguards than I
> ever before saw in all my life. I then saw Parson Baines of
> Exton standing up in his chair and actually spitting in Lord
> Cochrane's poll, while the latter was bending his neck out to
> speak. Lord Cochrane looked round and said 'By G— Sir, if
> you do that again I'll knock you down.' 'You be d—d' said
> Baines 'I'll spit where I like'. Lord Cochrane struck at him.
> Baines jumped down, put his two hands to his mouth in a
> huntsman-like way and cried 'Whoop! Whoop!' till he was
> actually black in the face. One of them trampled upon my
> heel as I was speaking. I looked round and begged him to
> leave off. 'You be d—d' said he 'you be d—d, Jacobin.' He
> then tried to press on me, to stifle my voice, till I clapped my
> elbow into his ribs and made 'the spiritual person' hiccup.
> There were about twenty of them mounted upon a large
> table in the room: and there they jumped, stamped, hallooed,
> roared, thumped with canes and umbrellas, squalled, whistled
> and made all sorts of noises. As Lord Cochrane and I were
> going back to London, he said that, so many years as he had
> been in the navy, he never had seen a band of such complete
> blackguards.

Whatever the truth about the attack on the Prince Regent, the government, already panicked by the success of the 2d *Register* and the
Spa Fields meetings, appointed two secret committees which quickly
produced reports confirming the existence of not just one plot, but
several. The plotters' aim, they reported, was 'to infect the minds of
all classes of the community, and particularly of those whose situation
most exposes them to such impressions with a spirit of discontent and
disaffection, of insubordination and contempt of all law, religion and
morality, and to hold out to them the plunder and division of all

property, as the main object of their efforts, and the restoration of their natural rights; and no endeavours are omitted to prepare them to take up arms on the first signal for accomplishing these designs'.

The result was the passing of a Bill suspending Habeas Corpus and declaring public meetings illegal unless authorised by a magistrate – the so-called 'Gagging Act'. Although there was alarm at the much-exaggerated reports of insurrection, behind it lay a more potent fear of the radical press, and especially *Cobbett's Register*. Wilberforce, who had been a member of the House of Commons Secret Committee, was so alarmed that he urged his family to 'pray in earnest against sedition, privy conspiracy and rebellion'. Orator Hunt, he wrote, 'is a foolish, mischief-making fellow, but no conspirator, though the tool of worse and deeper villains. Cobbett is the most pernicious of all.'

Events had followed the same sequence as in 1809, and after Newgate Cobbett could be fairly sure of what was coming next. Only this time there might not even be a trial. Imprisonment was inevitable. But before that there came, once again, the possibility of a deal: 'A proposition to see Lord Sidmouth and to retire to my estate with a compensation for the loss of income from my writings.' Later, in 1830, Cobbett wrote: 'If I had a mind to touch the public money I might have remained in safety and with ten thousand pounds in my pocket: or at least such an offer was made to me, by a gentleman whose word and authority I firmly believed. The sole condition was *future silence*.' Whatever the temptation, Cobbett felt that life was 'scarcely worth preserving with the consciousness that I walked about my fields, or slept in my bed merely at the mercy of a Secretary of State'.

But in the meantime Cobbett and Hunt had made approaches to the Whigs in the persons of Lords Grey and Holland to form some kind of alliance against the Tories, an idea which, according to Holland, originated with Lord Cochrane. Lord Holland, nephew of Charles James Fox, was a kindly, avuncular figure of liberal instincts who occupied a key position in the Whig hierarchy. He had an interview with Cobbett to discuss the idea, and although he was impressed – 'his upright figure indicated the drill of a soldier, his ruddy complexion and homely accent the subsequent character of a farmer' – he prudently declined to take things further. 'Cobbett,' he wrote, 'was alarmed at the threatened suspension of the Habeas Corpus. He very unaffectedly acknowledged his distrust of his own nerves, and a dread of behaving meanly and basely if arrested; he therefore hinted an intention, which he afterwards executed of retiring to America.' (Not surprisingly in view of his savage attacks, before and afterwards, on the Whigs, Cobbett himself never referred to this meeting with Lord Holland.)

In the meantime Cobbett gave no immediate reply to the government's offer, and deliberately leaving them in suspense decided to flee the country just as he had done in 1792 prior to the court martial. He would leave London by night and would say nothing about his plans – not even to Henry Hunt, who had arranged to meet him for a political rally at Devizes. (Hunt was 'thunderstruck' when he heard the news of Cobbett's flight, though when he thought about it, he recalled that 'there was something *mysterious* in Mr Cobbett's conduct when I last saw him which was a few days before in London'.) Once his mind was made up Cobbett summoned Nancy from Botley to Catherine Street and explained the situation to her. 'As soon as she was in the room,' Anne wrote, 'Papa put his two hands on her shoulders, said, "Nancy I must go to America."' Nancy must have been well used to such crises by now. At any rate, Cobbett reported, 'she did not utter a single plaintive accent; a few big tears rolled down her face; she resumed her smiles in an instant'.

The family sat up till 4 a.m., when Cobbett with his two sons William (nineteen) and John (sixteen) left in a post-chaise for Liverpool. It was Saturday, 22 March 1817. By night-time they had reached Lichfield. The next day they set off for Liverpool, and by now Cobbett was relaxed enough to enjoy the scenery:

Of the whole country through which we passed, we were more delighted with the ten miles from Dunchurch to Coventry in Warwickshire. The road very wide and smooth, rows of fine trees on the sides of it; beautiful white-thorn hedges and rows of ash and elm dividing the fields; the fields so neatly kept; the soil so rich; the herds and flocks of fine fat cattle and sheep on every side; the beautiful homesteads and numerous stacks of wheat! Every object seemed to say; here are resources! Here is wealth! Here are the means of natural power, and of individual plenty and happiness! And, yet, at the end of those ten beautiful miles, we entered that city of Coventry, which, out of twenty thousand inhabitants contained at that very moment, upwards of eight thousand miserable paupers.

As we passed onwards through Staffordshire and Cheshire all the same signs of wealth and of the sources of power, on the surface of the earth struck us by day; and, by night, those more sublime signs, which issued from the furnaces on the hills. The causeways for foot-passengers, paved, in some instances, for tens of miles, together; the beautiful rows of trees shading those causeways; the canals winding about through the valleys, conveying coal, lime, stone, merchandise of all sorts; the immense and lofty woods of the hills, every object seemed to pronounce an eulogium on the industry, skill and perseverance of the people. And, why, then, were those people in a state of such misery and degradation?[15]

The Cobbetts reached Liverpool at about 10 p.m. on 24 March. Three days later they were able to board the *Importer*, bound for New York. In the custom house a scene took place which anticipated Oscar Wilde's famous riposte that he had 'nothing to declare but his genius'. When Cobbett went through customs with his friend Mr Casey, the latter was asked whether Cobbett had anything saleable about him. Casey replied, 'Oh, yes Sir! He bears about him his mind, had he been disposed to sell that, he need not have left this country for another.' The boat was very crowded and during the six-week voyage they were obliged to witness the slow death 'of a lingering disease' of the captain's brother, a fellow passenger. In addition there was an acute water shortage and the ship was twice struck by lightning. To avoid contact with fellow passengers the Cobbetts spoke French among themselves. In spite of everything they arrived in New York spick and span on 5 May 1817.

6

AMERICA REVISITED

WITHIN A DAY of landing in New York Cobbett had found a farm on Long Island at Hyde Park (now New Hyde Park), about eighteen miles from New York City. The house was in a run-down state, but it came with four hundred acres of land which Cobbett was determined to farm. He and his two sons moved into a local inn while the house was made habitable.

Cobbett, as always, was determined to make the most of his situation. 'Go and kick an ants' nest about,' he once wrote, 'and you will see the little, laborious, courageous creatures instantly set to work to get it together again and if you do this ten times over, ten times more they will do the same. Here is the sort of stuff that men must be made of to oppose those who by whatever means get possession of great and mischievous powers.' Only a fortnight after landing in America he was writing home to Nancy: 'The boys are very well indeed. John as fat as a Sussex pig. We are at a beautiful place called *Hyde Park*. A fine park, orchards, garden and fields and woods, *for a year* – A fine house too, but out of repair . . . A million of kisses to dear Nancy [Anne] and Ellen and Susan and James and Little Dick, and ten millions to your dear self from your affectionate husband Wm Cobbett.'

Inevitably, Cobbett's departure to America had led to a spate of critical comment in England. 'What do you think of Cobbett's running away?' Miss Mitford wrote to her painter friend Sir William Elford.

'Were you surprised at it? I was not . . . I was sure that he would never expose himself to a second imprisonment. He has courage but he has no fortitude. He would fight, I dare say, but he does not know how to suffer.' There was truth in this, but Miss Mitford, who knew Cobbett in his Botley days, would have known how temperamentally unfitted he was to being confined within the walls of a prison. After two years in Newgate he himself knew this better than anyone.

Sharper criticism came from some of the younger, more radical spirits in the reform movement, notably Thomas Wooler (1786?–1853), a Yorkshire-born debater and satirist who had launched his latest paper, the *Black Dwarf*, early in 1817. The very first issue of Wooler's paper, before Cobbett's departure for America, had contained some disrespectful remarks on his apparent failure to support the principle of universal suffrage. But now Wooler, seeing himself perhaps stepping into the great man's shoes once he had gone into voluntary exile, launched a ferocious assault headed 'Trial and Desertion of Corporal Cobbett'. 'The powers of Mr Cobbett,' he wrote, 'were great, but he seems to have wanted that most valuable of requisites for public life: a resolution that could look dangers and even death, steadfastly in the face.' The following week, Wooler resumed the attack: 'Fear alone has been his leading principle . . . speaking of his farewell *address* as a mere composition, it is truly contemptible . . . he must have been seasick when he wrote it . . . Mr Cobbett carries with him the contempt of every manly mind in England . . . Silly old man!'

Cobbett was used to being attacked from the right, but this was the first time he had been mauled by a left-wing adversary. Stung by the *Black Dwarf* articles, he replied at length in his *Register*, listing all those eminent writers like Paine and Voltaire who had been forced to flee their country when threatened by the government of the day:

> If it be cowardice to do what I have done and what so
> many eminent and immortal patriots have done before me,

everything must be cowardice, which embraces the most distant consideration of a personal safety . . . In the estimation
of Mr WOOLER it must be cowardice to take shelter from a
thunderstorm; tis cowardice to avoid being buried by a falling
house; it must be cowardice to lower sail in a hurricane; it
must be cowardice to resort to a surgeon in the case of a
broken leg; in short, this is such superlative nonsense in Mr
WOOLER, that it takes away and fixes in his own bosom,
whatever there could be intended as a sting in his calling me
'a silly old man.'

The description had plainly wounded Cobbett, and he was still sniping
at Wooler two years later, accusing him of writing 'intolerable nonsense'. Wooler in turn replied with mock pomposity that he would
not be induced to enter into controversy with Mr Cobbett during his
absence. When he returned, he said, he would be 'ready to defend
himself from any attack Mr C. may deem it advisable to make'.

The government press meanwhile had circulated the story that
Cobbett had fled to America in order to escape his creditors. It was
perfectly true that Cobbett's finances were in a chaotic state. He still
owed large sums to Sir Francis Burdett, and the Botley house was
heavily mortgaged. But the truth of the situation was that he went to
America partly so as to be able to go on earning in order to be able
to pay off his debts (rather than to avoid settling them), and at the
same time be able to support his large family. Yet the difficulties were
overwhelming. Cobbett could continue to write the *Register* from
Long Island, but he would now have to rely on the newspapers for
information, and he was deprived of one of the essentials of good
journalism – topicality. It took six to eight weeks for the papers to
reach him from England, and an equivalent length of time for his copy
to get to the printers in London. As the *Black Dwarf* put it in another
of its occasional swipes at Cobbett: 'To write from America is of some
service certainly because all that Mr Cobbett writes must be of some
value but I have observed that the distance and the time that must

elapse must always take much from its value and more from its utility. We might play at chess at that distance very well if we were not anxious to finish the game.'

None of this would have mattered if things in England had been peaceful. But the two years of Cobbett's exile were highly eventful. In June 1817, shortly following his arrival in New York, a group of two hundred Derbyshire protesters led by one Jeremiah Brandreth set out for Nottingham, where they were arrested and Brandreth charged with killing a farm labourer on the way. He was eventually put on trial and executed along with several others. Countless reformers were arrested, including Cobbett's critic Wooler. Bamford had been imprisoned following the ill-fated hunger-march by the 'Blanketeers' earlier in the year. There were strikes in the north and in the Midlands, and despite the government's efforts the agitation (almost always peaceful) continued for months, culminating in the climactic demonstration at St Peter's Field, Manchester, on 16 August 1819, known as 'the Peterloo massacre'.

Cobbett missed out on all this excitement, and it was inevitable that in his absence other pamphleteers like Wooler and the young Richard Carlile would be able to steal a march on him simply by being on the spot, even if they could never hope to match the extent of his appeal. All the same, he was able to resume publication of the *Register* in July 1817 with six long and powerful pieces headed 'The Last 100 Days of English Freedom', giving an account of the events leading up to the 'Gagging Acts' and the suspension of Habeas Corpus. But in the meantime, with the greater amount of spare time available and the urgent need to make money, he took the decision to start writing books. He would begin by giving an account of his impressions of America. Not only had he found a house within a day of landing in New York, he simultaneously began to keep a diary in the style of Gilbert White, though with typical Cobbett touches:

1817 May.

5. Landed in New York.

6. Went over to Long Island. Very fine day, warm as May in England. The peach trees going out of bloom. Plum trees in full bloom.

7. Cold, sharp, East wind, just like that which makes the old debauchees in London shiver and shake.

This diary, which eventually formed the first part of his book *A Year's Residence in the United States of America*, was published the following year, in 1818. The book marks the emergence of a new Cobbett, recognisable as the author of *Rural Rides*, who alternates his views on the countryside and farming with political asides and the occasional diatribe against one of his pet hates, whether it was potatoes or Lord Castlereagh. In so far as he had a political purpose in his book, it was to emphasise the prosperity of Americans compared with their British counterparts. But he stressed in his introduction that he had no special desire to encourage people (farmers in particular) to emigrate to the United States – as some Tory economists were encouraging them to do. He himself had no such intention to settle permanently there. 'I myself,' he wrote in his introduction, 'am bound to England for life. My notions of allegiance to country; my great and anxious desire to assist in the restoration of her freedom and happiness; my opinion that I possess, in some small degree at any rate, the power to render such assistance; and above all the other considerations, my unchangeable attachment to the people of England and especially those who have so bravely struggled for our rights; these bind me to England: but I shall leave others to judge and act for themselves.'

It was not just these abstract sentiments that prevented Cobbett from emigrating permanently. In this book, for the first time he describes the English countryside which meant so much to him. Cobbett had no artistic imagination. He lived at the same time as the great Romantic poets – Wordsworth, Keats, Shelley, etc., all of whom were readers of the *Political Register* – but there is nothing to suggest that he ever read a word of theirs in return. Painting and music were also a closed book to him, and he frequently complained of farmers who spent money on such useless things as pianos. But he remained throughout his life intensely responsive not only to landscape but to all natural phenomena – including trees, flowers and birds:

> There are *two things* . . . which are almost wholly wanting here, while they are so amply enjoyed in England. The *singing-birds* and the *flowers*. Here are many birds in summer, and some of very beautiful plumage. There are some wild flowers, and some English flowers in the best gardens. But, generally speaking, they are birds without song, and flowers without smell. The *linnet* (more than a thousand of which I have heard warbling upon one scrubbed oak in the sand-hills in Surrey, the *sky-lark*, the *goldfinch*, the wood-lark, the *nightin-gale*, the *bull finch*, the *black-bird*, the *thrush* and all the rest of the singing tribe are wanting in these beautiful woods and orchards of garlands. When these latter have dropped their bloom, all is gone in the flowery way. No shepherd's rose, no honey suckle, none of the endless variety of beauties that decorate the hedges and the meadows in England. No *daisies*, no primroses, no cowslips, no blue-bells and no daffodils, which, as if it were not enough for them to charm the sight and smell, must have names too, to delight the ear . . .

One compensation was the abundance of game birds to be shot at. 'The woodcock shooting is just begun here,' he wrote in an open letter to Orator Hunt in October 1818. 'Anything of a shot will kill ten or twelve brace a day . . . You would kill a hundred brace a day . . . think of it. A hundred brace of woodcocks a day. Think of *that*! No alien acts here. No long-sworded and whiskered Captains. No Judges escorted from town to town and sitting under the guard of dragoons. No packed juries of tenants. No crosses. No Bolton Fletchers. No hangings and rippings up. No Castleses and Olivers. No Stewarts and Perries. No Cannings, Liverpools, Castlereaghs, Eldons, Ellenboroughs or Sidmouths. No

Bankers. No squeaking Wynnes. No Wilberforces. Think of *that*! No Wilberforces!'

If Cobbett had been hoping for any kind of official welcome from the Americans, he would have been disappointed. His earlier notoriety in Philadelphia had by now been forgotten, and there was no longer the same kind of enthusiasm for the victims of British oppression that had greeted his first-ever Aunt Sally, Dr Priestley. Cobbett had championed America in the recent war with Britain (1812–14), and some of his articles were reprinted in the States, but from the time he set foot in New York, the Americans ignored him. The only first-hand account of his lifestyle on Long Island is given by one Henry Bradshaw Fearon, a young British surgeon, a radical and one of a handful of authors (including Cobbett himself) who were writing books about America at this time which they hoped would be read by those, especially farmers, who were thinking of emigrating to the United States. Fearon had arrived in New York in August 1817. After a few days in the city he took a steam ferry-boat to Brooklyn and then travelled in intense heat in an open coach, like a fair-wagon, to Wiggins' Inn, a four-mile walk from Cobbett's farm. He was, he writes, struck by melancholy thoughts as he approached the house – 'a path rarely trod, fences in ruins, the gate broken, a house mouldering to decay'. Cobbett, as it happened, was not at home, but Mrs Churcher, his faithful English housekeeper, welcomed Fearon in, delighted, she said, to see an English face – 'instead of those nasty guessing Yankies', and conducted him to 'a front parlour which contained but a single chair and several trunks of sea-clothes'. Fearon returned early the following day, when he found Cobbett 'writing with his coat off'.

> This being the first time I had seen this well-known character, I viewed him with no ordinary degree of interest. A print by Bartolozzi [see page 45] executed in 1801 conveys a correct outline of his person. His eyes are small and pleasingly good natured ... To all his tone and manner resolute and deter-

mined. He feels no hesitation in praising himself and evidently believes that he is eventually destined to be the Atlas of the British nation. My impressions of Mr Cobbett are that those who know him would like him, if they can be content to submit unconditionally to his dictation. 'Obey me and I will treat you kindly: if you do not I will trample on you' seemed visible in every word and feature.

Despite the generally respectful tone of Fearon's account, he was trampled on all the same. Cobbett was especially outraged by the suggestions in this account that his surroundings were run-down and squalid. 'All is false,' he wrote. 'The house is a better one than he ever entered. The path, so far from being trackless, was as beaten as the highway.' Yet he in his letters home had said himself that the house was 'out of repair'. He told Nancy on 19 June 1817: 'As to our living *here* in a way suitable to my state in life, the thing is out of the question. I will make no alteration in any respect. Simply to preserve *life* and *health* is all that reason or common sense, will permit me to go to the expense of.' It may well have been the rather primitive conditions that resulted in Nancy Cobbett's premature departure from Long Island. She had sailed from England with her remaining children in late 1817 but stayed only a few months before returning home. In his *Emigrant's Guide* (1829) Cobbett advised husbands thinking of emigrating that they would need 'that quality which enables a man to overcome the scruples, the remonstrances, and the wailings of his wife. Women, and especially Englishwomen, transplant very badly.' It is fair to assume that, as usual, Cobbett was writing from personal experience.

If Cobbett had no special interest in improving his house, the same did not apply to the land. Wherever he went in his nomadic existence, whether in New Brunswick, Philadelphia, Botley, or now on Long Island, almost the first thing he did was to create a garden. His skill in this department is attested to by Mary Russell Mitford:

'Few persons excelled him in the management of vegetables, fruit and flowers. His green Indian corn, his Carolina beans – his water melons could hardly have been exceeded at New York. His wall-fruit was equally splendid, and much as flowers have been studied since that day, I never saw a more glowing or a more fragrant garden than that at Botley with its pyramids of hollyhocks and its masses of china-asters, of clover of mignonettes and of variegated geraniums.'

The American climate, with its very hot summer, was not ideal for gardening, and Cobbett lamented the almost total lack of the cottage gardens which made England so attractive. Still, he had no shortage of water:

A large rain-water cistern to take the run from the house, and a duck-pond to take that from the barn, afforded an ample supply. The rains came about once in fifteen days; they came in abundance for about twenty-four hours; and then all was fair and all was dry again immediately. [The summers] were very, very hot. The thermometer 85 degrees in the shade; but a breeze. I worked in the land morning and evening, and wrote in the day in a north room. The dress became very convenient, or, rather a very little inconvenient affair. Shoes, trousers, shirt and hat. No plague of dressing and undressing! I never slept better in all my life. No covering. A sheet under me, and a straw bed. My window looked to the East. The moment Aurora appeared, I was in the orchard. How I pitied those who were compelled to endure the stench of cities! The dews were equal to showers: I frequently, in the morning, washed hand and face, feet and legs, in the dew on the high grass.[1]

His son James described him riding round his estate in a wagon drawn by two oxen – 'he with only a shirt, a pair of nankin trousers, yellow buckskin shoes and a broad brimmed straw hat'.

Cobbett was delighted with his harvest of fall pippin apples, and by September he had finished his crop of Indian corn and was busy nurturing his cabbages, mangel wurzels, turnips, beets, carrots, parsnips and parsley. All this in addition to making his own candles and caring for a collection of pigs, sheep, cows and poultry.

In January 1818 Cobbett set off by coach for Philadelphia in an attempt to secure some $4000 which he claimed had been unjustly taken from him by the federal government for allegedly violating an undertaking to be of good behaviour following the Yrujo libel action of 1797 (see pages 33–4). As well as offering him the chance of recouping a large sum at a time when he was short of funds, this gave Cobbett an opportunity to travel and gain some useful material for his book. Philadelphia he found 'greatly augmented', though its streets were still full of pigs, and he was pleased to meet some old friends. He was then obliged to go to the new town of Harrisburg, where the legislature was sitting and where he discovered, as do all litigants, that he was obliged to hang around for days waiting on the lawyers. 'Tired to death of the tavern at Harisburgh,' he wrote in his diary on 27 January 1818. 'The cloth spread three times a day. Fish, fowl, meat, cakes, eggs, sausages; all sorts of things in abundance . . . Here we meet altogether: senators, judges, lawyers, tradesmen, farmers and all. I am weary of the everlasting loads of meat. *Weary of being idle.* How few such days have I spent in my life!'[2]

Eventually the Senate rejected Cobbett's petition and he left Harisburgh 'very much displeased'. After a few days in Philadelphia he set off for New York. He had to wait for a coach at Trenton, New Jersey, which he said he would 'have liked better, if I had not seen so many young fellows lounging about the street, and leaning against door-posts with quids of tobacco in their mouths or segars [sic] stuck between their lips and with dirty hands and faces'.

Trenton aside, Cobbett's view of America and Americans was distinctly favourable, in contrast with his previous impression in 1796. He was struck by the prosperity of the country, the almost complete absence of beggars. During his stay he met only two, he said, and one

of them was Italian and the other an Englishman from Croydon. Of
five thousand people at a race meeting, not one was shabbily dressed.
'How can a man be a pauper,' he wrote, 'where he can earn ten
pounds of prime hog meat a day, six days in every week?' This
obvious prosperity he contrasted with conditions at home. There were
few taxes, no tithes or game laws ('People go where they like and, as
to wild animals, shoot what they like'). 'What can any gentleman want
more than New York?' he wrote. 'Hotels, Courts of Justice, museums,
picture galleries, great booksellers shops, public libraries, playhouses
and in short, an over-stock of all sorts of amusements and of fineries
with the most beautiful streets and shops in the world and without a
single beggar, public prostitute, pickpocket or Jew.'

In the state of New York, he noted, there was no law of criminal
libel which had been used so effectively to clamp down on the press
in England. Truth was a sufficient defence, provided 'that the publication was made with good motives'. In the state of Connecticut, the
constitution affirmed that 'In all prosecutions and indictments for *libel*
the TRUTH *may be given in evidence*, and the *jury* shall have the
right to determine *the law* and *the facts.*'

Objections were made that this degree of liberty would lead to
invasion into personal privacy, to which Cobbett replied, in one of
his many very shrewd observations on the practice of journalism:
'Amongst the persons whom I have heard express a wish, to see the
press what they called free and at the same time to extend the restraints
on it, with regard to persons in their private life . . . I have never, that
I know, met with one who had not some *powerful motive* of his own
for the wish, and who did not feel that he had some vulnerable part
about himself.' The greater freedom of the press was only one aspect
of the democratic atmosphere of America which appealed especially
to him. He liked the service in the inns – 'civil but not servile' – he
even got on with the Quakers he met in Philadelphia (though he was
to turn on them later in life). He appreciated another thing: 'for, many

and striking as are the traits, that distinguish the American character, none is so striking and none exalts it so much, as the respect and deference of the male toward the female sex. They talk to us about French *politeness*; and we hear enough of the sentimental trash of romances, where Princes and Nobles are the heroes. But in no part of this whole world are the women so kindly and respectfully treated by the men as in America.' As for the American women he admired everything about them except the state of their teeth, caused in his opinion by eating too much sugar, which, he said, 'always tends to the destruction of the teeth. In America, where sugar is very cheap, a prodigious quantity of it is used in all sorts of ways. The pies are made so sweet that a stranger cannot eat the sweet meats, fruits of all sorts, even down to the Siberian crab are preserved in sugar. And these sweet meats are eaten even in labourers' houses, in quantities that it would surprise you to see. This is the cause, and I believe it is the sole cause of that lamentable defect in a considerable part of the females of America; who in all other respects are, perhaps, the most beautiful of their sex.'[3]

The only severe criticism he made was of American drinking habits. Travelling by coach from Trenton to Brunswick, New Jersey, he noted that his driver 'would have been a very pleasant companion, if he had not drunk so much spirits on the road. This is the *great misfortune* of America! As we were going up a hill very slowly, I could perceive him looking very hard at my cheek for some time. At last he said "I am wondering, Sir, to see you look so *fresh*, and so *young*, considering what you have gone through in the world." Though I cannot imagine *how* he had learnt who I was. "I'll tell you", said I "how I have contrived the thing. I rise early, go to bed early, eat sparingly, never drink anything stronger than small beer, shave once a day, and wash my hands and face clean three times a day, at the very least." He said that was *too much* to think of doing.'

Even if sober, few people could have matched Cobbett's energy and his phenomenal industry. By 8 May 1817, three days after landing at New York, he had sent off the copy for an issue of the *Register* (published eventually in July). He began writing his book on America immediately, and in November he was able to inform his English paper-supplier Mr Tipper that he had begun work on his *English Grammar*. Cobbett's stated aim was to help 'in the acquirement of book-learning all those against whom the Borough-mongers have, in a great degree, closed the door to such learning and whom they have the insolence to denominate the "Lower Orders"'. Although the *Grammar* took the form of a series of letters addressed to his fourteen-year-old son James, they were really intended to be read by working people. In a letter addressed to the 'Blanketeers', those hunger-marchers from Manchester who had been stopped in their tracks by government troops in January 1817, he wrote how impressed he had been by speeches made by working-class men at various reform meetings – 'but when these same persons came to put their thoughts to paper, which was necessary in the case of resolutions and petitions, there appeared, in their writings many things very ridiculous, for the want of good grammar'. He instanced the case of a long letter he had received from a journeyman stocking-weaver from Nottingham in January 1817. Everything about it was admirable – the ideas, the figures of speech 'apt, consistent, beautiful and striking. But there was throughout the whole, such a deficiency in point of grammar, and promiscuous mixture of capitals and small letters; such misuse of points in all sorts; such discord amongst nouns and pronouns and verbs – that this piece of writing . . . which would have done honour to the mind and heart of any man living, would have excited the ridicule of ninety-nine persons out of a hundred.'

In compiling his *Grammar* Cobbett remembered the difficulties he himself had experienced when, as a young soldier of seventeen in the Woolwich barracks, he tried to master the subject without assistance from anyone. He had relied entirely on Bishop Lowth's *Short*

Introduction to English Grammar (1762), which he learned by heart but initially found very hard to understand because of the lack of proper 'definitions'. Thus, the Bishop had defined a verb as follows: 'A verb is a word which *signifies to be, to do, or to suffer.*'

'That is all!' Cobbett wrote:

> I was seventeen years old when I first read this definition. I had a fair share of natural capacity; I was animated with a most ardent desire to learn; and yet, this definition so puzzled and so disgusted me that I was on the point of abandoning my pursuit . . . what was I to learn from an account so loose, so laconic, so vague as this? I do not know how this definition may have stricken other young minds, but I really thought that any word which was descriptive of *pain*, or *suffering*, of any sort, was a verb, such as a *toothache, fever, ague, rheumatism, gout* . . . I was a young man, a private soldier animated with the double ambition of shining as a scholar and as a soldier . . . I was naturally industrious, persevering and sanguine . . . Yet, even with these motives and with this character, I was a hundred times, upon the point of committing the Bishop's book to the flames.

No one could have been left in the dark when Cobbett came to illustrate the various parts of speech, partly because he was incapable of writing anything without allowing his personality and his prejudices to intrude. 'For once,' he announced of his *Grammar*, 'I have written a book without politics in it.' But it wasn't true. Thus, as an example of what constitutes a sentence, he writes: 'The people suffer great misery'; nouns of number are illustrated by 'Mob, Parliament, Rabble, House of Commons, Regiment, Court of Kings Bench, Den of Thieves'. To show a typical solecism he writes: 'The gang of borough-tyrants is cruel and are also notoriously as ignorant as brutes.' It was thanks to these frequent jokes and barbs that Hazlitt called the *Grammar* 'as entertaining as a story book'.

When it came to writing, Cobbett had little awareness of how exceptional his ability was. Intensely egotistic, he remained oblivious of the diversities of human talents and achievement. He discovered, for example, at some stage in his life that he was allergic to mushrooms (though he was, like his contemporaries, ignorant of the nature of allergy). 'I had not long eaten them,' he wrote, 'before my whole body, face, hands and all was covered with red spots or pimples, and to such a degree, and coming on so fast that the doctor who attended the family was sent for.' But it did not occur to Cobbett that he might be unusual in his reaction. 'I do not advise anyone to cultivate these things,' he concluded. In the same way, with writing, he considers himself a typical specimen of the human race. Like any other self-educated man he had never competed with his contemporaries for prizes, scholarships or university degrees. It was perhaps natural for him to think that anyone could do what he had done, once he or she had mastered the elementary rules.

His view of writing was entirely practical. 'Language,' he said, 'is made use of for one of three purposes; namely, to inform, to convince, or to persuade.' Literature, poetry, fiction or drama did not come into it. He was thinking, as usual, only of his own experience. When he described the actual process of composition he wrote about himself with little apparent awareness of how much he differed from the rest of us. 'Thoughts come much faster than we can put them down on paper,' he said. 'Use the first words that occur to you . . . put down your thoughts in words just as they come.' This is not very helpful advice to an aspiring writer, but it does give a picture of Cobbett's own experience, the spontaneity of his journalism and his ability to write with exceptional fluency without alterations or afterthoughts. It explains too the occasional lapses, the repetition of words which a more leisurely writer would correct in reading over his text. But Cobbett, the master stylist, had no interest in style. 'I do not understand what *elegance* in writing means,' he said. Had it been otherwise he could never have produced such a huge, unequalled body of work during his lifetime.

Apart from explaining the simple elements of grammar, Cobbett had another aim – to dispel the mystique attached to a classical education and the idea that only someone who had studied Latin and Greek could be considered educated or 'learned'. 'I have always contended,' he wrote, 'and have now proved that a knowledge of those languages is, generally speaking, of no use, and that as the acquiring of that knowledge costs much time and money, it is, generally speaking, *worse than useless.*' Even if he conceded that it might have its uses, he was determined to show 'that even a thorough knowledge of these "learned languages" does not prevent men from writing *bad English*'.[4]

To prove his point, he included in later editions of the book examples of bad writing taken from the books and speeches of a number of eminent public figures like the Duke of Wellington and Lord Castlereagh, not merely to disparage their bad grammar but as proof that, in his view, they were unfit to hold high office:

> He who writes badly thinks badly. Confusedness in words can proceed from nothing but confusedness in the thoughts which give rise to them. These things may be of trifling importance when the actors move in private life; but when the happiness of millions of men is at stake, they are of importance not easily to be described.

Cobbett had a great deal of sport at the expense of Dr Johnson, or 'Old Dread-Devil' as he habitually called him. Though he admired Johnson in many respects, and often quoted him to good effect, he never forgave him for having defined the word 'pensioner' in his dictionary as 'Slave of State hired by a stipend to obey his masters', and then having himself accepted a pension from George III, thus anticipating the ranks of the Southeys, the Giffords and other 'base men' who had betrayed the writer's calling. If Cobbett, as so often, over-laboured the point, he was on surer ground when he criticised Johnson for his clumsy writing, deriving the moral that clever people, great scholars, were not necessarily able to express themselves clearly. He seized upon the frequently used expression 'than whom', as in 'Cromwell, than whom no man was better skilled in artifice', as an example of bad grammar: 'It is a very common parliament-house phrase and therefore presumptively corrupt'; but it is a Dr Johnson phrase too: 'Pope, than whom few men had more vanity'. The Doctor did not say, 'Myself, than whom few men have been found more base, having in my Dictionary, described a pensioner as a slave of state, and having afterwards myself become a pensioner.'

Published in December 1818, Cobbett's *Grammar of the English Language* was a phenomenal success, proof not only of his writing skills but of the overwhelming demand for self-improvement at this time among the working people of England. The first edition of five thousand copies was sold out in a fortnight, and two further editions were published in the next four months. By 1825 Cobbett was boasting that over 55,000 copies had been sold 'without ever having been mentioned by the old shuffling bribed sots, called Reviewers'. By 1829 he had sold 100,000 *Grammars*.

Having successfully instructed his fellow countrymen in the basics of English grammar, Cobbett turned to a project that had been on his mind since his arrival on Long Island – teaching the Americans how to garden. Ever since he was a little boy Cobbett had been a compulsive gardener. He was just as keen on flowers as on vegetables, as he told his readers in *The American Gardener* (1821): 'Some persons may think that *flowers* are things of no *use*; that they are nonsensical things. The same may be, and perhaps with more reason said of *pictures* . . . for my part, as a thing to keep and not to sell, as a thing, the *possession* of which is to give me pleasure, I hesitate but a moment to prefer the plant of a fine carnation to a gold watch set with diamonds.'

By our standards, some of Cobbett's views on gardening were highly eccentric. He refused to accept that pollen played any part in fertilising the female plant, and preached that watering flowers and vegetables was 'a thing of very doubtful utility in any case, and in most cases, of positive injury'. Still, we have Mary Russell Mitford's testimony that Cobbett was a superb flower gardener, and his personal insistence that it was all his own work. He was very firm on the subject of hired gardeners, who had to be kept in their place:

> Every gardener thinks that every one who employs him, as far as relates to gardening, is a natural born fool. He will allow him to be, and indeed he will boast of his being, the greatest of orators, the greatest of generals, the most valiant of admirals, the most profoundly wise of lawgivers, the most heavenly of heaven-born ministers, the most pious and learned of bishops, the most learned of all learned lawyers and, if a physician, capable almost, of raising the dead to life: but in matters of gardening he will insist that he is essentially a fool . . . One of the consequences of this way of thinking is that gardeners, if the master be of a character that makes it perilous to flatly contradict him [i.e. somebody like Cobbett], hear, with very little interruption, all that he has to say . . . they receive his directions very quietly, then go away, and pay no more attention to them than the whistling of the winds.

As far as the Americans were concerned, they seemed to Cobbett's eye to be in need of instruction about many aspects of gardening. Rhubarb, for example, was unknown, not to mention broccoli, a particular favourite of Cobbett's because it was in season early in the year – 'for at that season the people of New York are carrying wild dock leaves from market at three or four cents a handful!' Another thing he urged on the Americans was hedges, especially of hawthorn:

> the hawthorn is the favourite plant of England: it is seen as a flowering shrub in all gentlemen's grounds; it is the constant ornament of paddocks and parks; the first appearance of its blossoms is hailed by old and young as the sign of pleasant weather . . . And why should America not possess this most beautiful and useful plant! She has English gew-gaws, English

Play-Actors, English cards and English dice and billiards; English fooleries and English vices enough in all conscience; and why not English hedges, instead of post and rail and board fences? If, instead of these steril [sic] looking and cheerless enclosures the gardens and meadows and fields, in the neighbourhood of New York and other cities and towns, were divided by quick-set hedges, what a difference would the alteration make in the look, and in the real value too of those gardens, meadows and fields!

Apart from the *Grammar* and *The American Gardener*, while still in America Cobbett worked on a new edition of his earlier book *Le Maître Anglais*, for teaching French people English, and began a companion volume for teaching the English French, which was eventually published as a *French Grammar* in 1824. Then there was a *History of the Laws and Constitution of England* and a *View of the Present State of the Income, Debt and Expenditure of the Kingdom*, neither of which was ever completed, if indeed started. He did however make some progress with a life of Thomas Paine, a project especially dear to Cobbett, who was anxious to atone for his earlier attack. (Cobbett also planned at one stage to publish Paine's complete works in cheap form, but nothing came of this.)

After ten years in France, Paine had returned to America, which he regarded as his home, in October 1802. He had earlier been released from prison in Paris and was a bitter and disillusioned man. In America, instead of being treated with respect as one of the heroes of the Revolution, he found himself under constant attack especially for his religious views (Paine was a Deist, someone who believes in God but rejects the divinity of Jesus Christ). He continued to correspond with his friend Thomas Jefferson, who became President in 1801, but Congress rejected his appeal for financial compensation and he was even refused the right to vote in the presidential election of 1805.

When Paine eventually died in 1809 the only people at his

graveside, apart from his Quaker friend Wilbert Hicks and two black men who wanted to thank Paine for his efforts to abolish slavery, were Mme Margaret Bonneville and her son Benjamin. Margaret Bonneville with her husband Nicholas, a journalist, had cared for Paine for five years at their house in Paris following his release from prison. At Paine's suggestion she later followed him to America with her children, though her husband was detained for insulting Napoleon. Paine's critics sought to discredit him by suggesting that he was a drunk, and also that Mme Bonneville had been his mistress; but there is no proof of this. Paine helped her with money out of gratitude for her hospitality in Paris, and made her his executor, leaving her all his manuscripts.

Having joined with such gusto in the persecution of Paine as a young man in Philadelphia, Cobbett now, in 1818, felt the urge to make amends to someone he recognised as a very great Englishman. Cobbett was never a republican, and had little sympathy with Paine's religious views (he claimed never even to have read *The Age of Reason*, in which Paine outlined his belief that Jesus was 'a virtuous and amiable man' and not the son of God). But he had originally been won over by Paine's economic theories, and by this stage in his life he no doubt identified himself with a man whose career in many ways mirrored his own, a man who set out to benefit his fellow men and met with nothing but ingratitude and imprisonment.

In 1818 Cobbett publicly announced his intention of writing a life of Paine, and this brought him into contact with Margaret Bonneville, now reunited with her husband and living in New York. Mme Bonneville was herself working on a biography in an attempt to rebut all the false stories that had been circulated about her friend and benefactor – '*L'indignation*,' she wrote, '*m'a fait prendre la plume.*' Cobbett agreed to pay her $1000 for all her material and also agreed, according to her account, to publish it in England without alteration. In the event he rewrote the entire work, but it was never published in his lifetime, presumably because of opposition from the Bonnevilles.*

Paine had asked in his will to be buried in the Quakers' graveyard, but as the final insult the Quakers refused permission because of his religious views, and he was buried on open land near his farm at New Rochelle on Long Island. A wall was erected round the grave but this was soon being vandalised by pious Americans, as were the actual gravestones. Ten years after Paine's death the grave was in a neglected state, and Cobbett was writing in the *Register* (1 May 1819) of his hope to 'see an Act of Parliament to cause his bones to be conveyed to England and deposited in the stead of those of Pitt'.

Shortly after this was published Cobbett was forced to deal with more immediate questions. On 20 May 1819 his house burned down. 'I should have gone to New York,' he wrote, 'and remained there till the time of my departure for England; but, when I considered the interruptions which such a removal would occasion, and when I thought of the injury that these and the air of the city might be to my literary labours, I resolved on making a sort of thatched tent, in which I might enjoy tranquillity and in which I might labour without intermission – from this tent made of poles, thatch and English newspapers, I had the honour to address many "Registers". Happiness never depends upon mere place. It depends little more on good raiment. My diet all came from my own fields and my cow was my vintner and brewer. I was asleep on my straw by nine o'clock and I was in my orchard before four o'clock.'

Cobbett prided himself on his constitution – 'the strongest that God, in his bounty, ever gave to man, a constitution which has enabled me to experience not the smallest inconvenience from being wet to my skin for many hours together and suffering my clothes to dry upon my back; a constitution that makes me feel no change in passing from

* Cobbett's 'Life' was published as an appendix to Moncure Conway's 1892 biography of Paine.

one climate to another; that enables me to sleep upon a feather bed'. In the height of the American summer, he wrote, when the temperature was ninety-eight degrees, 'I have gone, in my shirt and trousers and stood under the drip of the house while a thunder shower sent down the water upon me by hogsheads. I called it a shower bath. The perspiration was washed away, by the rain from the clouds. This I have repeatedly done; and it never gave me the slightest cold.'[5]

With such simple habits Cobbett was perfectly happy in his improvised tent. But he could not have stayed in it once the weather cooled. He moved to New York and prepared to return to England. In September, he reported to his readers:

> I have just done *here* a thing, which I have always, since I came to this country, vowed that I would do; that is *taken up the remains of our famous countryman* PAINE!, in order to carry them to England! In his old age and last days he was most basely treated by the republican rulers and by many beside. The Quakers, even the Quakers refused him a grave! And I found him lying in a corner of a rugged, barren field! . . . our expedition set out from New York in the middle of the night, got to the place (22 miles off) at peep of day; took up the coffin entire; brought it off to New York, and just as we found it, it goes to England!'[6]

Returning with Paine's bones from two years' exile, Cobbett was intensely gratified by his reception in England. After a three-week voyage 'over a sea almost as smooth as beautiful Long Island Lake' he arrived on 21 November in Liverpool, where he was greeted by a huge crowd of supporters. In Bolton, he learned, a town crier had gone round the streets with a bell announcing the good news that 'Our countryman William Cobbett is arrived at Liverpool in good health.' The man was later arrested and taken before the magistrate.

After a few days Cobbett set out with his sons William and John for Manchester, where a celebration dinner had been arranged.

However, at Irlam, ten miles from the city, he was told that the authorities had issued an order banning him from entering Manchester. Anticipating another demonstration on the scale of Peterloo, the magistrates had taken extraordinary precautions. Hussars were posted on the roads into the city to give warning of Cobbett's approach, and 'several pieces of cannon' were brought into the centre of the town. In compliance not only with the magistrates but with reformers in Manchester who urged the public not to give 'the friends of St. Peter's another opportunity of shedding innocent blood', Cobbett turned back and set off for London. Near Coventry he was followed by a crowd of supporters, and when he stopped the coach he was, he wrote, 'surrounded by several thousands of persons of both sexes, the females forming a very beautiful battalion, many of them with children in their arms, in one part of the circle, not mixed among the men, while other persons were running towards us not only along the track of the chaise from the city but in all directions over the fields and meadows. This was not a meeting. There had been nothing done to call it together. It was spontaneous, it was collected of itself, by the mere sound of my name. Never did I behold any spectacle in my whole life that gave me so much pleasure as this.'[7] After stopping in London to attend the traditional dinner at the Crown and Anchor, he arrived home in Botley where, despite the expected opposition of Reverend Baker, there were scenes similar to those of 1812 when he was released from Newgate.

Cobbett returned to find the reform movement in turmoil and his own place in it uncertain. Two events had aroused the conscience of the middle classes, at the same time confusing the reformers. The first was the so-called Pentridge Rising of June 1817, which resulted in the exposure of a small army of government spies not merely keeping tabs on suspected revolutionaries but acting as *agents provocateurs* and deliberately fomenting unrest. At the trial of the Pentridge rioters it was shown that their abortive coup had been instigated by the government spy William Oliver, a revelation that shocked all who read about it. Cobbett had been fully informed of this in America, and had written at length in defence of the deluded revolutionaries who were either executed or transported. He had no first-hand knowledge before landing in Liverpool of the Peterloo massacre of August 1819, when a huge but peaceful demonstration of eighty thousand men and women in Manchester was broken up by sabre-wielding cavalry who killed eleven people, including a woman and a child, and wounded over four hundred more. Orator Hunt, who had summoned the meeting and was in the process of addressing it when the attack occurred, was now under arrest along with several others.

This single, dramatic atrocity, condoned and excused by Sidmouth and other ministers, was to have lasting effects on the political situation in England. In the reform movement, the pamphleteers to the left of Cobbett were encouraged. But many, already demoralised by the real possibility of spies infiltrating their meetings, were left frightened and confused. From now on the feuds and disagreements grew more frequent and intense. Cobbett, never the easiest of collaborators, played his part as well as anyone in these disputes. The other side of the coin was the effect of Peterloo on moderate, middle-class opinion. As so often in English history there was a widespread feeling that 'something must be done'. The Tory government led by Lord Liverpool merely helped to encourage the feeling. Refusing to contemplate any question of reform, Liverpool could only repeat the traditional cry, 'the state of the Press. This is really the root of the evil.' It followed that the only policy was further repression.

To any reasonable person it was clear that these measures would only make things worse, and that the need of some version of reform was urgent, if only to prevent outbreaks more serious than Peterloo – which had started out as an entirely peaceful and disciplined demonstration. Yet for the Whig intelligentsia, their natural snobbery dictated that if reform was to be undertaken, then it was best left to well-bred, well-educated persons like themselves. In this they were at one with Tories such as Wilberforce, who believed that men like himself ought to do something 'to rescue the multitude of the hands of the Hunts and Thistlewoods [see pages 174–5]'. The disdain for Cobbett was common even to those of a radical reforming tendency. 'I contemplate Cobbett and Hunt,' Jeremy Bentham wrote, 'with much the same eye as the visitor of M. Carpenter [dealer in microscopes] contemplates the rabid animals devouring one another in a drop of water.' Byron exactly echoed these sentiments, along with the feeling that political issues were best left to those like himself who had learned Latin at a good school – 'Why our classical education should teach us to trample on such unredeemed dirt,' he wrote to his friend Hobhouse in April 1820. Sydney Smith, the witty, enlightened clergyman, the friend of Henry Brougham, Lord Holland and other leading Whigs, put the point perfectly at about the same time in a letter to Edward Davenport: 'The attack upon the present order of things will go on; and unfortunately, the gentlemen of the people have a strong case against the House of Commons and the borough-mongers as they call them. I think all wise men should begin to turn their faces reform-wards. We shall do it better than Mr Hunt or Mr Cobbett. Done it *must* and *will* be.'[8]

If the crowds that had greeted Cobbett were looking for leadership in the days of doubt and uncertainty that followed Peterloo, they were to be disappointed. Cobbett, always opposed to violent resistance and still worried about his personal freedom, had absolutely no wish to advocate any kind of armed uprising, let alone to make a martyr of himself. In the *Register*s of this period there is scarcely a mention of Peterloo. Even when the Female Reformers of Bolton, in one of many welcoming addresses sent to him along with a silver pen and inkstand on his return to England, refer to this as a time 'when the blood of Britons shed in the exercise of constitutional rights crieth aloud from the ground for justice', Cobbett makes no reference to the massacre in his reply. 'It is difficult not to conclude,' E.P. Thompson writes, 'that Radical leaders themselves were alarmed at the character of their following in the industrial centres.' Cobbett had no new message to give except to urge the continuation of petitions for reform, whilst he impressed on them his confident belief that sooner or later, because of the growing national debt, the economic system would collapse. 'My earnest hope,' he wrote, 'is that people will place their grand reliance on the Debt . . . It is the *most effectual* as well as the safest way, to let the truth exhaust itself, while we hold the rod and line and the hook.'

It was not the most inspiring message to rally the faithful. But Cobbett had new problems of his own. The sixth of the Six Acts passed in Liverpool in 1819 decreed that 'whereas pamphlets and printed papers containing observations upon public events and occurrences tending to excite hatred and contempt of the Government and Constitution of these realms as by law established . . . have been lately published in great numbers and at very small prices . . . these shall be deemed . . . newspapers . . . and to be subject to the same duties of stamps as newspapers are now subject unto'. This edict, aimed primarily at Cobbett, effectively spelled the end of the mass-circulated 2d *Register*, resulting in an 80 per cent fall in sales and a further blow to his personal finances. Everything called for retrenchment, and it is not surprising to find an entire issue of the *Register* at this time devoted to a lengthy diatribe against the evils of coffee and tea, and the following issue containing an equally lengthy defence of Tom Paine's religious position.

In the meantime Cobbett's proposals to honour the memory of Paine were reluctantly jettisoned. He had intended to have a funeral ceremony with twenty wagonloads of flowers strewn in front of the church, the erection of a bronze statue in Thetford (Paine's birthplace) or Botley, a public dinner to be held on Paine's birthday and even the sale of gold rings containing a lock of Paine's hair (presumably

A contemporary view of Cobbett digging up
the remains of Thomas Paine

removed from his corpse). But the public response was apathetic when
it was not actually hostile. Amongst reformers in the period following
Peterloo there was perhaps a feeling that there were more urgent
matters to attend to, whilst to the general public Paine's support of
the French Revolution and his Deism, which Cobbett insisted on
regarding as a forgivable eccentricity on the part of the great Englishman, were still held against him. Cobbett was satirised and cartoons
were published of him lugging a huge coffin round the country. 'No
one dared to move a pen or tongue in my defence,' he wrote. 'All the
hypocrites in the nation, all the bigots, all those who live by the taxes
were open mouthed against me and my relicts.'[9] In the end he was
forced to abandon all his plans, and the bones were to remain in his
possession until his death. What happened to them after that has
never been determined, so that Tom Paine was left eventually without

a final resting place in spite of Cobbett's efforts. It was a more fitting end to the story of someone who thought of himself as the friend of all mankind, and not the citizen of any particular country.

7

QUEEN'S COUNSEL

T HINKING ON PAPER as he so often did in the *Register*, Cobbett
wrote in December 1819: 'What remains to be done must be
more of an occasional nature: must be called forth by events and acts
as they arise before one.' This is the cautious, pragmatist Cobbett,
who to all intents and purposes was aware that he had said all he had
to say on the subject of the debt, the paper money and reform, and
could now only wait on events. There was to be no shortage of events
in 1820.

They began on 29 January, when King George III, who had long
been insane, finally died at the age of eighty-two. His death had two
immediate consequences, both of which directly affected Cobbett.
One was the general election which automatically ensued on the death
of the monarch. The other was the revival of the long-running saga of
Princess, now Queen, Caroline, which was to run its course in a series
of sensational events during the coming year.

The announcement of the election could not have come at a worse
time for Cobbett. Whilst he was in America he had persuaded himself
that he would do more good for the cause of reform by becoming an
MP – 'ten thousand times as much as I am able to do with my pen
only'. He anticipated, correctly, that there would be fresh curbs on
press freedom and that he would be better able to publicise his views
speaking in Parliament, where he would be protected by privilege and
where the government-subsidised press would be obliged to print his

speeches. He announced his intention to stand for Parliament at the first opportunity in the *Register*. At the same time, on his return to England he had announced that in order to circumvent the new stamp duty he was going to launch a daily newspaper, *Cobbett's Evening Post*. Yet the first issue was published on 29 January, the day of George III's death, which meant that Cobbett would now be obliged to devote all his energies to his election campaign, which readers of the *Register* were helping to sponsor via a special reform fund launched in the paper. Not surprisingly, the newspaper was a short-lived affair, and folded after only three months.

In the *Register* of 25 March Cobbett gave a full account of his election campaign in the form of an open letter to his sixteen-year-old son James: 'The moment the King's death was announced,' he began, 'I announced my intention to stand for *Coventry*, which is a city containing about twenty thousand souls and the business in which is principally watch-making and ribbon-weaving.' Compared to many constituencies Coventry had a large electorate – about three thousand 'freemen', those who had served seven years or more in a trade in the city. The quantity of voters and the fact that most of them were poor led Cobbett to think that he had every chance of winning the seat. But he had little idea of what lay in store. For a start, he discovered that many of the voters were no longer residents of Coventry. Hundreds were now living in Birmingham or London, and if Cobbett wanted their vote he would have to pay their expenses – 'these out-living Freemen require not only to be taken to Coventry, but to be entertained there and on the road and to be paid for their time into the bargain'. He had arranged a meeting in London to address the freemen, and was not impressed. Though 'some of them acted a most honourable and patriotic part, others of them appeared to be as selfish and greedy and base a crew as I ever set eyes on'.

Undeterred, Cobbett set out by post-chaise for Coventry on 28 February, 'the coldest night of the winter', along with his daughter

Anne and his brother-in-law Frederick Reid. They breakfasted at Daventry, but when they reached Dunchurch, eleven miles from Coventry, they were met by messengers who warned Cobbett 'that I should certainly be murdered if I attempted to enter the city'. It emerged that Cobbett's opponents, anticipating defeat if he was allowed a free rein, had hired a gang of heavies to see him off. 'They therefore got together on the morning of Tuesday the 29th of February, a parcel of men, whom they made partly drunk, and whom they gave orders to go out, meet me at the bridge, about a mile from the city and if I refused to return to London, *fling me over the bridge.*'

Learning that his own supporters had dispersed the gang, Cobbett decided to press on. The two pub landlords at Dunchurch refused to supply him with a coach, but he managed to commandeer a gig and set out for Coventry with Anne. Four miles from the town they were met by parties of young men with laurel in their hair and branches in their hands – the by-now traditional badges of organised reformers. Gradually the numbers grew, and by the time he reached the city in the evening there was a crowd, he estimated, of about twenty thousand people to greet him. Cobbett, who had acquired a coach, got up on the footboard and took his hat off to acknowledge the cheers. It was a freezing day, he was suffering from a cold, and for two hours he processed slowly through the streets. The result was that he lost his voice, which 'proved, in the end, an evil, which I have lamented more than any other misfortune of my life: or rather, than all other misfortunes put together. The loss of the election was a mere nothing, when compared with the *loss of my voice*, which was nearly as complete as if I had been dumb from my birth.'

The tactics of the opposition were apparent that night when the windows of the house where the Cobbetts were staying – 'a melancholy, comfortless place' – according to Anne, were smashed and a number of his supporters were attacked by gangs armed with knives. There followed a lull of a few days before the arrival in the city of

Cobbett's opponents, the then sitting Members (both Whigs) Peter Moore and Edward Ellice. Both were rich, as one had to be at that time to secure a seat in Parliament. Moore was a clergyman's son and a former radical. Prior to becoming an MP, Cobbett wrote, he had 'come home from India with a great parcel of money, got, of course, in the usual way in which money is got in those regions'. He was 'a singularly mean looking man, with not the smallest portion of talent, but with a great deal of impudence, and an apparently utter insensibility to the feelings of shame'.

Ellice, later a Whip in Lord Grey's government, was a more formidable figure and also the richer of the two. A Scotsman, he worked in the fur trade business founded by his father and had, in his youth, been a radical and a follower of Sir Francis Burdett. 'Ellice is a very tall man,' Cobbett wrote, 'as big as Mr Hulme about the shoulders and breast, but with a frame tapering downwards. This great, bulky body is surrounded by a head as disadvantageous in appearance as any that I ever saw in my life. The eye, set in a shallow socket, is large, round, dull, and of downward cast. Very much like that of the chubby, good-tempered, honest Jew, who sells cakes and oranges on board the steamboat which crosses from NEW YORK to BROOKLYN. The voice of Ellice is what we may call *soft* and *fat*. He has nothing of the *keenness* of 'Change Alley about him. He would seem to have taken lessons to acquire the Bond-Street *croak*. In short imagine a great *schoolboy of forty*, and you have my man fully before your eyes.'

Polling at that period lasted for several days, with the running count being announced day by day. Cobbett was ahead on the first day, and this caused consternation in the Moore/Ellice camp. Ellice himself even considered leaving town, but was eventually persuaded to remain. Voters were meanwhile being bombarded with a mass of anti-Cobbett broadsheets. All the old smears were revived. Cobbett – 'That Demon of Discord' – mistreated his farmworkers, he had fled to America to avoid paying his debts, he was 'a WRETCH who dares to tell you he will pledge himself never to touch a farthing of the public money at the same time he is spending money not a farthing of which but what has been extorted from the pockets of those he describes as being in a state of starvation'. More predictable was the attempt to brand Cobbett as an apostle of Paine – 'Mad Tom' – in other words an enemy of Christianity, and a promoter of irreligion. Cobbett was able to give as good as he got in this kind of propaganda war. He could always get the better of his opponents in any battle of words because he was able to write more cleverly and more entertainingly. Nor did he have any scruples about hitting below the belt. Ellice, he suggested, was a Jew whose real name was Elias, and 'Who are they who set about these underhand calumnies of irreligion? Mr Ellice a stock-jobber and Mr Moore who until of late was, for years, the Head Manager of a *filthy playhouse*,* to which there belongs *three hundred common* prostitutes who have *free admission tickets*, in order that they may be there to entice young men to go thither! Is not this immoral? Is not this irreligious! Never have I, in all my life, or any one of my family entered that infamous playhouse; that shocking scene of debauchery and prostitution.'[1]

But the war of words was a side issue compared with the campaign of physical intimidation used against anyone intending to vote for Cobbett. On the third day of polling, he writes, 'I . . . saw about twenty of my voters actually turned away from the polling place, and ripped up behind and stripped of their coats, and sometimes, even of their waistcoats!' Despite this, Cobbett was still leading Moore at the end of the day, and he saw Ellice leaving the booth 'in great dudgeon'. When he himself left he was obliged to walk through the 'bands of savages' who had been collected to frighten away his supporters, and found himself being jostled and punched. He was forced to defend

* Drury Lane Theatre.

himself with the help of a sharp-edged snuffbox, which 'cut the noses and the eyes of the savages at a famous rate', and eventually was pulled to safety by some of his friends. The following day (Friday), reinforcements were brought in from the country, 'fed and drenched at different houses', and with sheer force of numbers they simply drove away Cobbett's voters from the polling booth 'as if an army had made an attack on them'. A special band meanwhile was assigned to 'pour forth execrations' on Cobbett himself. 'The execrators', regularly supplied with gin and brandy, 'foamed at the mouth, till, in some cases, the foam extended itself widely down their dirty and long beards . . . One wretch, who had swallowed a great deal of gin, exhausted himself so much by straining his throat, that he at last fell down in a sort of fit, with the curses on his lips!'

Though Cobbett expresses his great indignation that such things could happen in his beloved England, another part of him was clearly enjoying the battle:

> The way I managed the brutes was well calculated to sting them and their employers to madness . . . My way was to stand and look upon the yelling beasts with a most good-humoured smile: turning my head now and then and leaning it, as it were to take different views of the same person, or same group. I now and then substituted something of *curiosity* instead of the general total *unconcern*, that was seated upon my face . . . Then, another time, when half a dozen fresh-drenched brutes were bursting forth close under my nose, I would stretch up my neck, and look, with apparently great curiosity and anxiousness towards a distant part of the crowd, as if to ascertain what was passing there; and this I would do with so much apparent earnestness and continue in the attitude so long, that the beasts really seemed, sometimes, as if they were going mad!

The following day Cobbett caused further annoyance to his opponents by insisting on keeping the poll open during the next week. That

Coventry Election.

STATE OF THE POLL,

AT THE

End of the Sixth Day, Tuesday, 14th March, 1820.

	ELLICE.	MOORE.	SEDITION.
London Votes Polled - - - -	140	140	109
Country Ditto - - - - -	214	212	78
Coventry Ditto - - - -	1069	1025	329
	1423	1377	516
Numbers Polled the Sixth Day - -	276	269	31

Total Number Polled -	1964
Majority for Ellice - - -	907
Majority for Moore - - -	861.

The Poll having been kept open by the *partizans of* SEDITION and their *secret abettors*, two or three days, without any prospect of success; and it appearing to be the wish of the FREEMEN and INHABITANTS, that each should have an opportunity of declaring his detestation of the principles of *Cobbett*, it is now determined by the Friends of MOORE and ELLICE, to keep the Poll open as long as there is a *resident* Freeman willing to Poll.

*_** Two days notice will be given of the CHAIRING DAY.

God save the King!

W. Rotherham, Printer, Fleet Street, Coventry.

A handbill gives the count after six days' polling in the Coventry election
('Sedition' = Cobbett)

evening the house where he and Anne were staying, belonging to his friend Frank Sargeant, was attacked by a gang of forty or so thugs. They broke open the front door while others climbed over a wall and tried to get in through the garden at the back. Cobbett, who was upstairs at the time nursing his cold with Anne, barricaded himself into his bedroom by moving the bed against the door while Mr Sargeant and his friends, armed with pokers and fire tongs, prepared to do battle downstairs. Cobbett had a sword and was taking off his coat, ready 'to give with a clear conscience, as hearty a thrust as ever was given by a man'. Fortunately it never came to that, as the intruders, after stabbing one man in the arm, made a swift retreat just as some constables were about to arrive. Edward Ellice was observed outside a neighbouring inn where a man came running from Sargeant's house and told him, 'We are working well, we have smashed all the windows and broke the shutter and we are going to kill him.' Tapping the man on the shoulder, Ellice replied, 'Well done, my lads, work away.'

Considering all this, it was remarkable that when the votes were finally counted, Cobbett did as well as he did. The result was as follows:

Ellice 1474
Moore 1422
Cobbett 517

Cobbett did not seem unduly depressed by the outcome. He may have lost the election, but the experience gave him another nail to drive into the coffin of 'The Thing'. His full account of the campaign, more amusing than indignant, gave his readers a vivid picture of the system in action, and was backed up by several affidavits from witnesses.

Still suffering from his cold, Cobbett returned to London to face a number of pressing personal problems. His debts had accumulated, and he was threatened with arrest for non-payment of bills, including one from his printer. 'The night we got back to London,' Anne recorded, 'to the house in Kings Road John and I went off to Mr. Reeves . . . to get him to come and see papa. Cold East wind and a dull dreary walk. Mr Reeves said "Come what's the use of his knocking his head against a stone wall. He has tried them all round and found none to rely upon. Better to take up again with where he started." '

After twice being arrested for debt, Cobbett eventually took his friend's advice and declared himself bankrupt. He was finally forced to sell Botley, which his family had never really liked, and move into a rented house in Brompton, near London – 'walled in from all roads, distant from all houses, nice garden, 4 acres of rich land for cows and pigs, surrounded by Nursery Gardens'. In order to become a bankrupt Cobbett had to spend five months in lodgings in Lambeth Road, near Kings Bench prison. 'It was very gloomy indeed,' Anne remembered. 'John took me over to the lodging Papa was in, in the Lambeth Road. Found Benbow* with him. Papa was very much cut down. It was a small dirty place in a dusty road, glaring with a spring sun and a cold wind.'

Anne found the streets of London full of troops brought in for the public execution of Arthur Thistlewood and others involved in the so-called Cato Street Conspiracy, who had been arrested in February. Thistlewood – one of the very few agitators of this period who can fairly be described as a Jacobin, albeit a very amateur and incompetent one – had previously been arrested following the Spa Field riots in December 1817, but was acquitted thanks to the damning evidence of a government agent, John Castle, who was shown to have played a leading role in instigating the riot. Undeterred by this brush with the law, Thistlewood formed a new plan, with the help of another of Sidmouth's agents, George Edwards, to assassinate the entire cabinet at a dinner party in Grosvenor Square. In fact there was never any

* Publisher of the *Political Register*.

dinner party – the government had inserted a bogus announcement in a London newspaper in order to incriminate Thistlewood's gang, who were all then arrested in an upstairs room above a barn in Cato Street, off the Edgware Road. This time the government knew better, and kept their agent Edwards well away from the trial. As was by now traditional, the prosecution along with the press asserted that the accused had all been led astray by 'seditious and blasphemous publications' – a theory that seemed to be confirmed when one of the witnesses, Thomas Chambers, was asked by the judge (Tenterden) what books he read:

> CHAMBERS: I read no books except the *Bible* and *Cobbett's Register*, and I believe I have read all of them.
> JUDGE: You could not read worse books than *Cobbett's Register*.
> CHAMBERS: I think, my Lord, I could not read a better; for, by following Cobbett's advice I have kept out of many hobbles and squabbles. *(Excessive laughing in the court.)*
> JUDGE: You may go.

Five men, including Thistlewood, were eventually convicted and publicly hanged at Newgate on 1 March. Cobbett, who had no sympathy with Thistlewood's politics, and who strenuously denied ever having met him when accused by Charles Dundas (Lord Amesbury) of being his associate, was all the same greatly impressed by his courageous bearing at his execution. 'Albion is still in the chains of slavery,' Thistlewood proclaimed from the scaffold. 'I quit it without regret.'

As with Peterloo, where the authorities had been alarmed primarily by the order and discipline of the thousands of demonstrators, it was the calm, defiant demeanour of the Cato Street conspirators which provoked an overreaction. Thousands of troops were massed in the streets around Newgate and barricades erected to prevent onlookers from getting near the scaffold and hearing the speeches of the condemned men. All these precautions had the opposite effect to that intended. The savagery of the executions, which included the decapitation of the dead men after they were hanged, provoked new anti-government feelings and did nothing to diminish the people's hostility towards the Liverpool ministry, which had done its best with the help of the press to portray the conspirators as a gang of dangerous desperadoes and atheists.

> Thus terminated a plot [Cobbett wrote] which produced a very great effect in this nation . . . such a horrible design, a design to inflict an indiscriminate killing on thirteen or fourteen men, the perpetrators being not only sane and sensible men, their justification of their conduct from first to last: their persisting in spite of the remonstrances of the judge that it was a duty to their country that they intended to perform, and finally the bravery with which they met their death; these all put together, could not fail to produce the deep impression which they did produce upon the minds of the whole nation, especially as they had been so recently preceded by the transactions at Manchester* which were still fresh in everyone's mind . . . From that day, the tone of the sons of corruption became less insolent and audacious. Everybody observed this, and every one said it to his neighbour.[2]

The Cato Street affair had one beneficial effect for Cobbett, in that it brought him into contact with a young doctor called Thomas Wakley, later a famous medical reformer and founder of the *Lancet*. The dead conspirators had had their heads cut off by a man in a black mask using a surgeon's knife, and later the rumour circulated that the masked man was a doctor lodging in Argyll Street, where, as it happened, Wakley lived. Four months after the execution a gang broke into Wakley's house, knocked him down, stabbed and kicked him, and set fire to the building, which was gutted. The villains were never traced and Wakley was unable to practise for months as a result of

* Peterloo.

his injuries. During this period he went to Cobbett for help, and the two became great friends. Wakley began to turn his attention to reform, and in 1823 with Cobbett's help and encouragement founded the *Lancet*, which included in its first issue a savage attack on the former Prime Minister William Pitt, with no reference to medicine that any reader could discern.

Only a month after the Cato Street executions, Queen Caroline landed in England. Since her departure in 1814 she had been travelling all over Europe in the company of her Italian lover Bartolomeo Bergami. They were closely followed by the spies of her husband the Prince Regent gathering evidence of adultery for the divorce he was determined to obtain. When she made it plain that she was returning to England and claiming her rights as lawful Queen, Liverpool sent the Whig lawyer Henry Brougham and William Huskisson to meet her at St-Omer in France. They proposed a deal whereby the Queen would agree not to come to England in exchange for an annuity of £50,000. Advised by the radical Alderman Wood, the man who had helped Cobbett when he was sent to Newgate, the Queen rejected the offer and embarked for Dover.

She landed on 6 June, to be greeted with extraordinary scenes of popular enthusiasm. 'The joy of the people,' Cobbett wrote, 'of all ranks was boundless and they expressed it in every possible way that people can express their joy. They had heard rumours about a lewd life and about an adulterous intercourse. They could not but believe that there was some foundation for something of this kind, but they, in their justice, went back to the time when she was in fact turned out of her husband's house, with a child in her arms, without blame of any sort having been imputed to her. They compared what they had *heard* of the wife with what they had *seen* of the husband; and they came to their determination accordingly.'[3]

As the Queen set foot in England cannons were fired from Dover Castle, the horses were taken from her carriage and she was dragged through the streets accompanied by waving flags and blaring trumpets. All the way to London she was escorted by young men on horseback while bells rang out from village churches. In London itself she was greeted by vast crowds and, as usual, the mob went round smashing the windows of anyone who refused to illuminate their houses in her honour. For the next months wherever she went there were massive demonstrations in her support. In September, during the divorce trial, the diarist Creevey saw thousands of sailors – what seemed like the entire Royal Navy – marching to Brandenburgh House, the Queen's temporary home at Hammersmith, to present an address to Her Majesty.

After years of suppression it seemed as if the people at last had an outlet through which to express their hostility towards the King and the Tory government. Cobbett, who with Anne had watched the Queen's procession into London from Shooters Hill, was now to throw himself wholeheartedly into her campaign. He had always sympathised with her, simply as a woman who had been harshly treated by the King and his ministers. But he was honest enough to admit that there was more to it than that:

> I had been two years in jail and had paid a thousand pound fine besides, for an act which merited the applause and admiration of all good men, and the King had my thousand pounds in his pocket. I had been driven across the Atlantic; I had been stripped of every farthing I had in the world; I had been torn from my farm, to earn which I had worked like a horse for twenty years; I had been made a bankrupt, and was then in the rules of the Kings Bench, in consequence of these two houses and this King, having passed laws to enable SID-MOUTH and CASTLEREAGH to put me in a dungeon at their pleasure. I will not pretend that the feeling created by these injuries had no effect upon my conduct here; and, for what purpose has God placed resentment in the breast of man, if it be not to prevent oppression, by showing those who possess

power that they are not always safe to exercise it in the doing of wrong? How would it be possible for justice long to continue in the world, if those who have power were *always safe* from the resentment of the oppressed?[4]

If Cobbett felt a personal resentment, it was not apparent in his writing. In keeping with his aim, previously outlined, to make use of all events in the cause of reform, he sensed immediately, with his extraordinary political instinct, how important the Queen's arrival in England was going to be. 'Here is a new and great event,' he wrote on 10 June, only four days after she set foot in Dover, 'and in the state in which we are placed *every* event, no matter what it be, may be looked upon as of importance to us; because it may lead to some change or other; and it is next to impossible to suppose any change that would do us any harm, while it is always *possible* that a change may do us good, be the change what it may, and come how it may, and when it may.'

Whatever happened, the vital thing was for Caroline to stay in England. In a series of passionate letters over the next few days following her arrival in London, Cobbett urged her to stand her ground. If she returned to France, that would be taken as an admission of her guilt. Writing in the third person as 'the humble individual . . . who begs leave to address Her Majesty the Queen', he begged her to resist all attempts to make her compromise: 'He implores Her Majesty to be convinced that no terms, no conditions, no qualifications can, in the public opinion, remove the impression which consenting to abandon the country must necessarily make.'[5]

'The Queen's affair' revived Cobbett's spirits and gave him new hope. 'We were poor all the while,' Anne wrote. 'Papa, John and I often and often dined on cauliflowers or salad. But we were in high spirits. I, for my part think papa would never have got thro' that hard time so well, if it had not been for the Queen's affair.' Anne, with her brother John, helped Cobbett distribute placards which were posted up all over town. But they had to be careful. 'We did not keep any of these in the house,' she writes, 'we were afraid'.

Cobbett's obsessive interest in the issue of Queen Caroline was by no means unique. For several months the affair occupied the attention not only of the press but of almost everyone in the country, regardless of age or class. As Hazlitt wrote:

> It was the only question I ever knew that excited a thorough popular feeling. It struck its roots into the heart of the nation, it took possession of every house or cottage in the Kingdom; man, woman and child took part in it, as if it had been their own concern. Business was laid aside for it, people forgot their pleasures, even their meals were neglected ... The arrival of the Times Newspaper was looked upon as an event in every village, the Mails hardly travelled fast enough; and he who had the latest intelligence in his pocket was considered the happiest of mortals.[6]

For his part, Cobbett filled issue after issue of the *Register* with all the speeches being made in Parliament, and printed in full the 'loyal addresses' which were being sent to Caroline from all over the country bearing thousands of signatures. Apart from all this, he used every opportunity to defend the Queen against the Tories and their cronies in the press. 'Never was there heard of in this world,' he wrote in an open letter to George Canning, 'persecution so implacable as that which has pursued this amiable, this unsuspecting, this unoffending, this excellent lady! She has been pursued by a spirit of persecution of the lowest and yet the most malignant description. A nasty, envious, jealous, grudging, bitter, venomous, grovelling, hate-engendered, soul-degrading spirit seems to have hunted her spirits as the dark and deadly minded polecat pursues the traces of the pheasant or the hare.'[7]

Cobbett was even prepared to defend the Queen's alleged lover Bartolomeo Bergami, on whom she had conferred the title of Count

(Bergami had wisely decided not to accompany her to England). But why shouldn't Caroline make him a count if she wanted?

> It would be a pretty principle, indeed to establish that men are taken from low and placed in high situations from bad motives in them that promote them. If this principle were applied to the persons promoted by His Majesty the King, where would the consequence of it end? There is the Right Honourable *William Huskisson*, whom you remember as a garcon apothecaire at Paris, and who used to stand with his hat off in Mr NEPEAN'S Hall waiting for answers to billets that he used to carry for him. There was the Right Honourable George Rose who was once a slop-server, but who was thought worthy of being visited in his house by the late King and Queen. I see some persons whose wives are now giving most splendid and sumptuous entertainments, and who are visited by whole troops of the nobility: I see some persons of this description who were not many years ago carrying orange baskets and pencil boxes about the streets, and who have grown up out of the paper money system as toad stools arise out of the trunk of an old rotten tree.[8]

Cobbett could not resist taking a crack at George Canning, whose mother had been on the stage. Was Bergami the social inferior of the cabinet minister, who was 'the son of a play actress, that had to resort to a pension from the public after she left the stage? . . . COUNT BERGAMI'S origin was scarcely lower than this; and yet, Sir, we have seen a man of this origin, not only cut a great figure, but take upon himself to speak most contemptuously of what he has been impudent enough to call the lower orders of the people'. Cobbett appeared to be sincere in arguing that the Queen was innocent of the charge of adultery. Later he took the view that in the light of her husband's behaviour, his bigamous marriage and numerous affairs, the question was irrelevant. But in 1820 when the King was still alive it was impossible for any journalist to make such points. Cobbett had to content himself by reminding his readers that Caroline had been accused of this sort of thing before, in 1807, and that the charges had been dismissed by a panel of peers. What was to stop the same thing happening again? And this time the charge was of such 'a vague and uncertain character the sort of proof upon which it rests must be poor and insignificant compared with that which was offered and given on the former occasion'.

As the trial of the Queen approached, Cobbett's old Aunt Sally William Wilberforce took it upon himself, as keeper of the nation's conscience, to intervene and attempt a last-minute settlement of the issue. He obtained the consent of the House of Commons to an address to be delivered to Caroline proposing on behalf of MPs that in return for her leaving the country she would be allowed to keep her royal status and be given money, even a special yacht to convey her to the Continent. But nothing was said about her insistence that her name be restored to the Church of England's liturgy – a concession which George IV adamantly refused to make. In yet another letter Cobbett urged Caroline to reject Wilberforce's package:

> Mr Wilberforce's notion is clearly seen through by the public, who have no doubt that it is intended to effect by supplication that which it is perceived cannot be effected by threats . . . The writer of this paper presumes humbly to express an opinion that the Answer to his Address should explicitly reject the advice contained in it . . . An answer of this description, would, it is believed, put a stop to the efforts of Mr Wilberforce.[9]

He could not conceal his delight at the treatment given to Wilberforce and his three fellow MPs when, wearing special court dress, they called on the Queen the following day at Alderman Wood's house in Portman Street. A large crowd had collected outside, and while the negotiations were in progress kept up a chant of 'Turn them out!', at the same time, according to Cobbett, 'making use of other expressions very little flattering of the deputation'. When the MPs eventually emerged, the Queen having politely rejected their proposals, they had to run the gauntlet of the angry protesters: 'A most dreadful rush,' Cobbett wrote in his open letter to Wilberforce, 'accompanied with expressions which I do not choose to put upon paper, was made by the people towards the door of the first carriage into which you all four jumped with great agility.' Wilberforce returned home to Kensington, where he burst into tears on seeing a humble moss rose in his garden: 'Oh the beauty of it, oh the goodness of God in giving us such alleviations in this hard world . . . And how unlike the Queen's countenance.'[10]

After the ignominious failure of the Wilberforce mission, Lord Liverpool reluctantly began proceedings against Caroline, which took the form of a Bill of Pains and Penalties which had to be passed through both Houses of Parliament. Before the trial began, the Queen sent a long (three-thousand-word) letter to her husband which was published in all the newspapers and caused a further sensation. Rumours flew about as to its authorship. Alderman Wood was mentioned. Dr Samuel Parr, a learned schoolmaster and scholar who had once been a friend of Cobbett's first Aunt Sally Dr Priestley, was also suspected of writing it.

Even in his *History of the Reign of George IV*, published in 1832 when the King and Queen were both dead, Cobbett did not like to reveal that it was he himself who wrote the letter. His children were sworn to secrecy, and it was only after his death that James revealed the truth. The significance of the letter from Cobbett's point of view was that it gave him *carte blanche*, in the person of the Queen, to attack the King – something he could not do writing in the *Register* under his own name for fear of prosecution. Even so, we note that he held back from referring to George's various infidelities, not to mention his bigamous marriage, the kind of thing that 'a woman scorned' would have done in the circumstances. Cobbett would have remembered the fate of Leigh Hunt and his brother, who had been imprisoned for two years in 1813 for casting aspersions of this kind on the King (then the Regent). Not only that, but Sidmouth's infamous Six Acts, introduced in the previous year, specifically defined as a seditious libel any language intended to bring into hatred or contempt the King or either House of Parliament. Even though the letter was officially written by the Queen, when it was published the government-financed *Courier* called it a libel, while the *New Times*, which also received a subsidy from the government, said it contained 'seditious and treasonable doctrines'.

There were therefore very good reasons for Cobbett, already a convicted libeller and liable to banishment if convicted a second time, to go to any lengths to conceal his authorship. 'We were in absolute terror when the Queen's letter first appeared in the newspapers,' Anne wrote. 'Young Mr Bryant came over to us with one in his hand and read it out with great feeling, Papa and I affecting wonder and admiration the while. He the writer, I the copier. Papa got up and went away and tore up his rough copy.'

The letter was published in all the newspapers on 7 August 1820, and when printed separately was estimated by Cobbett to have sold an amazing two million copies, and an even larger number in America. The Queen herself was especially pleased with it, and when she had her portrait painted by James Lonsdale insisted that it should show her holding the letter in her right hand (the picture now hangs in the Guildhall in London). Almost equally popular as the letter was an anonymous pamphlet called 'A Peep at the Peers' which, according to Cobbett, sold 100,000 copies and went into several editions ('It was in every village in the Kingdom'). Dedicated to the Queen, its aim was to demonstrate the amount of patronage enjoyed by the members of the House of Lords and their relations, thus rendering them unfit to judge the Queen impartially. Cobbett, again, never claimed authorship of 'A Peep at the Peers'. It was not listed in the regular catalogue of his books in the *Register*, and he printed a number of letters from 'The Authors' to give the impression that the pamphlet was the work of others.

Cobbett would never admit it, but Anne, in her memories of this time, twice refers to their being afraid. In fact 'A Peep at the Peers' bears his unmistakable stamp, if only in the frequent use of italicised words and the references to some of his favourite bugbears, such as Edmund Burke. Along with a companion pamphlet, 'The Links of the Lower House', 'A Peep at the Peers' gives a clear and concise picture of the degree of nepotism and corruption endemic in the system and the links between the aristocracy, the armed services and the Church. For instance, the entry under the Prime Minister Lord Liverpool reads:

LIVERPOOL. E. First Lord of the Treasury £7000: Commissioner of Affairs of India £1500: Warden of the Cinque Ports £4,100: Clerk of the Rolls in Ireland £3,500. Half brother of Cecil Cope Jenkinson, Under Secretary Colonial and War Department £2,000. His cousin John Banks Jenkinson, Dean of Worcester and two church livings £2000. This man married a daughter of *Augustus Peckett*, Receiver-General of Customs £4000. One son of this Peckett is a Judge in India £4000. And another is Captain in Navy £700. A brother is a Major-General and Gentleman Usher to the late Queen, and has a pension; and a son of this one is Captain in Navy £700. Another sister of the Parson married a Mr. Cornwall and has a pension of £250. His relations Mrs Rickets and Miss Rickets receive, the former £411 and the latter £103.10s. This Earl is related to the *Bishop of Worcester*, whom see. His wife is sister of the Earl of Bristol and his sister is wife of Lord Verulam. See Whitworth. The Tutor of this Earl, Dr Ireland Dean of Westminster with two church livings worth altogether 3 or £4000 – £34,964.*

* Total paid from public funds.

In his letter Cobbett (in the person of the Queen) made much of these incestuous connections, to argue that the Lords would not give her a fair trial:

> Your Majesty is the *plaintiff*: to you it belongs to appoint and to elevate peers. Many of the present peers have been raised to that dignity by yourself and almost the whole can be, at your will and pleasure, further elevated. The far greater number of the peers hold, by themselves and their families, offices, pensions, and other emoluments solely at the will and pleasure of Your Majesty, and these, of course, your Majesty can take away whenever you please. There are more than four fifths of the peers in this situation, and there are many of them who might thus be deprived of the far better part of their incomes.

The bulk of the letter, however, consisted of a highly emotional protest in Cobbett's best purple prose, calculated to arouse the sympathy, especially, of female readers, and ending with a final magnificent flourish:

> I have now frankly laid before your Majesty a statement of my wrongs, and a declaration of my views and intentions. You have cast upon me every slur to which the female character is liable. Instead of loving, honouring and cherishing me, agreeably to your solemn vow, you have pursued me with hatred and scorn, and with all the means of destruction. You wrested from me my child, and with her my only comfort and consolation. You sent me sorrowing through the world, and even in my sorrows pursued me with unrelenting persecution. Having left me nothing but my innocence, you would now, by a mockery of justice, deprive me even of the reputation of possessing that. The poisoned bowl and the poniard are means more manly than perjured witnesses and partial tribunals; and they are less cruel, inasmuch as life is less valuable than honour. If my life would have satisfied Your Majesty, you should have had it on the sole condition of giving me a place in the same tomb with my child; but, since

you would send me dishonoured to the grave, I will resist the attempt with all the means that it shall please God to give me. CAROLINE. R.

The trial of the Queen finally opened in the House of Lords on 19 August, amid elaborate security precautions. Cobbett described how a number of witnesses, mostly Italian, Swiss and German, had been mustered by the government to support the charge of the Queen's adultery with Bergami – 'but the people of DOVER were with great difficulty prevented from sending [them] back again by water, without assistance of boats or ships'. When the foreigners reached London they found it impossible to obtain accommodation: 'For the safety of their own houses people drove them out as they would have driven out snakes.' Meanwhile no Italian in England could consider himself safe – 'the people of that nation were in actual peril of kicks and cuffs wherever they were seen'. Eventually it was decided that the only way of getting them to Westminster in safety was by water. Cobbett explained:

> There is an immense mass of building at Westminster called *'Westminster Hall,'* where the Houses of Parliament, the four courts of justice, and several other public offices, are included under one roof, covering an immense space, abutting on one side towards the THAMES, and having an open space between the building and that river. A part of this space is a spot called 'COTTON GARDENS.' Into this place, which had been fitted up with temporary buildings, for the purpose of cooking for the coronation-banquet (which coronation was to have taken place in July, if the Queen had not come), the witnesses had been brought from Holland, coming up the *Thames* in an *armed boat* and landed at night. Nothing could get at them on the land side, without battering rams or cannon. On the water side there was a wall of twenty feet high, and in the THAMES, just opposite, a vessel carrying from sixteen to twenty guns. At the distance of about six hundred yards to the north of the House of Lords, there was a barrack of foot

soldiers: another barrack, similarly finished at five hundred yards to the west; at a mile, a horse barrack to the west; at about two miles to the north, another horse barrack; a strong body of horse guards at about four hundred yards; a corps of yeomanry cavalry paraded the streets, with their swords drawn, to the east about four hundred yards; soldiers and police innumerable, constantly drawn up in every street and passage leading to the House.[11]

The scene inside the House of Lords has been captured in minute detail on a vast canvas, now in the National Portrait Gallery in London, by Sir George Hayter. It shows the small, forlorn figure of the Queen seated in a sea of male faces, many of them bewigged, with a few select spectators peering down from the upper galleries specially erected for the trial. The eye is drawn to the figure of Lord Grey, who with outstretched arm is in the act of cross examining the first and most important of the Italian witnesses, Theodore Majocchi, who had been the Queen's servant on her Continental travels. Majocchi later collapsed when he was subjected to a barrage of questions by the Queen's main counsel Henry Brougham, to most of which he replied, '*Non mi ricordo*' (I don't remember), a phrase that was a national joke for several years afterwards.

Cobbett in his account gives no credit to Brougham, though his final speech on behalf of the Queen was generally regarded as a triumph. As always, Cobbett paints himself as the central figure in the Queen's cause, with men like Brougham or Alderman Wood relegated to walk-on roles. Perhaps the highlight, from Cobbett's point of view, came when he finally had an audience with Caroline. The meeting was described by Anne in a letter to her brother James:

> My dear James, since I wrote the other letters which accompany this, Papa has been to Court and kissed the Queen's hand, and a very pretty little hand he says it is. We made the gentleman dress himself very smart, and powder his head, and I assure you he cut a very different appearance to what

he used to do on Long Island with the straw hat slouched over his eyes. He carried two addresses, one from the town of Warwick and the other from Bury St Edmunds (Baker's Town*). The Queen made him a little speech, in which she thanked him for the great services he had rendered her, and conveyed to him some handsome compliments about his talents and so forth. This was in public, of course, that is to say, her Chamberlains, Major Domos and Dames of Honour standing about. Her Chaplain, the gentleman who writes her answers for her (all that the Govr [i.e. Cobbett] has not written) told us the next day that when Papa left the room she turned round and said in her lively manner 'Well now, if that is Mr C no wonder such fine writing comes from him, he is the finest man I have seen since I came to England, aye, aye, if there be only a few such men as that to stand by me, I shall not care for the Lords.' All of which the Govr. says is nothing more than bare justice, for he says he saw no man there anything to compare to himself; you know the gentleman has by no means a contemptible notion of his person . . .[12]

Meanwhile at Westminster the case against the Queen rapidly collapsed, and when the Bill of Pains and Penalties had its third reading in the House of Lords the majority in favour was only nine. Liverpool was forced to give in and abandon the campaign. The news of his surrender spread rapidly through the country, and a massive celebration was soon under way. Cobbett hired a coach and drove round London with his children:

The streets were filled with people. It was dirt up to ones ankles on the horse road and in the causeways it was uncommonly dirty. In spite of this women as well as men crowded every street. The whole population seemed to be on foot; and not a face could I see that had not a smile upon it . . . From the extremity of Bishopsgate-Street down over London Bridge and through the Borough to Kennington; then again from

* Reverend Baker, the Botley parson.

Billingsgate to Kensington down Holborn-Hill along Fleet Street and the Strand, up the Haymarket and along Piccadilly; in all these streets . . . it was one place of illumination and one continued cry of triumph.

There was another characteristic in this rejoicing, well worthy of notice, namely that upon this occasion, an infinite number of guns and blunderbusses and cannons kept firing during the whole of this night, from sun set nearly till day light . . . To the noise of these was added that of squibs, crackers, rockets, fire-balls and all sorts of fireworks, so that not only in the street but also up in the air there was continual light over this immense space. All over the country church bells were rang, except of course in Botley. (Baker the parson whom I rendered so famous under the name of the '*Botley Parson*' had got the key of the church and would not give it up.)[13]

The Italian witnesses were burnt in effigy on bonfires, whilst 'At *Exeter* the rejoicing was such as must have charmed the bishop of that see.'

The remarkable thing about the non-stop series of demonstrations, culminating in the outbreak of this mass rejoicing following the Queen's acquittal, was that they were almost entirely peaceful and well-disciplined. This made it extremely difficult for the government to do anything to oppose them, or to fall back on the traditional propaganda about the 'lower orders' being whipped up into a revolutionary mood by seditious journalists like Cobbett. As one of those journalists, supposedly the most seditious of all, he experienced a new mood of freedom and elation. He had been afraid to acknowledge his authorship of the Queen's letter, and even when reporting the verbatim evidence of the Cato Street trial had used asterisks in some of the more inflammatory speeches of the conspirators. But now, after weeks of caution, the asterisks had been abandoned and he felt free to revert to his old knockabout style. He picked up on a story in the *Courier* which related how in the recent celebrations the Marquis of Buckingham, who had voted against the Queen, had been set upon by a mob when travelling through Aylesbury on the way to his seat at Stowe ('Though not in his own carriage the people discovered him,' the paper reported). The Marquis had been heckled by the crowd, objecting to his recent stance against the Queen, and had finally been allowed to go on his way 'amidst the most deafening groans'. Cobbett wrote:

> I must stop here to condole a little with the noble Marquis, who seems to have fallen in with a set of true-born radicals. Not to travel in his own carriage, and yet to be discovered by the people, must have been truly mortifying! And in Buckinghamshire too! To be placed in a state of *peril*; and to be rescued, probably by vile mechanic hands! The rabble rout rascals could not know it was the descendant of ROLLO, first Duke of Normandy, that they were thus handling! They could not know that it was a *Plantaganet* whose person they were placing in a state of peril! Alas! All respect for antiquity is disappearing! All veneration for noble blood, in spite of Sidmouth's circular and the Six Acts. Even these and Sidmouth's letter to the Manchester Magistrates and Yeomanry into the bargain, and a hundred other efforts made within the last three years and a half, not forgetting the example made in the Old Bailey in May last;* in spite of all these endeavours to keep alive in the bosoms of the people their reverence for noble families; in spite of all these, we see even in Buckinghamshire this noble Marquis actually mobbed and put in peril.[14]

'Nothing ever was, or ever will be more than a nine days wonder in England,' Cobbett once wrote. The euphoria did not last long. After a triumphant thanksgiving in St Paul's the Queen forfeited most of her support when, going back on all her previous pledges, she agreed to accept the government's offer of a £50,000 annuity. The following

* The trial and execution of the Cato Street conspirators.

year when she tried to break into George IV's coronation in Westminster Abbey she was rebuffed, and few people came to her support.
Shortly afterwards she fell ill and died – one of those convenient
deaths that so often come to the aid of the Royal Family. Her funeral
provided one last display of public feeling, and then, inevitably, she
was forgotten.

'The Queen's affair' is dismissed by some historians as an irrelevant and slightly farcical interlude following which events resumed
their normal and rather boring course. Such a view is quite mistaken.
It was not only one of the most extraordinary events in English history:
it had an enormous impact on politics and the course of the reform
movement. To that extent Cobbett had been right to recognise it as a
great opportunity. 'We owe a great deal to the poor Queen,' he wrote
to an American friend, Dr Taylor, in 1822. 'It was she that pulled
down the haughty foes of our freedom more than all the rest of us put
together . . . It was she that raised us from the very dust. The feeling
towards the THING now is much more of a *contempt* than *dread*.'[15]
At the time, he wrote in the *Register*: 'The truth is that the people
have been greatly changed, in respect of their opinions as to their
superiors in rank. The change has been going on from the beginning
of the French revolutionary War to this day. In 1793 the nation stood
in need of gentle treatment. Conciliation ought always to have been
the object of the Government. It never was, and it never has been, up
to the present hour. We have been under a government of lawyers
and lawyers know of no principle to govern by but that of fear; know
of no remedy but that of punishment.' Yet the *Courier* along with
other papers was still calling for more punitive measures, and once
more blaming the radical press: 'Again I say, it is worse than nonsense
to talk of bringing back the people to their former habits of cheerful
obedience by further assaults upon the press . . . A censorship would
only add to the evil. It would only render the people more callous
and the government more hated.'[16]

In fact the government's Six Acts had been made to look a non-sense. Sidmouth and Castlereagh had banned seditious assemblies and demonstrations of the Peterloo type, yet the government had not dared to act in the face of the vast demonstrations involving thousands of respectable people over weeks and weeks parading through the streets of London and other major cities. The Six Acts were supposed to put a stop to seditious libels. But numerous pamphlets, including William Hone's famous satires and Cobbett's own 'Peep at the Peers', had sold in their thousands and no prosecutions had been brought. As Cobbett himself wrote later, 'There was no law of libel for nearly a year; men talked in public and in print as if they were sitting by their fireside. All this gave a very rude shock to the whole of the governing power.' In February 1821 Castlereagh himself had lamented in Parliament that there were now so many libels being published that there was no time to take them all up. The King was not satisfied, and an organisation called the Constitutional Association (or the 'Bridge Street Gang' as the satirist William Hone called it) was formed to raise money in order to prosecute the 'scurrilous slanders and the most false inflammatory statements respecting public institutions and public men'. It was all very well, they said, when such libels had been read by 'the higher classes, which possessed the means of detecting their falsehood', but they were now in the hands of the lower orders – 'who are destitute of all means of arriving at the truth'.[17] Several MPs and peers including the Duke of Wellington and over a hundred bishops and clergymen subscribed to the Constitutional Association, but its legitimacy was questioned in Parliament and the few prosecutions which it brought were thrown out by juries.

On the wider reform front the Queen's affair had a number of important consequences. Some historians maintain that the reform campaign was eclipsed by the events of 1820, but Cobbett was much nearer the mark when he insisted that thousands who had hitherto been neutral had been persuaded by these events to join the movement.

Almost equally significant was the emergence of the Whigs as a popular party. Despite Cobbett's strictures on him, Brougham, the Queen's lawyer, became a national hero overnight, so popular that pubs were named after him. His success in the trial strengthened his hand in the party, helping to influence it towards reform. It was significant that immediately following the Queen's 'acquittal' three prominent Whig leaders, the Duke of Bedford and Lords Grey and Holland, began holding meetings at which they called for parliamentary reform. Even the Tories were forced, by the extent of the protests, to modify their hard-line policies and consider the need for a change of course. Cobbett said that after the Cato Street Conspiracy the 'Sons of Corruption' became 'less insolent and avaricious'. Events showed that this was even more true in the wake of the Queen's affair. The move towards the Reform Bill was slowly getting under way, but in the process William Cobbett was inevitably being sidelined by more influential figures who had adopted his ideas.

8

RURAL RIDER

I F COBBETT, like Queen Caroline, had died in 1821 he would be remembered by historians as a leading figure in the reform movement. But it is likely that he would be otherwise forgotten. What changed things was his decision the same year to set off on a series of journeys round England. So began those rural rides which, when his accounts were brought together in book form, made Cobbett an immortal, the author of a classic which has never since been out of print.*

Cobbett was quite unaware of the implications when he rode out of London with his son James on that misty October morning in 1821. As far as he was concerned it was an opportunity to see the state of the countryside at a time when he was once again becoming more and more involved with agricultural issues. And as an astute journalist he must have realised that his readers would welcome a change after an apparently endless series of diatribes on reform, the paper money and the national debt. It is unlikely that, at this stage, he had a book in mind.

Even the title *Rural Rides* came later. The first extract, written

---

* There are a number of different versions of *Rural Rides*. The first edition in book form was published in 1830. A new edition, edited by Cobbett's son James Paul, was published in 1853, including material from the *Political Register* not included in the first edition. Yet further matter from the *Register* was published in a three-volume limited edition by G.D.H. and Margaret Cole (1930). This also included Cobbett's *Tour in Scotland* (1832) and the account of his tour of Ireland in 1834. Recent editions consist of variations of the above.

from Burghclere, Hampshire, appeared under the simple heading of 'Journal', dated 'October 30, 1821, Tuesday (evening)':

> Fog that you might cut with a knife all the way from London to Newbury. This fog does not wet things. It is rather a smoke than a fog . . . The fog prevented me from seeing much of the fields as I came along yesterday; but, the fields of Swedish turnips that I did see were good; pretty good; though not clean and neat like those in Norfolk. The farmers here, as everywhere else, complain most bitterly; but they hang on, like sailors to the masts or hull of a wreck.

This journal was to appear irregularly in the *Political Register* for the next ten years as Cobbett travelled to and fro, usually on horseback, throughout the southern counties of England.

The year 1821 was a good time to do something different. Since 1820 the economic situation had improved, and the radical reform movement was in the doldrums. Orator Hunt was still in prison in Ilchester, but relations between him and Cobbett had cooled. Admiral Cochrane had gone to Chile to help that country's struggle for independence from Spain. The new breed of pamphleteers, Wooler, Carlile and the disciples of Paine, had come to regard Cobbett as something of a reactionary. Carlile himself referred to a 'disease in this gentleman to think well of past times and to see retrogression and not improvement in society'.[1] For his part Cobbett would always be at odds with the more radical reformers who, following Paine, were not only republicans but deists or atheists. Besides which, Cobbett had little interest in ideas or philosophy: he described one of Jeremy Bentham's books as 'puzzling and tedious beyond mortal endurance'. Richard Carlile he later demonised not only on account of his anti-Christian writings but because he had allied himself with Parson Malthus as an advocate of birth control, something that Cobbett regarded with abhorrence (though Nancy Cobbett, with fourteen pregnancies behind her, might have had a different view of the subject).

Poised between the radicals and the Whigs, with few political allies let alone a party, Cobbett more than ever resembled a one-man band. It was not a situation that he resented. On his return from America in 1819 he had written: 'I shall pursue my own cause singly. My banishment was productive of this advantage, among others, that it taught me to *depend on myself*. I am resolved to walk in the trammels of nobody; and to have no intimate connection, as to public matters, with any man.' It was an appropriate manifesto for Cobbett the rural rider, one man going forward alone on his horse.

In spite of all his setbacks Cobbett had never lost his love of England. It was this, rather than any political enthusiasm, that had inspired his early writings in America and that had brought him back in 1820. It was this too that made him reluctant, until quite late in the day, to encourage others to emigrate. Shortly before his death in 1835 he wrote in the *Register*: 'Is there any other country with homesteads, mansions, gardens, woods, such as there are in England? Are the post-chaises and coaches worthy of the name in any other country in the world? Does any other country present, and in such numbers, such bridges, churches and cathedrals?'[2] Coaches especially he loved, and horses:

> In every thing where horses are the chief instruments (and horses are second only to men) the English so far surpass all the rest of the world that there is no room for comparison. The man who has a mind to know something of England in this respect, should walk from the Tower of London to Charing Cross a little after day-light in the morning, while the streets are clear of people. He would often then see the teams of immense horses drawing up from the banks of the Thames, coals, timber, stone and other heavy materials – one morning last summer I counted, in various places, more than a hundred of these teams worth each of them, harness, wagon, load and

all, little less than a thousand pounds. The horses, upon an average, weigh more than a ton. But the finest sight in England is a stage coach ready to start. A great sheep or cattle fair is a beautiful sight; but in the stage coach you see more of what man is capable of performing. The vehicle itself, the harness, all so complete and so neatly arranged; so strong and clean and good. The beautiful horses, impatient to be off. The inside full and the outside covered, in every part with men, women, children, boxes, bags, bundles. The coachman taking his reins in hand and his whip in the other, gives a signal with his foot, and away go, at the rate of seven miles an hour the population and the property of a hamlet. One of these coaches coming in, after a long journey is a sight not less interesting. The horses are now all sweat and foam, the reek from their bodies ascending like a cloud. The whole equipage is covered perhaps with dust and dirt. But still, on it comes as steady as the hands on a clock.[3]

The long-lasting appeal of *Rural Rides* to later generations is in many ways due to the panorama it presents of an England before the Industrial Revolution transformed it, an England before the train, before the camera, the same country that can be seen in the large canvases of John Constable or the small engravings of Thomas Bewick. To his contemporaries Cobbett now emerged as someone more than just a pugnacious journalist, a writer who was likened to a guard dog by Heine and other, generally sympathetic, critics. In the far-off days at Botley Cobbett's neighbour Mary Russell Mitford, who watched Admiral Cochrane playing games in the garden with Cobbett's children, had seen that Cobbett had another side to him. 'Whenever he describes a place,' she wrote of his conversation, 'were it only to say where such a covey lay, or such a hare was found sitting, you could see it, so graphic – so vivid – so true was the picture.'

For the first time in the *Register* Cobbett now described the English countryside, thus putting on record his great love of England, so much at odds with the Sidmouth/Wilberforce view of him as a

dangerous revolutionary aiming to overthrow the country's institutions. The word 'beautiful' is one that occurs on almost every page
of *Rural Rides*. He applies it to the Valley of Avon in Wiltshire,
Peterborough Cathedral, the village of Selborne (made famous by
Gilbert White), the American partridge, Lord Folkestone's acacia
trees, the Romanesque doorway of Malmesbury Abbey, etc., etc. But
what gives these rural rides their unique flavour is the contrast between Cobbett's delight at the beauty of what he sees and the erup-
tion of anger and satire which can follow in abrupt succession. Thus
we find him riding through Romney Marsh in 1823 – 'This was
grass-land on both sides of me to a great distance. The *flocks* and
herds immense.' But scarcely has he described the scene than he flies
into a rage:

> I had baited my horse at NEW ROMNEY, and was coming
> jogging along very soberly now looking at the sea, then looking
> at the cattle, when my eye, in swinging round, lighted upon
> a *great round building*, standing upon the beach. I had
> scarcely had time to think about what it could be, when
> twenty or thirty others, standing along the coast, caught my
> eye; and if anyone had been behind me, he might have heard
> me exclaim, in a voice that made my horse bound, 'The
> MARTELLO TOWERS by —!' Oh, Lord! To think that I
> should be destined to behold these monuments of the wisdom
> of Pitt and Dundas and Perceval! Good God! Here they are,
> piles of bricks in a circular form, about three hundred feet
> (guess) circumference at the base, about forty feet high, and
> about one hundred and fifty feet circumference at the top.
> There is a door-way, about midway up, in each, and each has
> two windows. Cannons were to be fired from the top of these
> things in order to defend the country *against the French
> Jacobins!*

Generally speaking *Rural Rides* is a farmer's, not a Romantic's, view
of the country. In a typical passage, singled out as an example of fine

writing by Alan Hodge and Robert Graves in *The Reader Over Your Shoulder* (1943), a book, like Cobbett's *Grammar*, designed to correct bad English, he writes:

> The land in this, which is called the high point of Lincolnshire has generally stone, a solid bed of stone of great depth, at different distances from the surface. In some parts, this stone is of a yellowish colour and in the form of a very thick slate; and in these parts the soil is not so good; but generally speaking, the land is excellent; easily tilled, no surface water; the fields very large; not many trees; but what they are, particularly the ash, very fine and of free growth; and innumerable flocks of those big, long-wooled sheep from one hundred to a thousand in a good flock, each having from eight to ten pounds of wool upon his body. One of the finest sights in the world is one of these thirty to forty acre fields with four or five or six hundred ewes, each with her one or two lambs skipping about upon grass, the most beautiful that can be conceived, and on lands as level as a bowling green. I do not recollect having seen a mole-hill or an ant-hill since I came into the country; and not one acre of wasted land, though I have gone the whole length of the county one way, and am now got nearly half-way back another way.

Cobbett had at last been able to resume his own farming activities early in 1821 when, with the help of his oldest friend Major Codd, he acquired a four-acre smallholding in what was then the village of Kensington ('a little out of town'), on what is now the site of High Street Kensington Underground station. 'We have three cows,' Anne wrote to her brother James, 'and we are to have two more, and all except one of these are presents to Papa. A gentleman in Kent sent him two and two gentlemen whom Papa never even saw are going to send him a cow each . . . We are going to have an oven built so that you see we shall have our own home made bread and butter, our own pigs and moreover we have got a nice pigeon house – Now this is all vastly comfortable for folks that have been used to the country and within two miles of Hyde Park Corner.'[4] Encouraged by all this husbandry Cobbett published in 1821 one of his most entertaining books, *Cottage Economy*, a sort of plain man's guide to self-sufficiency telling him how to keep a pig, brew beer or make his own mustard.

In the meantime Cobbett had survived two libel actions: one brought by his former business partner John Wright (see page 111), which he lost; the other by Thomas Cleary, whom Cobbett had accused of forging a letter vilifying Orator Hunt, which he won, a victory that gave him special pleasure as Cleary had been represented in court by Henry Brougham, later Lord Chancellor in the Whig government. Born in 1788, Brougham (pronounced Broom*) was an ambitious Scottish lawyer whose advocacy on behalf of Queen Caroline had won universal praise from reformers, apart from Cobbett, who never acknowledged his contribution. He was a brilliant man of immense energy and industry both as a writer and speechmaker and, partly for that reason, Cobbett saw him as a rival and treated him always with especial scorn and banter – 'a very greedy hunter after place and he dislikes me naturally as a rat dislikes the cat which guards the bacon and cheese'. Like all the leading Whigs Brougham was an intellectual snob, but he was in his way as devoted to the cause of reform as Cobbett himself, another reason why the latter did his best to disparage him. Besides which, Cobbett always tended to be harder on self-made politicians like Brougham or Canning than on such patrician figures as Grey or Russell.

Wright had been awarded £1000 damages, but Cobbett was rescued, as so often, by a rich friend, George Rogers, a carter of Southampton who paid Wright £700 in an agreed settlement. It was to be the start of a more prosperous period in Cobbett's affairs.

---

* Thomas Creevey the diarist insisted on calling him 'Bruffam'.

He was now released from bankruptcy, and he had dismissed his printer William Benbow and, with the help of his son John, taken over the entire business of the *Register*, which according to Anne was expected to bring in two thousand a year. The printing works was established in an outbuilding of the farm. 'This arrangement has only been made three weeks,' Anne wrote to James in New York in January 1821, 'and you cannot think how merry it has made us all. Papa declares he never was so happy in his life, for now he says he feels some encouragement to labour, for he knows we shall not be robbed any more.'[5]

Cobbett's happier mood is reflected in the pages of *Rural Rides*, which apart from the occasional angry outburst is written in a generally good-humoured and jocular style, in keeping with that twinkling half-smile which observers described and which John Doyle caught in his drawings of Cobbett. It was not just that his personal circumstances had improved. Since his return from America Cobbett had been living for much of the time in the shadow of Sidmouth's Six Acts and the threat of banishment if found guilty once again of libel. Thanks to Queen Caroline that threat seemed to have receded. Sidmouth himself, who according to Creevey had taken to the bottle, retired in 1822 and was succeeded as Home Secretary by the young Robert Peel. Peel had his failings, but he was sensible enough to realise that the libel prosecutions over the last ten years had achieved nothing. They were discontinued and only revived by a new Home Secretary, Lord Melbourne, in 1831.

In August 1822 came the astonishing news that Lord Castlereagh, the Foreign Secretary and Sidmouth's spokesman in the House of Commons, had committed suicide by cutting his throat with a penknife at his country seat at North Cray in Kent. At the time it was reported that he was suffering from acute depression, but in his book *The Strange Death of Lord Castlereagh* (1959) H. Montgomery Hyde has convincingly argued that he was also the victim of a gang of blackmailers. They had compromised him with a transvestite prostitute, whom Castlereagh picked up in the street only to discover when they undressed in a nearby brothel that 'she' was a man. The incident occurred very shortly after a major scandal involving the Protestant Bishop of Clogher (County Armagh), who had been caught *in flagrante* with a guardsman in the back room of a pub off St James's Street by a little girl who peeped through a window and saw the two men, in Cobbett's words, 'engaged in a way not to be described'. Though the Bishop was arrested and given bail (which he later broke and fled to Scotland), his name was suppressed by the papers until Cobbett revealed his identity in the *Political Register*, noting at the same time that some years previously, in 1811 in Dublin, one James Byrne, a coachman then working for the Bishop, had been found guilty of falsely accusing his employer of making an immoral proposition to him and had been whipped through the streets of the city and given a two-year prison sentence.[6]

The arrest of the Bishop caused a sensation in London – Cobbett himself devoted pages of the *Register* to the affair – and Castlereagh became convinced that he too would be exposed and possibly arrested; in the end he committed suicide. Cobbett, who would have known nothing of the blackmail, was nearer to the mark than the official diagnosis of depression when he wrote of Castlereagh's death: 'What makes the bankers, money-jobbers and merchants cut their throats so gallantly? The dread of humiliation ... the dread of being humbled ... the dread of being brought to sweep those streets through which the throat-cutters have rolled with such insolence in their carriages.'[7]

The death of Castlereagh, this distinguished statesman who had played a dominant role in the Congress of Vienna at the end of the Napoleonic War, provoked an extraordinary outburst of public rejoicing. His death, says the French historian Elie Halévy, 'was hailed by the entire body of Liberals and Revolutionaries both in England

COBBETT'S WEEKLY REGISTER.

Vol. 43.—No. 8.] LONDON, SATURDAY, August 24, 1822. [*Price 6d.*

Published every Saturday Morning, at Six o'Clock.

TO THE

BOROUGHMONGERS.

On Castlereagh's cutting his Throat, and on their own probable Fate.

———

Steyning, Sussex, 21 August 1822.

BOROUGHMONGERS,

THE last time I addressed you I did it from Long Island. It was in a few months after I had fled across the sea to avoid the dungeons of Sidmouth. It was in the memorable year 1817, when the *Petitions for Reform* were answered by Bills to enable the Ministers to shut whom they pleased up in any prison that they pleased and for any length of time that they pleased. It was in the year of *Sidmouth's Circular.* It was in the year of the *hanging* of the brave *Cashman.* It was in the year when the *stern-path* man said, that the *funds had risen* in consequence of the passing of the dungeon and the gagging bills. It was, in short, in the year of your *most insolent* triumph; though you have always been insolent when the people have been suffering from oppression. It was in the year when one of the most hardened and infamous of you said, that such a *fuss* need not be made about the dungeoning; for, what was it? It was, at most, the *abstracting* of a *few dozen* of individuals *from society.* The cold-blooded and insolent tyrant, who uttered those words, is a fair specimen of the *whole of you.*

Your affairs are a little changed now. I told you they would change. Read my letter, that

P

Printed and published by C. CLEMENT, No. 183, Fleet Street.

The *Register*

204

and on the continent as if it had been the death of a tyrant'. Byron was inspired to celebrate it in a tasteless verse,* and when the coffin was carried into Westminster Abbey for burial there were cheers from the thousands of bystanders. More than any other minister this haughty Irish aristocrat had become identified in the public mind with all the repressive policies of the Tory government – Peterloo, the Six Acts, etc. Cobbett exulted in his death, writing an open letter to an imprisoned reformer, Joseph Swann, sentenced to four years for selling seditious pamphlets:

> CASTLEREAGH HAS CUT HIS OWN THROAT, AND IS DEAD! Let that sound reach you in the depths of your dungeon; and let it carry consolation to your suffering soul! As to compassion, as to *sorrow*, upon this occasion how base a hypocrite I might be to affect it! Nay, how base a hypocrite to disguise my satisfaction! . . . The ruffians who continue to praise this man, tell us that the history of his life is found in the measures of the Government for the last twenty seven years; and that is true enough . . . it is written in a mass of pauperism, hitherto wholly unknown in England, and it is written in starvation to Ireland amidst overproduction. As to his family and connexions, look at the immense sums which they are now receiving out of the fruit of the people's labour. And as to any compassion that we are to feel for them, we will feel it when an end to the sufferings of Reformers and their families will leave us a particle of compassion to bestow on anybody else.[8]

'We are told, that, at the grave,' Cobbett wrote, '*Lord Liverpool* seemed deeply sunk in grief, wept much and "shook his head". Well he might: it was a season for serious reflection.' Following so closely on the Cato Street Conspiracy and the Queen Caroline demonstrations,

---

* 'Posterity will ne'er survey
A nobler grave than this:
Here lie the bones of Castlereagh:
Stop, traveller and —!'

the reaction to Castlereagh's death was another blow to Liverpool's administration, which was already licking its wounds, uncertain as to how to react when repression had been seen to fail.

'The Government is comparatively gentle,' Cobbett had written in July to a friend in New York, 'very *tame* from what it used to be.' He was feeling still more free to speak his mind once again, and to forget the asterisks. The *Register*s following Castlereagh's death were as savage as anything he ever wrote. Not only that, but after months of being cooped up in lodgings he was at last able to engage in that physical work which was so essential to his well-being. 'He is uncommonly well,' Anne told James on 17 January 1821, 'and in good spirits and in good humour with everybody and everything except this vile rascal Benbow.' It is interesting to note that Cobbett, who so often railed against the piano as a plaything of the *nouveaux riches*, wasteful of time and money, did not object to his children now having one in their new home: 'We have got a piano,' Anne wrote, 'and there he sits of an evening and hears the girls play and sing, and very often, with the Roses or the Codds we make a little dance and Papa will go to bed in the next room and always tells us not to stop on his account, and sometimes we dance or play and sing while he is snoring, and sometimes he will listen for an hour or two after he is in bed to the music with his door open.'

Nancy had bought him a new dressing gown, Anne remembered, 'For she thought it would be so *easy* and pleasant to sit writing in . . . and he did wear it for a little while but never liked it.' Cobbett was quite fussy about his clothes:

> He was so particular about neatness and *lightness* (the last being the opposite of slovenliness) that he, at that time, did not carry a pocket handk[erchief] because it stuck out of his dress . . . of a piece with neatness in dress, was his great, his rigid particularity in not letting books or papers come into contact with other things, such as eatables or drinkables

especially . . . He was not careful to have nice furniture in his study, but all the things in it were to be kept strait [sic] and in order, no confusion. What few papers he had (and they were few) used to be folded, endorsed and tied up neatly. He did not keep letters, that is to say in the later years of his life.[9]

Cobbett did not have the acreage at Kensington to plant crops. 'But I see no reason,' he told James, 'why I should not, as I have the land, and so well situated, form a nursery . . . I take great delight in trees and gardens, and it gives me great pleasure to introduce and spread things of this sort.' He now concentrated on selling the seeds and seedlings of trees, and particularly in popularising his favourite acacia tree (the American locust). With the help of James in New York he imported quantities of seed, which he advertised at intervals in the *Political Register*: 'The outward appearance of this tree,' he wrote in his guide to trees and tree-planting, *The Woodlands* (1825), 'its beautiful leaves and flowers, are pretty well known in most parts of England but it remained for me to make known the properties of the wood.' The wood is exceptionally hard and was widely used in America for making posts as well as in shipbuilding. Cobbett sold over a million acacia seeds and no fewer than 13,600 trees to his friend Lord Folkestone, who planted them all over his Wiltshire estates at Coleshill and Longford Castle – 'They are the most beautiful clumps of trees that I ever saw in my life,' Cobbett wrote on his rural ride in 1826. 'What a difference in the value of Wiltshire if all its *elms* were *locusts!*' A few of these trees survive to this day (2003), though all the elms have died as a result of Dutch elm disease (a small instance of Cobbett's prophetic powers), but though there were some specimens that grew to a great height, the tree never thrived as it did in America or on the Continent, where it could reach sixty to seventy feet. In the end, with its graceful leaves and white blossom, it came to be planted more for its ornamental value – 'Acacia Avenue' becoming shorthand for leafy suburbia.

Cobbett wrote copiously to persuade farmers to grow maize as he himself had done on Long Island. Modestly labelling it 'Cobbett's Corn', he extolled its value as a staple food in preference to potatoes. Since the beginning of the century he had been conducting a campaign against the potato, which the government of the day was trying to popularise as a substitute for bread. Cobbett saw this as a trick, a nutritional version of the paper money. Pages of his *A Year's Residence in the United States of America* are devoted to a hilarious diatribe against 'Ireland's lazy root', with its tendency to *'debase the common people* as everything does which brings their mode of living to be nearer that of cattle. The man and his pig, in the potato system live pretty much upon the same diet, and eat nearly in the same manner, and own of nearly the same utensil.' Cobbett even managed to drag Milton's *Paradise Lost* and Shakespeare into the argument by insisting that, like the potato, they owed their popularity solely to the dictates of fashion:

> Now, Sir, what can induce the American to sit and hear with delight the dialogues of Falstaff and Poins and Dame Quickly and Doll Tearsheet? What can make them endure a ghost *cap-a-pie*, a prince who for *justice* sake, pursues his uncle and his mother, and who stabs an old gentleman in sport, and cries out 'dead for a ducat! dead!' What can they find to 'delight' them in punning clowns, in ranting heroes, in sorcerers, ghosts, witches, fairies, monsters, sooth-sayers, dreamers; in incidents out of nature in scenes most unnecessarily bloody . . . If I were to judge from the high favour in which these two books seem to stand, I should conclude that wild and improbable fictions, bad principles of morality and politics, obscurity in meaning, bombastical language, forced jokes, puns and smut, were fitted to the minds of the people. But I do not thus judge. It is *fashion*. These books are in fashion. Everyone is ashamed not to be in the fashion. It is the fashion to extol potatoes and to eat potatoes. Everyone joins in extolling potatoes, and all the world likes

Above William Wilberforce (1759–1833): 'prince of hypocrites'.

Below Henry, Lord Brougham (1778–1868), Lord Chancellor, 'Lord Crackskull': 'he is the weazel, he is the nightmare, he is the indigestion'.

Above Dr Benjamin Rush (1745–1813): 'the noted bleeding physician of Philadelphia'.

Above The Reverend Thomas Malthus (1766–1834): 'Parson I have, during my life, detested many men; but never any one so much as you.'

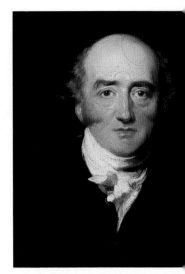

Above George Canning (1770–1827), Foreign Secretary and Prime Minister: 'impudent spouter'.

Above Henry Addington, First Viscount Sidmouth (1757–1844), Prime Minister and Home Secretary: 'the Doctor'.

Below Spencer Perceval (1762–1812), Prime Minister: 'the little pale-faced lawyer'.

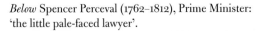

Above Lord Castlereagh (1769–1822), Foreign Secretary: 'shallow-pated as

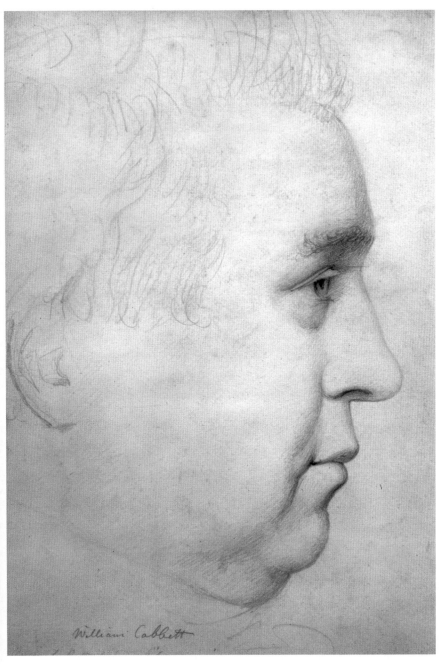

Cobbett in about 1816. Pencil drawing by Adam Buck.

Queen Caroline, wife of George IV, by James Lonsdale. The Queen is holding the letter 'For His Majesty the King' written for her by Cobbett and included in the painting at her request.

Nancy Cobbett in about 1830, by an unknown artist.

Cobbett enters Parliament in 1833. Detail from 'March of Reform' by
the political cartoonist 'H.B.' (John Doyle).

'You May Know a Man by the Company he Keeps'. The newly elected Cobbett takes his seat on the front bench, by Doyle (see pages 267–8).

The reformed House of Commons, 1833, by Sir George Hayter (detail).
Daniel O'Connell in the foreground, leaning forward, Cobbett on his right.

potatoes or pretends to like them which is the same thing in effect.

There was a good deal of deliberate exaggeration in all this, as Cobbett had a wide knowledge of Shakespeare and quoted him more often than any other writer. He also, in his book *The English Gardener*, which he adapted in 1828 from the American version, included detailed instructions on how to grow potatoes. Cobbett was more generally concerned to rebut the arguments of those politicians who were trying to turn the potato into a staple food. In Ireland, where the campaign was most successful, his arguments were more than vindicated by the terrible potato famine eight years after his death. As so often, what seemed at the time his wildest, most comical ideas were found to have been oddly prophetic.

Cobbett's seed-selling activities were conducted on missionary rather than profit-making lines. He saw himself as the benefactor of the community rather than a mere businessman, and as a result almost all his farming and nursery activities lost money. At the same time the trade in seeds brought him in touch with a great many farmers, most of whom would already have been familiar with his writings on agricultural topics. When Cobbett began his rural rides he often addressed large meetings of farmers in different parts of the country and stayed with farmer friends: William Budd at Burghclere, William Palmer of Bollitree in Herefordshire, or Joseph Blount, a Catholic landowner at Hurstbourne Tarrant in Hampshire, where Cobbett's initials can still be seen carved in the brick wall of Blount's house.

It was natural, when farmers began to agitate for political reform in the early 1820s, that Cobbett should ally himself with their cause. He did not agree with all their demands, opposing in particular the need to maintain a high price for corn, but it gave him another opportunity, as Queen Caroline had done, to make things difficult for the Tory government.

During Cobbett's lifetime farming had changed dramatically. An expanding population, the growth of big towns and the improvement in transport via roads and canals, turned agriculture into a highly profitable business. At the same time great advances were made in farming methods, such as the drill ploughing advocated by Jethro Tull, whose book *Horse Hoeing Husbandry* Cobbett republished in 1822 with a long introduction by himself. During the war years farming boomed, but after 1815 and the coming of depression prices fell, and in spite of the Corn Law of 1815, introduced to stop the import of cheap corn from abroad, many small farmers who had borrowed heavily in the boom years were bankrupted. A new kind of farmer had arrived, more interested in making money than in the welfare of his workforce. 'Scores of stock jobbers who did not know a fox from a deer or a hare from a pole cat are now become country squires,'[10] Cobbett wrote. This is one of the recurrent themes of *Rural Rides*. As Cobbett travels round the country he sees farms and estates in disrepair, fallen into the hands of 'Jews and Jobbers and eaters of taxes' or absorbed into big estates. At Burghclere in Hampshire,

> one single farmer holds by lease, under LORD CARNARVON, as one farm, the lands that men, now living, can remember to have formed *fourteen farms*, bringing up, in a respectable way, *fourteen families*. In some instances these small farmhouses and homesteads are completely gone, in others the buildings remain, but in a tumble-down state: in others the house is gone, leaving the barn for use as a barn or as a cattle-shed; in others the out-buildings are gone, and the house, with rotten thatch, broken windows, rotten door-sills, and all threatening to fall, remains as the dwelling of a half-starved and ragged family of labourers, the grand-children, perhaps of the decent family of small farmers that formerly lived happily in this very house. This, with few exceptions, is the case all over England . . .

Cobbett's concern lay always with the labourers, the real victims of the changes that were taking place, who had already been battered by the enclosures and the Speenhamland System. The old paternalistic system which Cobbett had been brought up in was disappearing. He looked back to a time when farmers and their labourers had lived under the same roof and shared their meals together – as they had done at Botley. But 'since the piano-fortes and the parlour bells and the carpets came into the farmhouse, the lot of the labourers has been growing worse and worse'. Wages fell, starvation was not unknown, and there were isolated outbursts of rick-burning. Sooner or later it would lead to a revolt.

Riding near Reigate in 1825, Cobbett went to a sale at a farm which had belonged for many years to a family called Charington:

> Everything about this farm-house was formerly of the scene of *plain manners* and *plentiful living*. Oak clothes chests, oak bed steads, oak chest [sic] of drawers and oak tables to eat on, long, strong and well supplied with joint stools. Some of the things were many hundreds of years old. But all appeared to be in a state of decay and nearly of *disuse* . . . This Squire Charington's father used, I dare say, to sit at the oak-table along with his men, say grace to them, and cut up the meat and the pudding. He might take a cup of *strong beer* to himself when they had none; but that was pretty well all the difference in their manner of living . . .
>
> I could not quit this farm house without reflecting on the thousands of scores of bacon and thousands of bushels of bread that had been eaten from the long oak-table which, I said to myself, is now perhaps, going, at last, to the bottom of a bridge that some stock-jobber will stick up over an artificial river in his cockney garden. '*By – it shan't*', said I, almost in a real passion; and so, requested a friend to buy it for me; and if he do so, I will take it to Kensington or to Fleet-Street, and keep it for the good it has done in the world.

The change in the relationship between master and worker was partly caused, in Cobbett's view, by an overall shift in the way the rich classes now regarded the poor. The old name 'the commons of England' had been replaced by the contemptuous and insulting expression 'the lower orders' (a usage that he endlessly harped on when attacking politicians). 'In short,' he wrote, 'by degrees beginning about fifty years ago the industrious part of the community, particularly those who create every useful thing by their labour, have been spoken of by everyone possessing the power to oppress them in any degree in just the same manner in which we speak of the animals which compose the stock upon a farm. This is not the manner in which the forefathers of us, the common people, were treated.'[11]

Richard Carlile could accuse him of thinking 'well of past times', but Cobbett had sensed for some time not only that a healthier, more democratic society had once existed in England, but that 'The Thing' had devised all kinds of propaganda to disguise the fact – what became known as the Whig interpretation of history, of which Macaulay was later the outstanding exponent. As defined by Chesterton in his study of Cobbett this went as follows:

> The revival of learning had led to the Reformation or sweeping away of the superstition that had been the only religion of the ruder feudal time. The enlightenment favoured the growth of democracy; and though the aristocrats remained, and remain still, to give dignity to the state with their ancient blazonry of the Conquest and the Crusades, the law of the land is no longer controlled by the lords but by the citizens. Hence the country has been filled with a fresh and free population, made happy by humane and rational ideas, where there were once only a few serfs stunted by the most senseless superstitions.

As usual with Cobbett, his conclusions were based largely on what he saw with his own eyes. As he went on his rural rides he looked at the soil and the farms, but also at the churches, impressed not only by their beauty but their size. A village with only a scattering of cottages had a church that could hold two or three hundred people. How could the likes of Malthus maintain that the population was growing at an alarming rate and would have to be diminished by birth control?

The old propaganda was powerful and effective. Even today the expression 'the Middle Ages' is used as shorthand for a time of barbarism and superstition. People say without thinking, 'We're not living in the Middle Ages,' to boast how enlightened and civilised they have become. Cobbett did not have to read any books to realise that this was nonsense. Visiting Salisbury on his ride of 1826, he went into the cathedral early in the morning:

> When I got into the nave of the church, and was looking up and admiring the columns and the roof, I heard a sort of *humming*, in some place which appeared to be in the transept of the building. I wondered what it was, and made my way towards the place whence the noise appeared to issue. As I approached it, the noise seemed to grow louder. At last, I thought I could distinguish the sounds of the human voice. This encouraged me to proceed; and, still following the sound, I at last turned in at a door way to my left, where I found a priest and his congregation assembled. It was a parson of some sort, with a white covering on him, and five women and four men; when I arrived, there were five couples of us. I joined the congregation, until they came to the litany; and then, being monstrously hungry, I did not think myself bound to stay any longer. I wonder what the founders would say, if they could rise from the grave and see such a congregation as this in this most magnificent and beautiful cathedral? I wonder what they would say, if they could know to what purpose the endowments of this cathedral are now applied; and above all things, I wonder what they would say, if they could see the half-starved labourers that now minister to the luxuries of those who wallow in the wealth of those endowments . . . For my part, I could not look up at the spire and the whole of the church at Salisbury without *feeling* that I lived in

degenerate times. Such a thing could never be made *now*. We *feel* that, as we look at the building.

Cobbett would always have described himself as a Christian. He had been taught his creeds by his old grandmother, and certainly during the Botley years he had been a regular churchgoer. His writings show a wide knowledge of the Bible (both Old and New Testaments), and he strongly disapproved of atheists like Richard Carlile. As for Paine and others who sought to extract from the Gospels a purely human Jesus – 'a virtuous and amiable man' – Cobbett with his habitual common sense could see that it was an impossible feat. 'I cannot,' he wrote, 'and I will not separate the scripture into *false* and *true*. It is, and it must be, all of a piece. If the miracles took place, so did the incarnation. We are told of both in the same book, and we have no other authority for either – to deny, therefore, the fact of the divinity of Christ, is, I repeat it again, to deny the truth of the Christian system.'[12]

To what extent Cobbett accepted the truth of the incarnation is not clear from his writings. For him, Christianity was always a matter of works rather than faith. 'In estimating the religion of man,' he wrote, 'we ought to enquire what is their *conduct*, and not what is their *belief*.' Christ's concern had been with the welfare of the poor, and in Cobbett's view this meant the simple business of seeing that they had enough to eat. His special contempt was reserved for those assorted do-gooders who hoped to improve the moral standards rather than the physical well-being of the 'lower orders' by providing them with tracts, or, like Wilberforce, making sure that they refrained from unsuitable behaviour on Sundays. Wilberforce, who abhorred everything about Cobbett, saw religion partly as a political tool, a way of keeping the lower orders in their place. 'The high and noble may be restrained by honour,' he wrote, 'but religion only is the law of the multitude.' His friend Hannah More (1745–1833) who had been a member of Dr Johnson's circle, produced 'cheap Repository Tracts', verses, chapbooks and moral fables for children, promoting the message that poor people should accept their lot in life and be prepared to suffer in silence. One of More's stories, singled out by Cobbett, was titled 'The Life of Peter Kennedy who lived on and saved money out of eighteen pence a week'. Another told of the death of 'the Evangelical mouse who *though* starving would not touch his master's cheese and bacon'. Some idea of the banality of Hannah More's verses for the 'lower orders' can be gleaned from the lines she penned at the time of the Spa Fields meetings of 1817, shortly before Cobbett's hurried departure to America:

> What follies what falsehoods were uttered in vain
> To disturb our repose by that Jacobin Paine
> Shall Britons that traitor who scorned to obey
> Of Cobbett and Hunt now become the vile prey?
> That 'England expects you should all do your duty'
> Is a phrase, I am sure, that cannot be new t'ye
> But can you your hero so sadly affront
> To confound the great NELSON with Cobbett and Hunt.

Enraged by her flow of pious humbug, Cobbett dubbed Hannah More 'the old bishop in petticoats', and in 1818 wrote a savage satirical parody of her verse:

> Come, little children list to me
> Whilst I describe your duty
> And kindly lead your eyes to see
> Of lowliness the beauty
>
> 'Tis true your busy backs are bare
> Your lips too dry for spittle
> Your eyes as dead as whitings are
> Your bellies growl for Vict'al
>
> But, dearest children, oh! believe
> Believe not treach'rous senses!

215

'Tis they your infant hearts deceive
And lead into offences

When frost assails your joints by day
And lice by night torment ye
'Tis to remind you oft to pray
And of your sins repent ye

At parching lips when you repine
And when your belly hungers
You covet what, by right Divine
Belongs to Boroughmongers

Let dungeons, gags & hangman's noose
Make you content & humble
Your heavenly crown you'll surely lose
If here on earth you grumble.[13]

The love of England which he so often proclaimed determined
Cobbett's loyalty to the national Church, however much he disapproved of its clergy. But it was that same patriotism which also led
him to defend Catholicism because it had been for nine hundred years
the official religion of England, the religion not only of those who
built the cathedrals but of King Alfred – 'perhaps the greatest man
that ever lived' – William of Wykeham and other famous men whose
memory he revered. Though Cobbett wrote little about specific Catholic doctrines, there were many aspects of the Church which he
strongly approved – notably the celibacy of the priesthood. Being
unmarried, William of Wykeham had used his revenues to provide a
school at Winchester and other benefits to the community,

> but in speaking of the diocese, in which I am born, and with
> which I am best acquainted, I may say, that it is certain that
> if the *late Bishop of Winchester* had lived in Catholic times,
> he could not have had a wife and that he could not have
> had a *wife's sister* to marry Mr EDMUND POULTER, in

which case, I may be allowed to think it possible, that MR
POULTER would not have quitted the *bar* for the *pulpit*, and
that he would not have had the livings of Meon-Stoke and
Soberton and a *Prebend* besides; that his son *Brownlow
Poulter* would not have had the *two livings* of Buriton and
Petersfield; that his son CHARLES POULTER would not have
had the *three livings* of Alton, Binstead and Kingsley; that his
son-in-law OGLE would not have had the living of Bishop's
Waltham; and that his son-in-law HAYGARTH would not
have had the *two livings* of Upham and Durley. If the Bishop
had lived in Catholic times, he could not have had a son
CHARLES AUGUSTUS NORTH to have the two livings of
Alverstoke and Havant and to be a *Prebend*; that he could
not have had another son, FRANCIS NORTH, to have the
four livings of Old Alvesford, Medstead, New Alvesford
and St. Mary's Southampton and to be, moreover, a *Prebend*
and *Master of Saint Cross:* that he could not have had a
daughter to marry Mr WILLIAM GARRIER, to have had the
two livings at Droxford and Brightwell Baldwin, and to be a
Prebend and a *Chancellor* besides; that he could not have
had Mr William Garrier's brother THOMAS GARRIER for a
relation, and this latter might not, then have had the livings
of Aldingbourn and Bishop's Stoke; and that he could not
have had another daughter to marry Mr THOMAS DE GREY,
to have the four livings of Calbourne, Fawley, Merton and
Rounton, and to be a *Prebend* and also an *Archdeacon* besides!
In short, if the late Bishop had lived in Catholic times it is a
little much to believe, that these *twenty four livings, five
Prebends,* one *Chancellorship,* one *Archdeaconship,* and one
Mastership, worth, perhaps all together more than *twenty
thousand pounds a year,* would have fallen to the ten persons
above named.[14]

Nepotism on a grand scale such as this was a feature of the Church
which made it the religious equivalent of the unreformed House of
Commons, and like MPs, parsons had very little contact with the
'lower orders' and knew scarcely anything of their lives. The poet

Walter Savage Landor wrote in 1836: 'There is no Church and never was there one in which the Ministers of religion have so little intercourse with the people as the English. Sunday is the only day that brings them together and not in contact. No feelings are interchanged, or sorrows or joys or hopes communicated.'[15] Many clergymen never went near their parishioners, leaving their curates to get on with it. Then there was the small matter of tithes, the system surviving from the Middle Ages whereby farmers were obliged to hand over a tenth of their produce (either in money or in kind) to the Church. As Cobbett never tired of repeating, the tithes had originally been intended to help the poor and needy, whereas now they were used by the clergy for their own benefit.

Cobbett's own experience of clergymen had not prejudiced him in their favour. Quite apart from the abuse of the tithes, they had allowed themselves to become part of 'The Thing', allies of the Tory Party, helping to keep the 'lower orders' in their place and stamp out any dangerous signs of radicalism. Cobbett had listened to the Botley parson preaching against reform and seen the Hampshire clergy spitting on his friend Admiral Cochrane in Winchester. He was well aware that many parsons also acted as magistrates and as such had played a prominent part in enforcing the Gagging Acts, like the Shropshire vicar who reported to Sidmouth in 1817 that he had sentenced two men to be flogged for selling the *Political Register*. All this was a far cry from the Christian tradition of helping the poor which he felt had prevailed prior to the Reformation.

Cobbett's feelings about cathedrals, the Middle Ages and the Reformation had been confirmed by the publication in instalments at this period of the *History of England* by John Lingard (1771–1851) – Lingard was a Catholic scholar, the friend of a number of Whigs like Brougham, who aimed in his history to give the Catholic side of the Reformation story but in an essentially moderate spirit, so as not to offend his mostly Protestant readers. Cobbett seized on his findings because they seemed to confirm what he had felt in his bones for some time: that the continuing prejudice against Catholics (especially the Irish) was unjustifiable, that the Reformation, which he came to view as one of the most shameful episodes in English history, had been converted by scholars and schoolmasters into a beneficial and necessary reform, and, above all, that the present-day aristocracy in many cases owed their wealth to lands and money that had been confiscated from the Church and given to their ancestors by the 'wife-killing founder of the Church of England, Henry VIII'.

Where Lingard had deliberately refrained from over-critical comment, Cobbett had no such scruples. Even the Catholic historians like Lingard and those who came after him would make a point of admitting that the monasteries in the sixteenth century were not wholly free of abuses, though never on such a scale as to justify their dissolution. Cobbett would not go so far. As usual he saw things in black and white – the monks were saintly figures helping the poor and the sick. Henry VIII and his henchmen Cranmer and Cromwell were unspeakable ruffians and villains. 'What man,' he asked, 'with an honourable sentiment in his mind, is there, who does not almost wish to be a *foreigner*, rather than be the *countryman* of CRANMER and of Henry VIII?'

Equally vile and obnoxious were those historians who had sought to whitewash these 'butchers' and 'ruffians'. Cobbett may have deplored Dr Johnson's inability to write grammatical prose, but he shared with him a deep-seated prejudice against Scotsmen, and especially those 'Scotch feelosofers', the economists and the Whig critics of the *Edinburgh Review*. The eighteenth-century Scottish philosopher David Hume had written what was then the standard *History of England* in several volumes. Hume gave the generally accepted view of the monasteries which Cobbett himself had hitherto supported. 'It is safest to credit,' he had written in volume four of his *History*, 'the existence of vices naturally connected with the very institution of monastic life . . . The supine idleness also and its attendant profound ignorance, with which the converts were reproached, admit of no question. No manly or elegant knowledge could be expected among men whose life, condemned to tedious uniformity, and deprived of all emulation, afforded nothing to raise the mind or cultivate the genius.'

'I question,' Cobbett replied, 'whether monk ever wrote sentences which contain worse grammar than these contain.' It did not take him long, with the help of mainly Protestant sources, to show that the 'malignant' Hume's picture of the monastic life was nonsense, and that aside from their good works and their schools the monks had produced countless manuscripts of unmatched beauty. He also pointed out that Hume, who had accused the celibate monks and nuns of being 'cursed with hearts more selfish and tempers more unrelenting than fall to the share of other men', had himself never had a family or a wife, and that he was 'a great fat fellow, fed, in considerable part, out of *public money*, without having merited it by any real public services'.

Today *Rural Rides* is by far the best-known and most widely read of Cobbett's books. But in his day the now forgotten *History of the Protestant Reformation* (1824) was much more popular not only in Britain but abroad. Cobbett claimed that he had sold 640,000 of the original part-works, and it was published in translation in France, Spain and Italy, and in Australia and America. In the *Register* Cobbett quoted a letter from a New York bookseller:

> Every person who reads anything on religion, or English history, has read it, and is talking about it. It's read by all sorts. And such is the demand for it that it is now stereotyping in this city, and, also, two separate translations of it are making into the Spanish language; one by a Mexican, and the other by an Irishman . . . I have just heard from a bookseller, who has come today from Philadelphia that they are stereotyping

it there. This is a thing heretofore unheard of, of any book,
in this country, except the Bible. I am confident from what I
see, that millions of them, almost will be sold on this continent.[16]

Such was the success of Cobbett's *History* that once again the authorities felt the need to 'write him down', as they had on a number of
previous occasions. A great many, mostly anonymous, pamphlets were
produced, the most popular being a series that contained Cobbett's
earlier anti-Catholic writings which used the trick of looking as if he
himself had published it. But Protestant apologists continued to try
to refute his arguments even after his death, and anti-Cobbett books
appeared in 1852 and again in 1869.

In spite of its extraordinary success the *Protestant Reformation*,
like almost all of Cobbett's books, was once again ignored by the
'shuffling bribed sots called Reviewers'. The intellectual snobbery of
the time decreed that someone who wrote so rudely, someone who
could describe the distinguished philosopher David Hume as 'a great
fat fellow', could not possibly be taken seriously as a historian. The
common reaction was put by the Whig diplomat Sir Henry Lytton
Bulwer who, though an admirer of Cobbett, wrote after his death that
'his two volumes are not to be regarded as a serious history'. (Ruskin,
a more considerable critic, described the history as 'the only true one
ever written, as far as it reaches'.) But even from a purely factual point
of view, as Abbot Gasquet observes in his introduction to the 1896
edition, Cobbett is generally very accurate. He relied for his facts on
John Lingard, and even occasionally used almost the same wording. It
was not the facts that upset the critics like Bulwer, but the conclusions
Cobbett drew, describing, for example, that national hero Queen
Elizabeth I as a cold-blooded murderer. Even the Abbot felt obliged,
for the sake of his Victorian readers, to omit 'the author's nicknames
and occasional strong or coarse expression'.

Cobbett later published a second part to the Reformation history consisting of a catalogue of all the abbeys and priories in the British Isles that had been confiscated or destroyed by Henry VIII and his successors. He was assisted in this task by an Irish priest, Father Jeremiah O'Callaghan. Father O'Callaghan had fallen foul of his Bishop in County Cork by conducting a single-minded campaign against usury, which he claimed was contrary to the law of God and a practice that had traditionally been condemned by the Church, St Augustine and other authorities. Forbidden to officiate as a priest, O'Callaghan travelled to Canada where he wrote a book entitled *Usury or Lending at Interest*. Finding himself *persona non grata* even in Canada, he decided to go to Rome and present his case in person to the Pope. On his way he stopped off in London and left a copy of his book in Cobbett's Fleet Street office. Cobbett was greatly taken by the book (which he later published), and also by its author when he finally met him. O'Callaghan, who obtained no support from the Vatican, returned to London where Cobbett engaged him to teach Latin to his sons. In 1828 Cobbett reprinted O'Callaghan's book, dedicating it to the Quakers, on whom in his preface he launched an extraordinarily vehement attack for practising usury:

> There you sit; there you consider and re-consider how you shall go to work to monopolise, to forestall, to rake wealth together by all manner of cunning and sharping tricks; and how you can contrive to live snugly and be as sleek as moles without ever performing one single thing that ought to be called work . . .
>
> You far exceed the Jews in point of turpitude, for they do work in certain ways; they collect old clothes; they patch shoes, they carry about pencils and oranges; and though they cheat like the Devil, still a considerable part of them do some sort of labour; whereas your whole sect live without labour and by preying constantly, from the beginning to the end of your lives upon the vitals of all those who labour. That you may receive your reward in dispersion over the earth of

poverty, rags, and hunger, is the sincere wish of WM. COBBETT.

Such a passage shows that in his support for Christianity, the Catholics and the poor Cobbett remained blissfully indifferent to any charges relating to a possible lack of charity on his part.

9

THE FINAL PROSECUTION

COBBETT'S FINAL PROSECUTION for libel in 1831 echoed that of 1810 in one important respect. In both instances he was sued for coming to the defence of a section of the community that he particularly admired and with whom he had close personal connections – in the first case soldiers who had been unjustly flogged, in the second farm labourers who were being arrested all over the country following the wide-scale rick-burning and the smashing of threshing machines.

Cobbett never forgot – nor could his readers, because he was constantly reminding them – that he had himself started life as an unpaid labourer, scaring the crows on his father's farm. Later at Botley he employed labourers, as he did on Long Island, at Kensington and now at Barn Elm on the south of the Thames, where he bought a farm in 1826. In accordance with the old tradition he kept his workers – four men and four boys – in the house, where they had free board and lodging. He stipulated that they all had to come from the country, be used to farmwork or be the children of farm labourers, and they had to wear smock frocks and nailed shoes – 'so that they were all clod hoppers'.

'For many years,' he wrote in December 1830, at the height of the rick-burning, 'there existed the *fashion* of looking on the working people, and particularly the labourers in husbandry, as an *inferior race* of human beings, and to treat them as such. They are the *contrary*

Cobbett's farm at Barn Elm

of this: they are the superior race and they always have been. They are laborious, willingly so; they are content as to their station in life; they are unpresuming, they are honest, they are sincere . . . and he who says the contrary is a base and infamous slanderer. It has been amongst the greatest delights of my life to see them happy, and amongst my most ardent desires to contribute towards that happiness. I have admired their character and their conduct ever since I was able to estimate them, and especially since I had the means of comparing them with those of the labourers in other countries, and I could willingly strike dead at my feet the insolent brutes who speak contemptuously of them and who fatten at the same time on their toil; who live in luxury on the fruit of their sweat and blood.'

The crisis in the countryside which erupted in widespread rioting and rick-burning in 1830 had a very simple cause – hunger. And the hunger in turn had an equally simple cause – low wages. Although it came to a head in 1830, the unrest had been bubbling away for some years. As long ago as April 1822 Cobbett had reported in the *Register* that stack-burning was going on in Suffolk: 'The mail coach is said to have passed in one night *seventeen fires* in this county.' It was, in its way, an agricultural form of Luddism, where desperate men with no political or union power drew attention to their conditions in the only way they could. The difficulty for the authorities, as Cobbett saw clearly, was that they could hardly blame it all on the agitation for reform as they had done on previous occasions. The result was that 'the cause of these acts of violence and revenge is always carefully kept out of sight'.

Cobbett knew perfectly well that the main cause was 'unsatisfied hunger', and he knew it, as he knew so many things, because he had seen it with his own eyes. On his rural ride near Petersfield in 1825 he cross-questioned a man who was hedging by the side of the road how much he was paid per day. The answer was eighteen pence – not enough, Cobbett noted, to buy sufficient bread for himself and his family, and less than was given to criminals in prison – 'In the gaols, the convicted felons had a pound and a half each of bread a day to begin with: they have some meat generally and it has been found absolutely necessary to allow them meat when they work at the tread-mill.' A single man working on the land in Sussex had seven pence a day – 'just seven pence, less than one half of what the nearest foot soldier in the standing army receives; besides that, the latter has clothing, candle, fire and lodging into the bargain'.

Cobbett was well aware of the practical as well as the moral benefits of ensuring that farm labourers were well fed. As a man who was more sensitive and imaginative than most of his political contemporaries, he also had a better idea than they did of what it was like to be hungry. In a moving passage in *Rural Rides* he describes how, setting out with his thirteen-year-old son Richard one morning without any breakfast,

The way seemed long and when I had to speak in answer to Richard, the speaking was as brief as might be. Unfortunately, just at this critical period, one of the loops that held the strap of Richard's little portmanteau broke; and it became necessary . . . for me to fasten the portmanteau on before me, upon my saddle. This, which was not the work of more than five minutes, would, had I had a breakfast, have been nothing at all, and, indeed, matter of laughter. But now it was *something*. It was his '*fault*' for capering and jerking about 'so'. I jumped off saying 'Here! I'll carry it *myself*!' And then I began to take off the remaining strap, pulling, with great violence and great haste. Just at this time, my eyes met his: in which I saw *great surprise*; and feeling the just rebuke, feeling heartily ashamed of myself I instantly changed my tone and manner, cast the blame upon the saddler, and talked of the effectual means which we would take to prevent the like in future.

Now, if such was the effect produced upon me by the want of food for only two or three hours . . . If the not having breakfasted, could, and under such circumstances, make me what you may call 'cross' to a child like this, whom I must necessarily love so much . . . how great are the allowances that we ought to make for the poor creatures, who, in this once happy and now miserable, country are doomed to lead a life of common labour and half starvation.

For five or six years prior to the outbreak of rioting in 1830 Cobbett had predicted that something of the kind was going to occur. It was not just the shortage of food in what looked like, to the outside observer, a land of plenty. The labourers had been degraded in a variety of ways which included their being treated in some cases as beasts of burden, harnessed to carts and dragging stones. They were viewed by their employers 'not as men and women, but merely as animals made for their service and sport'. But Cobbett's plea for sympathy would fall on deaf ears when those 'poor creatures' he described in *Rural Rides* took matters into their hands in the autumn of 1830. In Kent threshing machines, which put men out of work, were smashed even during that summer, and a month or so later the trouble spread throughout the county and into Sussex. Threatening letters from a mysterious Captain Swing (the rural equivalent of Ludd) were sent to farmers and landowners. Like Ludd, Swing was never identified, but the letters and the night sky lit up by burning ricks and barns were enough to inspire alarm and even panic.*

In general however the rebellion was a disciplined one. Following the burning of ricks or the smashing of machinery the gangs of labourers would descend on the farmer, demanding higher wages. Many farmers were sympathetic, and some even joined the rioters. They tended to blame low wages on the rents and tithes, in which case the village rector might find himself facing an angry crowd of workmen. What is undeniable is that throughout months of unrest involving many hundreds of labourers not a single person was killed.

Robert Peel, later Prime Minister, who had replaced Sidmouth as Home Secretary when the latter retired in 1822, was a superior character altogether, but his attitude to any form of political disturbance was no different from Sidmouth's. 'I beg to repeat to you,' he told the Kent magistrates, 'that I will adopt any measure – will incur any expense at the public charge – that can promote the suppression of the outrages in Kent and the detection of the offenders.' Peel was also keen, if not desperate, to implicate Cobbett in the disturbances. This feeling was shared by many of those, magistrates and others, who flooded the Home Office with letters demanding the prosecution of Cobbett. Peel's reply to one of them survives in the Home Office files: 'My dear Sir – If you can give me the name of the person who heard Cobbett make use of the expression to which you refer you would probably enable me to render no small public service by the prosecution of Cobbett for Sedition – Very faithfully yours, Robert Peel.'

* One of those to receive threatening letters – though not from Swing – was Shelley's father Sir Timothy, a reactionary Tory MP living at Horsham in Sussex. It carried a crude drawing of a knife with a warning to 'beware the fatal dagger'.

Illustration from a pamphlet accusing Cobbett of inciting farm labourers to riot

In November 1830, however, Peel along with the Prime Minister Wellington and his Tory colleagues, resigned. They were replaced, for the first time since 1807, by a Whig administration, headed by the seventy-year-old Lord Grey – 'this cold, proud, honourable, courageous man', as the Hammonds describe him. In spite of all he had said about them, Cobbett had high hopes of the Whigs, convincing himself that they were men of a different stamp from those they had replaced.

> They are not a fierce crew of hard lawyers such as we have seen in power before. The *chief* [Grey] is a mild and kind man, very fond of his own family, and who is likely to make the case of the labourers his own . . . Though Lord Melbourne did take part against us in 1817, he is not a ferocious fellow, he is a good-tempered man, and not inclined to be bloody.

There is Lord Holland who never gave his consent to an act of cruelty; and there is Lord Althorp, too, who has never dipped his hands in blood, nor crammed victims into the dungeon; and the Lord Chancellor [Brougham] with all his half-Scotch crotchets, has, at any rate, no blood about him.

As so often happened, Cobbett, with his natural instinct to think the best of people, was to be utterly disillusioned. The Whigs proved very quickly that when it came to the suppression of disorder they could be every bit as brutal as the Tories, if not more so. Cobbett, in other words, should have remembered his many previous reiterations that there was nothing to choose between the two parties.

Brougham, whom Cobbett had commended for having 'no blood about him', had been very quick to remedy the defect. On 2 December he told the House of Lords: 'Within a few days from the time I am addressing your Lordships, the sword of justice shall be unsheathed to smite, if it be necessary, with a firm and vigorous hand, the rebel against the law.' Melbourne, who had taken over from Peel at the Home Office, was that most dangerous of statesmen, the literary man who has strayed into politics. He was a wealthy dilettante who dabbled in theology, a man whose life had been saddened by a handicapped son and a wife, Lady Caroline Lamb, who was besotted with Lord Byron. For all his intellectual gifts and his knowledge of classical literature, Melbourne had no more understanding of the farm labourers' revolt than did Sidmouth or Castlereagh. In his view the main job of the government was merely to prevent crime. He therefore ordered troops into all the worst-affected areas and instructed local magistrates, many of whom were acting as mediators between the farmers and their workmen, to desist. Their duty was to enforce the law and impose the harsh penalties that were laid down (the law of 1827 prescribed seven years' transportation for the destruction of a threshing machine, the death penalty for firing a rick). Special commissions were now set up to try the hundreds of labourers who had taken part in the disturbances and the judges, taking their cue from Melbourne, showed no mercy. After two months of rioting three men were executed and 457 transported for various terms – all this despite the loss of not a single life. It was one of the most savage and reactionary suppressions by any government during the nineteenth century, and it led to bitterness in the countryside which in some instances lingered on into the twentieth. It was presided over by a man, Melbourne, who has been held up as a charming and civilised minister and is remembered as the kindly avuncular 'Lord M' who coached the young Queen Victoria in the art of statesmanship.

As happened so frequently in the past, the gentlemen in the House of Commons were unable to grasp the simple fact that starving farm labourers – those ignorant and illiterate 'lower orders' – could resort to violence of their own accord. There had to be 'a plot', and there had to be radical agitators urging them on to commit their crimes. Once again Cobbett found himself the chief suspect, despite the fact that he had frequently expressed his horror of violence. In December Arthur Trevor, the MP for the rotten borough of New Romney, asked the Attorney General to prosecute Cobbett, whom he accused of 'exciting the population to disturbance and discontent'. Peel had been looking for evidence to connect Cobbett directly to the riots, and Melbourne, his successor, was no different. He too was being bombarded with petitions from magistrates urging drastic action against Cobbett. But, like Peel, he needed evidence to prove incitement. 'Nothing is so difficult to prove as the utterance of words,' he replied to High Sheriff of Sussex Mr Sanctuary on 6 January 1831, 'so it might be very difficult to found a prosecution upon any proof which could now be obtained; at the same time it would be of considerable importance to obtain such proof as it would throw new light upon the character and proceedings of the individual in question' (i.e. Cobbett).[1]

A Hampshire magistrate, Mr Drummond, had advised the Home

Secretary to use informers to get the necessary evidence, but Melbourne was wise enough, in the light of the previous scandals involving government agents like Oliver and Edwards, to reject the proposal. At the same time he was foolish enough to involve himself in an intrigue every bit as devious and compromising as those which so discredited his Tory predecessors, and one which later gave Cobbett a useful stick with which to beat him.

Cobbett had lectured at Battle in Sussex in October 1830 to 'the chopsticks of the country', as he called the farm labourers. The following month Thomas Goodman, a cooper earning fifteen shillings a week (twice the average pay of a farm labourer), was convicted of setting fire to a Battle farmer's barns on five separate occasions. He was sentenced to death. Some days later Reverend H.J. Rush, a curate from Crowhurst, several miles from Battle, obtained a confession from Goodman which was published on the same day as the MP Arthur Trevor passed his motion calling for Cobbett's prosecution: 'I, Thomas Goodman, never should have thought of douing aney sutch thing if Mr Cobet had never given any lectures; I believe that their never would bean any fires or mob in Battle nor maney other places if he never had given aney lectures at all.' The confession was reported in *The Times*, which had for some time been supporting the Whig opposition and which had very close links with a number of ministers, especially the Lord Chancellor Brougham.

In his *Register* Cobbett was easily able to show that the confession was false, and that the two or three hundred people who had been at the Battle meeting would confirm it. But the matter did not stop there. On 30 December three Sussex magistrates went to Horsham, where Goodman was awaiting execution, and procured a second, more detailed, confession:

> I Thomas Goodman once heard of one Mr Cobbit going A
> Bout gaving out lectures at length he came to Battel and gave
> one their and there was a gret number of peopel come to hear

him and I went he had verrey long conversation concerning the state of the country . . . and he said it would be verry proper for every man to keep gun in his house espesely young men and that they might prepare themselves in readiness to go with him when he called on them and he would show them which way to go and he said that peopel might expect firs their as well as others places. This is the truth and nothing but the truth of a Dying man

Thomas Goodman.

A third, even longer, confession going over the same ground was later printed by *The Times* on 7 January 1831. In it Goodman embellished his account of Cobbett's Battle lecture, which he claimed 'made A verrey great imprision on me and so inflame my mine that i from that time was determined to set stacks on fire'.

The course of events was following a familiar pattern. First there was the attempt to discredit Cobbett with the help of the press and the fraudulent confessions, two of which were published and circulated as a separate pamphlet. Then, when the campaign proved counter-productive, the confessions so easily disproved, there remained the possibility of prosecution. In the meantime, however, Melbourne committed a fatal error by securing a royal pardon for Goodman, who was sentenced instead to transportation to Tasmania. Thus the Home Secretary was implicated in what looked like a blatant miscarriage of justice. He cannot have been so foolish as to think that Goodman could have appeared as a witness against Cobbett in court. So what had he hoped to achieve? The only consequence was to provide Cobbett with invaluable ammunition for his defence in any subsequent prosecution.

The Constitutional Association known as the Bridge Street Gang had already been complaining in 1822 about the lack of prosecutions for libel and blasphemy being initiated by the government. William Hone's scathing satire 'The Political House that Jack Built', with cartoons by George Cruickshank, had sold thousands of copies, as had Cobbett's 'A Peep at the Peers'. Yet no action was taken in spite of the Six Acts being in force when Robert Peel became Home Secretary in 1822 – he seems to have accepted the obvious fact that libel prosecutions and imprisonments achieved nothing beyond turning the accused into heroes and martyrs. The Whigs' decision to resort once again to the law was the result of a renewed panic brought about not just by the Swing riots but also by the second French Revolution of July 1830, which resulted in the downfall of Charles X, whose Bourbon dynasty had been restored to the throne following the defeat of Napoleon. All kinds of wild rumours were current about the farm disturbances, including the suggestion that they were being organised by Frenchmen. For a brief period the old nightmare of Jacobinism returned to haunt the governing classes, and they resorted to the same old remedies that had failed so often in the past. As far as Cobbett was concerned it was a tactical blunder to prosecute him at the very time when the Whigs were at last engaged in a campaign for political reform against powerful opposition from the King, the Tories and the Lords. Cobbett, a hugely influential figure with an enormous following in the country, was their natural ally at such a time. Instead of which they embarked on a course that seemed bound to alienate him.

Richard Carlile, whom Cobbett had attacked for advocating birth control, was put on trial for libel in January 1831 and sentenced to two years' imprisonment. Proceedings were launched against Cobbett the following month (17 February), accusing him of seditious libel in the *Political Register* of 11 December 1830. The offending passage occurred in a lengthy article headed 'RURAL WAR':

> . . . But without entering at present into the *motives* of the working people, it is unquestionable that their acts have produced good, and great good too. They have been always told and they are told now, and by the very parson that I have quoted above, that their acts of violence, and particularly the burnings *can do them no good* but add to their wants, by

destroying the food that *they would have to eat.* Alas! they know better; they know that one threshing-machine takes wages from ten men; and *they* also know that they should have none of this food: and that *potatoes* and *salt* do not burn! Therefore, this argument is not worth a straw. Besides, they see and feel *that the food comes,* and comes *instantly* too. They see that they do get some bread, in consequence of the destruction of part of the corn; and while they see this, you attempt in vain to persuade them, that that which they have done is *wrong.* And as to one effect, that of *making* the parsons reduce their tithes, it is hailed as a *good* by ninety-nine hundredths even of men of considerable property; while there is not a single man in the country who does not clearly trace the reduction to the acts of the labourers, and especially *to the fires*; for it is the terror of these, and not the bodily force, that has prevailed.

Cobbett himself seems to have been quite unconcerned about the prosecution ('Indignation is the main feeling of us all,' his son John wrote, 'women as well as men'):

When the news of the indictment was brought to my house in Bolt Court, by a reporter of 'The Star' newspaper, about eight o'clock in the evening, and when the servant came up and told me of it, after I was in bed, I prayed to God to protect me, turned myself round and fell fast asleep. The next morning I went home to Kensington and sat down with my family whom I found at breakfast; the whole group heard of my resolution with delight. They had made up their minds to the same thing before my arrival. Not a tear, not a sigh, not a sorrowful look did this dreadful menace produce, if I except one little mark of anxiety which discovered itself in my wife on the morning of the trial. She had got me a pair of new silk stockings to wear on that day: and when I put them on, I found them too short and spoke rather hastily about it, whereupon she made a little bit of a cry . . .[2]

His mood of optimism persisted until 7 July, when the case was due to be heard at the Guildhall in the City of London. The night before he slept soundly for seven hours, got up as usual at four o'clock, gave instructions to the workers in his Kensington nursery and set off for Bolt Court:

> Arrived there and found breakfast ready for me and a good many friends; and now mind, ate about half a pound of good fat leg of mutton, roasted the day before, and no bread or anything else with it, and no salt, and never drank one drop of anything that whole day until after the conclusion of my speech, when I drank two stone bottles of milk, out of a horn given me by a pretty little American lady, the wife of Mr Cooke, the portrait painter.[3]

Cobbett set out for the Guildhall by coach with his friends Sir Thomas Beevor, Mr Blount of Hurstbourne Tarrant, his lawyer Mr Edward Faithful and Mr William Palmer. 'I beseech you *to come*,' he wrote to Palmer. 'Pray make a shift to do it. It is a monstrous fight and I ought to have my friends about me.' One of his sons rode in the box with the coachman. They found the hall so crammed with people that it was hard to get in. Cobbett claimed there were two or three thousand people present. They included the Prime Minister, Earl Grey, and a number of cabinet ministers – Brougham, Melbourne, Durham, Goderich and Palmerston – whom Cobbett had compelled to attend by subpoena: 'There they sat, ranged in a row, to hear my defence.'

'The moment I entered,' he wrote, 'there was a great and general clapping and cheering for some time. When I got to my station, I, in order to produce silence, turned round, and, addressing myself to the audience, said "Be patient, gentlemen, for if truth prevail, we shall beat them."' Such a provocative start drew an immediate rebuke from the prosecuting counsel, the Attorney General Sir Thomas Denman. 'I feel it my duty,' he began with typical legal pomposity, 'to advert to some circumstances which have taken place and which are calculated in a material degree to interfere with the due administration of Justice. I allude to the fact that the defendant having thought proper, within a few minutes of the present time to enter this court at the head of a large number of persons . . . and that, after this court was assembled, while his Lordship was waiting in the ante-chamber he has thought proper to make an address to those people stating that, if truth prevailed he was sure of an acquittal, which sentiment has been received with shouts of applause by the persons assembled.'

His protest duly noted, Denman proceeded to quote at length from the *Political Register*, with particular emphasis on Cobbett's notion that the violence was producing benefit for the rioters: 'Therefore the people are told that the threshing machines might be consumed not only without depriving them of food, but with the immediate effect of putting food into their mouths. They are told that the effect of making the parsons reduce their tithes being hailed as a good by ninety-nine hundredths, even of men of considerable property, is a plain reason for acts of violence.' Under the law as it stood there was no need for Denman to prove that Cobbett's writings had led to acts of violence. No witnesses were produced and no reference was made to Thomas Goodman and his three confessions. Finally it was Cobbett's turn to address the jury.

When, against the advice of his friends, he had conducted his own defence in the libel trial of 1810, it was generally agreed that he put up a very poor performance. Ten years later however, when he acted as defendant in two libel actions, the picture was very different. 'Then,' wrote one observer, 'having by practice during the interval, acquired considerable ease of speaking, his appearance was more than respectable – it was very effective. His style was also abundantly characteristic and racy: it had great originality – it suited the man – it possessed nearly all the merits of his written productions, and it was set off by a kind of easy, good humoured, comic delivery, with no little archness both of look and phrase.'[4]

In 1810 Cobbett had been continually thrown as he struggled to make his case by the interruptions from the judge, Lord Ellenborough, who ruled that much of the evidence he tried to introduce was inadmissible. By 1831 the law had not been changed. Brougham had at one point introduced a Bill to allow a defendant to prove the truth of what he had written, but it was rejected by the House of Commons. All the same, Cobbett found to his relief that the judge on this occasion, the Lord Chief Justice Lord Tenterden, was more amenable. Although a firm opponent of reform, Tenterden was a moderate and reasonable judge by the standards of the day, and had even been commended more than once in the *Political Register*. Whether or not it was on account of his age – he was seventy, with only a year to live – he made little attempt to put Cobbett down.

Cobbett was a journalist of genius partly because he was able to seize on some pertinent fact, some remark made by a politician, and harp on it remorselessly, knowing that it would register in the minds of his readers and influence them towards his point of view. It was not a question of simplifying the issue but of finding something that would illustrate it in a remarkable way. He approached his defence in the same spirit – ignoring for the time being the specific passage that had been singled out, knowing that he was on weak ground, and instead launching into a general attack on the Whigs:

> You may have read in the newspapers of the vast affection which our present Whig Government have for the liberty of the press. They never proceed by information! Oh! no: they have a monstrous regard for the liberty of the press! And their Attorney General – Sir Thomas Denman, he also has a particular affection for the liberty of the press. 'Oh! Denman is an honest fellow; *he* will not, on any account, touch the liberty of the press.' But mark what has happened. What do you think? The Whigs have got themselves crammed into office and will you believe that this Whig Government will with their Whig Attorney General have actually carried out

more state prosecutions during the seven months that they
have been in office, than the former ministers, the Tories,
have done for the preceding seven years. The Tories, the
haughty and insulting Tories, if they showed their teeth, at
any rate, they did not venture to bite. But if this Whig Government retain their offices for twelve months, the jails must
unquestionably be enlarged.[5]

Cobbett proceeded to demonstrate very convincingly how, while prosecuting himself and Carlile, the Whigs had been prepared to ignore
libels in friendly newspapers like *The Times* or the *Courier*, 'which
are the tools, the dead tools of the Whig Government'. With his eye
no doubt on Lord Tenterden, he singled out an article in the *Courier*
which had attacked the 'degraded' judiciary, claiming that the only
reason the judges opposed reform was that they feared their salaries
would be reduced if it came about.

So long as the judge allowed him to roam far and wide, Cobbett
had been handed his defence on a plate by the Whigs. First the House
of Commons motion put down by Arthur Trevor, followed by the
three confessions by Thomas Goodman printed in *The Times*, which
in turn were followed by Goodman's reprieve. All this pointed to a
political prosecution. In answer to Goodman's confession Cobbett was
able to produce an affidavit signed by 103 people who had attended his
lecture in Battle stating that Goodman's allegations were totally false.
The signatories even included the Battle farmer whose barn Goodman
had burnt down.

Another defendant might have left it at that, but Cobbett, with his
eye for the telling detail, chose to link the Goodman story with another
– the story of Henry Cook, a nineteen-year-old ploughboy from the
village of Micheldever in Hampshire. Cook had joined a gang of
labourers who had gone round the local villages demanding money
from farmers and parsons. At one farm Mr William Bingham Baring
JP had grappled with the leader of the gang, who was threatening to

break the threshing machines, whereupon Cook aimed a blow at him with a sledgehammer and struck his hat. Though some witnesses claimed Baring was felled to the ground, he could not have been badly injured as he was seen the following day walking in Winchester. Nevertheless Cook, who put up no defence, was sentenced to death and hanged.

Apart from the contrast with Goodman's pardon, there were two reasons why Cobbett should have been especially outraged by this course of events. One was that they occurred in Hampshire ('that county which I know so well and which is dear to me from many causes'), not far from his birthplace at Farnham and his former home at Botley. Secondly, they involved a member of the Baring family, who symbolised for Cobbett the new order that had taken over in the countryside. The Barings, of whom there were many, were mostly merchant bankers who had amassed wealth during the recent war against Napoleon by lending money to the government. With their money they had bought estates, especially in Hampshire. 'The Barings are now the great men in Hampshire,' Cobbett wrote on his rural ride of 1823 – and later, 'they are everywhere, indeed, depositing their eggs about, like cunning old guinea-hens in sly places, besides the great open, showy nests that they have'. The Barings were not only loan-jobbers but boroughmongers as well. Bingham Baring was the eldest son of Sir Alexander (first Lord Ashburton), a Tory MP and owner of two boroughs (Thetford and Callington). (It was Bingham's wife who later bewitched Thomas Carlyle, much to the distress of his wife Jane, who echoed Cobbett's sentiments when she wrote: 'The Barings are everywhere. They get everything. The only check upon them is that they are all members of the Church of England, otherwise there is no saying what they would do.')

'The Attorney General and his colleagues,' Cobbett continued, 'know nothing of the state of the country, nothing of the feelings of the country people ... When Cook was taken home in a coffin, the people went to the confines of the parish to meet his corpse: indeed I may say the whole parish went to meet it. I feel more than I can express and you will have the goodness to excuse me.' The court report states: 'Mr Cobbett here made a slight pause, and then proceeded.'

> Gentlemen, six young women dressed in white, went to hold up the pall which a tradesman had gratuitously lent. Twelve young men went out to the bearers, and the corpse was conveyed two miles, to a place where it was interred in solemn silence. This is the important thing which I wish to impress upon the mind of his Lordship who is trying this case; upon the minds of the Noble Lords sitting by his side; upon the mind of the Attorney General, if he be susceptible of any feeling, upon your minds, Gentlemen of the Jury: namely that these transactions will never be wiped out of the minds of the labourers, until my advice be followed by the ministers, which is to bring those unfortunate men back to their families and their children, whom they have either imprisoned or transported.[6]

(This prediction was true. The rioters were not pardoned, and the Hammonds reported in their book *The Village Labourer*, published in 1911, that according to villagers at that time the snow never lay on Cook's grave in Micheldever churchyard.)

The story of Henry Cook had aroused strong feelings, and not only in Hampshire. The result was that the government and its news-papers had been forced, once again, to resort to lies. A correspondent at the friendly *Times* had reported on 3 January 1831: 'The fate of Henry Cook excites no commiseration. From everything I have heard of him, Justice has seldom met with a more appropriate sacrifice. He shed some tears shortly after hearing his doom, but has since relapsed into a brutal insensibility to his fate.' Relying on this and further reports in *The Times*, Denman had announced in the House of Commons that Cook was not even a poor ploughboy, as had been claimed.

He 'was a carpenter earning thirty shillings a week at the time when he joined the outrages ... He struck down, with a sledgehammer, one of the family of his benefactor; repeated the blow; and, but that he was prevented by one more faithful than himself, an individual whose arm was broken in the attempt to save the victim, a valuable life might have been lost to the community.'

Cobbett now produced an affidavit from John Cook, the boy's father, who was present in the court, and another from one of Alexander Baring's servants who had witnessed the attack (such as it was), refuting all Denman's claims: 'Now, this shows to what lengths he will go. He found this libel in the Times newspaper and "Ah!" said he "I know it is false; but as my friend Brodie* put this in and as that paper is praising me and my party, I will not prosecute, though it is such an atrocious lie upon this young man."' Cobbett declared that as far as Goodman was concerned, he could if he wished have proved very easily that his confessions were false as soon as they were published. There were many witnesses who had been at the Battle meeting who would have supported him. He however pointed out that if Goodman had been publicly shown to be a liar he might very well have been hanged, and he had no wish to be responsible for the death of the young man, whatever lies he might have told. He therefore did nothing until Goodman had been reprieved and transported to Australia:

> It is a very curious thing, that a man whom it was clearly proved had been guilty of five fires from private malice should be pardoned, while the life of poor Cook was taken, who did nothing but strike the rim of the hat of a man who had five relations having votes in Parliament: Mr Bingham Baring ... but this Goodman told a lie, and because he belied *me*, they spared him! If they had executed him, it would have been a proof that they did not believe his accusation against me; but because the Attorney-General did not put a stop to the

* Cobbett's nickname for *The Times*, after one of the newspaper's shareholders, Mrs Anna Brodie.

calumnies affecting my character; because he had plotted this prosecution against me, Goodman was pardoned. Here was mercy arising out of malignity; here was one of the highest prerogatives of the Crown prostituted for the purpose of propagating calumnies against one of his Majesty's most faithful subjects.[7]

This produced a burst of applause from the spectators, and Lord Tenterden threatened to clear the court if it happened again.

Later, Cobbett called the Home Secretary Lord Melbourne, the man primarily responsible for Goodman's reprieve, and asked him about the case.

> MELBOURNE: I recollect a man named Thomas Goodman who was sentenced to suffer death.
> COBBETT: Upon what grounds did he receive his Majesty's pardon?

At this the Attorney General immediately objected to the question, arguing that it was 'irregular and illegal'. Lord Tenterden agreed at once, thus effectively confirming Cobbett's suspicions. Cobbett then dismissed the five cabinet ministers on the grounds that he only wished to question them about Goodman's reprieve.

When it came to the actual passage complained of, he was on weaker ground. By saying that 'out of evil came good', and that the workers had benefited from the riots by gaining better wages, he appeared to be arguing that the end justified the means. He was saved, ultimately, by a piece of good fortune, the kind of thing that every hard-pressed litigant prays for. Some time previously Henry Brougham, now the Lord Chancellor, a man who was concerned in his own way just as much as Cobbett with helping to educate the 'lower orders', had formed a Society for the Diffusion of Useful Knowledge, publishing pamphlets – 'any work of useful tendency and sound principles' – on astronomy, animal physiology, the life of Galileo, etc. In December 1830, when the farm riots were at their height, Brougham had approached Cobbett asking permission to reprint the open letter he had addressed to the Luddites of Nottingham in 1816 urging them to refrain from smashing machinery. Ignoring the awkward fact that in 1831 he had said something rather different, namely that violence had produced results for the farmworkers, Cobbett seized on Brougham's request to republish his earlier pamphlet:

> This very publication of mine to the Luddites has been revived at the very time that the fires were raging in Kent . . . The Lord Chancellor applied in the name of a Society for the Diffusion of Useful Knowledge . . . and they wished to circulate it among those very labourers whom I am now charged with inciting to acts of violence. What times are these! This Diffusion of Useful Knowledge Society, with the Lord Chancellor at its head, came to quiet the labourers by some of the stuff out of 'Cobbett's sedition shop!' Nay, another member of that Society is my worthy friend the Attorney General: my worthy friend who accuses me of stirring up sedition, of stirring up the labourers to destroy property, applied to me for leave to publish my writings as a means of quieting the labourers! This is so monstrous that it will hardly be believed.[8]

According to the diarist Charles Greville it was the Brougham evidence (confirmed by the Lord Chancellor in person) that was responsible for Cobbett's eventual acquittal, but he grudgingly acknowledged that Cobbett made a powerful speech. It had lasted in all for four and a half hours and ended with a magnificent peroration, one of the finest pieces of invective in our political history:

> I have pointed out, and insisted upon, the sort of Reform that we must have; and they are compelled already to adopt a large part of my suggestions, and avowedly against their will. They hate me for this; they look upon it as I do, that they are married to Reform, and that I am the man who has furnished the halter in which they are led to church. For supplying that

halter, they have made this attack on me, through the Attorney General, and will slay me if they can. The Whigs know that my intention was not bad. This is a mere pretence to inflict pecuniary ruin on me, or cause me to die of sickness in a jail; so that they may get rid of me because they can neither buy nor silence me. It is their fears which make them attack me, and it is my death they intend. In that object they will be defeated, for, thank Heaven, you stand between me and destruction. If, however, your verdict should be – which I do not anticipate – one that will consign me to death, by sending me to a loathsome dungeon, I will to my last breath pray to God to bless my country and curse the Whigs and I bequeath my revenge to my children and the labourers of England.[9]

The trial had lasted from nine o'clock in the morning to seven in the evening. The jury sat all night but were unable to agree. The foreman, James Wilkinson, was an admirer of Cobbett, but John Seeley, a well-known bookseller, was equally strongly opposed to him. The result was deadlock, and at nine o'clock the following morning they sent a note to Lord Tenterden saying that they could not reach a unanimous verdict. 'Therefore the judge discharged them,' Cobbett wrote, 'and by that act an acquittal was pronounced, to the great joy of the audience (some of whom had remained in court the whole night to hear the verdict), to the joy of the friends of freedom in all parts of the Kingdom, and, I trust to the lasting benefit of the industrious, virtuous and hardly-used labourers of England, among whom I was born and bred, and to prevent whom from being reduced to live upon potatoes – the soul-degrading potato – and on water, instead of the bacon, bread and beer, of which our fathers had plenty.'[10]

It was Cobbett's finest hour, and a great blow to the Whigs – to Melbourne and Brougham especially. 'They have made a fine business of Cobbett's trial,' Charles Greville wrote in his diary.

His insolence and violence were past endurance but he made an able speech. The Chief Justice was very timid and favoured and complimented him throughout; very unlike what Ellenborough would have done. The jury were shut up the whole night and in the morning, the Chief Justice, without consulting either party, discharged them, which was probably on the whole the best thing that could have been done. Denman told me that he expected they would have acquitted him without leaving the box, and this principally on Brougham's evidence . . . This made a great impression, and the Attorney General never knew one word of the letter till he heard it in evidence, the Chancellor having flourished it off, as is his custom, and then quite forgotten it. The Attorney told me that Gurney overheard one juryman say to another 'Don't you think we had better stop the case? It is useless to go on.' The other, however, declared for hearing it out, so on the whole it ended as well as it might, just better than an acquittal and that is all.[11]

10

A GREAT EVENT

I N SPITE OF his defeat at the Coventry election in 1820, and in spite of the easier conditions for the press that prevailed, Cobbett had not abandoned his ambition to become a Member of Parliament. Like a number of people before and since he clung to the delusion that as an independent MP he would be able to exercise a great influence on the affairs of the nation.

The money problem had been solved thanks to the support of Sir Thomas Beevor, a wealthy young baronet of Hargham Hall near Norwich. Beevor, who accompanied Cobbett to the Guildhall for his trial, was happy to lend Cobbett large sums of money. He also, like Lord Folkestone, bought hundreds of Cobbett's acacia trees for his estate. In 1826 Beevor called a meeting at the Freemason tavern in London with the aim of getting Cobbett elected to Parliament, and a fund was established to raise the necessary money. The result was that Cobbett became a candidate for Preston at the election of 1826.

The Preston election was an almost exact repetition of the Coventry fiasco of 1820. Once again Cobbett travelled north, this time with three of his children and his faithful supporter Beevor, to be met by vast crowds whom he duly addressed in a speech lasting three quarters of an hour. When it came to polling, although there was not the same degree of intimidation as at Coventry, Cobbett's opponents (who included the future Prime Minister Edward Stanley, later Lord Derby) may not have been as openly hostile as Ellice and Moore, but they managed by all kinds of devious tricks to prevent Cobbett's supporters from voting, with the result that once again he failed to be elected. He was not in the least surprised or depressed, and declared that he had not had such a good time since he got married. Cobbett always enjoyed a scrap, and his experience gave him an opportunity, once again, to expose the corruption of the electoral system in the pages of the *Register*.

By the time Cobbett stood for the third and final time in 1832, the political map had been transformed. Liverpool, the long-serving Prime Minister and the surviving member of the infamous trio which included Castlereagh and Sidmouth, finally died in 1827. He was succeeded briefly by the 'impudent spouter' Canning, but he too died after only four months in office. In 1828 the Duke of Wellington, an arch-reactionary and opponent of any kind of reform, became Prime Minister and was soon involved in a controversy over the recurring question of Catholic emancipation. George IV died in June 1830, to be succeeded by his brother, the more accommodating William IV. The change of monarch, as always, entailed a general election, which took place in October amid rising alarm in governing circles over the farm labourers' riots and the revolution in France. The Whigs were returned to office under Lord Grey.

Cobbett, with his acute powers of foresight, had been predicting for some time that a great event was going to happen, but when Lord John Russell presented his Reform Bill to Parliament on 1 March 1831 he was probably as amazed as everybody else. The proposed reforms, which in effect abolished the rotten and pocket borough system, extended the franchise and weakened the hold of the aristocracy over the House of Commons, went much further than anyone had anticipated. All the same they did not go nearly as far as the campaigning radicals Hunt and Cobbett himself had demanded – universal suffrage, voting by ballot, one-year Parliaments. Should they now support the Whigs, or insist that the Bill as it stood was inadequate?

Cobbett's opponents, the Tory politicians, the judges, the hack journalists, too often took him at his face value – the belligerent, abusive egotist so frequently compared to a savage guard dog. That was the public image of the man, valuable from Cobbett's own point of view for ensuring that the sales of the *Register* were maintained. But perhaps because he was a farmer and used to making do with the best that he could get, what with all the vagaries of climate and the fickleness of nature, Cobbett had always been, behind his combative façade, a shrewd pragmatist, keenly concerned with advancing things by any practical means and if necessary by compromise. On the subject of reform, as long ago as 1819 he had written: 'I am for rejecting nothing that is tendered; I am for receiving anything as I would receive a shilling, a penny in part payment of a guinea.' Unlike some fellow radicals Cobbett, with his experience as the confidant of William Windham in his early career, had a sound understanding of the way politics worked. He would not have said so publicly, but he was no doubt well aware of the immense obstacles now standing in the path of Lord Grey, someone for whom he had considerable respect as a man, like Windham, unsullied by corruption. As the crisis neared its climax his support was total and unqualified. 'Every drop of honest blood in the nation has been roused for him,' he wrote on 12 May 1832, 'and *against* his false and perfidious foes in whom the people see *their own implacable and deadly enemies.*'

Cobbett had another powerful motive for compromise: his genuine abhorrence of violence. He saw his role to advocate, as always, the great benefits of reform whilst at the same time insisting on the need for peaceful means to achieve it. As for the first aim, in a remarkable passage in *Twopenny Trash** he wrote:

> It may be asked, will a reform of the parliament give the labouring man a cow or a pig; will it put bread and cheese

---

* Monthly extracts from the *Political Register* published between 1830 and 1832.

into his satchel, instead of infernal cold potatoes; will it give
him a bottle of beer to carry to the field, instead of making
him lie down upon his belly to drink out of the brook; will it
put upon his back a Sunday coat and send him to church,
instead of leaving him to stand lounging about shivering, with
an unshaven face and a carcase half covered with a ragged
smock-frock, with a filthy cotton shirt beneath it as yellow as
a Kite's foot? Will parliamentary reform put an end to the
harnessing of men and women by a hired overseer to draw
carts like beasts of burden; will it put an end to the practice
of putting up labourers to auction like negroes in Carolina or
Jamaica; will it put an end to the system which caused the
honest labourer to be fed worse than the felons in the gaols;
will it put an end to the system which caused almost the
whole of the young women to incur the insensible disgrace of
being on the point of being mothers before they were married,
owing to that degraded poverty which prevented the fathers
themselves from obtaining the means of paying the parson
and the clerk; will parliamentary reform put an end to this
which was amongst the basest acts which the Roman tyrants
committed towards their slaves? The enemies of reform jeer-
ingly ask us, whether reform would do these things for us;
and I answer distinctly that IT WOULD DO THEM ALL.[1]

But nothing would be achieved overnight, and in the meantime it was
necessary to be patient: 'We see land; and it would be foolish indeed
to jump into the sea of confusion and anarchy to reach it, when we
know, that, by quietly remaining on board, the ship would bring us
to it and land us in safety.' For a short time in May 1832, when the
Lords and William IV showed themselves adamantly opposed to the
Reform Bill, and when it looked as if the Duke of Wellington could
return as Prime Minister, many felt that if not anarchy then revolution
was a strong possibility. Well-organised civil disobedience was
planned, weapons were bought, huge demonstrations took place all
over Britain. Cobbett reported on 19 May:

To describe the agitation in London, and the anger of the people against the Lords, the Bishops, Wellington and particularly against the King is a task that no pen or tongue can perform. Every man you met seemed to be convulsed with rage: to refuse to pay taxes was amongst the mildest of the measures that were proposed at the general meetings: the language of the newspapers especially with regard to the King, Queen and other members of the Royal Family was such as to make them doubt the evidence of one's senses and yet it was a very inadequate representation of what was issuing from people's mouths. A cry for a republic was pretty nearly general; and the emigration [of the Royal Family] to Hanover formed the subject of a popular and widely-circulated caricature. Resistance in every shape and form was publicly proposed; and amongst the means intended to defeat the King and the new Minister was that most effectual of all means, a run upon the bank of Gold! which on Saturday the 12th May was recommended in a placard posted up all over London in the following words 'To stop the Duke, go for Gold'.*[2]

'There is a tremendous run upon the Bank,' Cobbett wrote to his friend William Palmer. 'The Old Devil cannot stand it many days.' He played little personal part in these events, and as they reached their climax, when the King at last capitulated and agreed to the creation of peers to get the Bill through the House of Lords, he retired to Godalming 'in order to get clear out of the hubbub of the noisy WEN'. Even here in 'this little quiet town of cleanly hearts' he witnessed signs of the hostility to the Royal Family, and especially William IV's German wife Queen Adelaide, who was known to be vehemently opposed to reform in the belief that if the Bill was passed she might meet the same fate as Marie Antoinette:

* A slogan coined by Cobbett's patron the cotton manufacturer John Fielden.

REMARKABLE RE-ACTION

AT Godalming in the county of Surrey

On Wednesday the 16th instant, the people of this little quiet town got a cart drawn by a horse and seated in it the representative of a MILITARY CHIEF; at his side the representative of a FROW.* The cart appeared to be accompanied, during the procession, by every creature in the town and also by numerous persons from the villages round about. The personages in the cart were a *living man and woman*! There was an erection, resembling a gallows, fixed to the cart, with a swing rail going over the heads of the culprits. The procession started from the bridge at the bottom of the town, going on slowly towards the market-place at the upper end of the town. At about every fifty yards of the progress, the executioner, armed with a pistol and a powder *shot the military chief*, who fell down backward in the cart, the *frow* hanging about his neck and screaming. At last the ceremony was concluded, by regularly putting ropes round their necks, white caps on their heads, and these being drawn down over their faces, the offending parties expiated their sins in a very becoming manner, first, listening attentively, with great apparent penitence, to a prayer of considerable length that was read to them and then committing their souls in due form, to the devil, hanging the legal length of time, and, being cut down, fell apparently dead into the bottom of the cart. The performers in this affair collected a good parcel of money, which they expended in drinking 'success to the Reform Bill.' The church-bells rang from morning to night, except when the offenders were hanging, when, as a matter of course, the *knell tolled*.

Such, and such like, has taken place in almost every sensible town in ENGLAND. This *ought to be translated and published in FRANCE*. Our neighbours ought to know the way that we go on in our little quiet country towns. I should have remarked that the FROW appeared singularly fond of the COMMANDER and kissed him, very affectionately, previous to their finally taking leave of this *miserable reforming world*.

* William IV and his German wife (i.e. *Frau*).

Looking back over the so-called 'Days of May' which ended eventually in the passing of the Reform Bill, Cobbett described it with his usual hyperbole as 'the most important event that ever took place in the world in my time'. But whether he genuinely believed that reform would produce the benefits for the working man that he had predicted is doubtful. He was however convinced, like many radicals, that the amount of money paid out in the form of grants and pensions to various placemen and hangers-on was responsible for the high levels of taxation, and that once the system was abolished all would be better off. Perhaps more important, to Cobbett's thinking, was the hope which he had stressed for many years in the *Political Register* that reform would bring new men into Parliament and so break the hold of the ruling oligarchy – the peers and landowners who had for so long held sway. But there was no guarantee of this. 'It is very much to be feared,' he wrote, 'that the habit of looking up to men of rank and wealth will prevail in the selecting of members of Parliament; and, if it prevail to any very great extent, the reform will produce no good effect.'

Cobbett was attacking the consensus, common to all ranks of society at that time, that government was something that was best left to the wealthy and well-educated, the same form of snobbery which led even the likes of Byron, Sydney Smith or Lord Holland to turn up their noses at Cobbett himself, a farmer's son ignorant of Latin and Greek. He imagined a conversation between himself and an elector:

COBBETT: Why do you want a man of rank or of wealth?
ELECTOR: Because he is more likely to be a clever man and to understand such matters on account of the superior education he has had.
COBBETT: Is the country in a state of ruin, misery and crime; is it not loaded with an irredeemable debt?
ELECTOR: Yes, certainly.
COBBETT: Have we not been governed entirely by men of rank and wealth?
ELECTOR: Yes, we certainly have.[3]

Cobbett pointed to the American example. Here was a country that was well governed, but where 'there is no *pecuniary qualification* whatever for a member of Congress: very poor men are frequently chosen, and very rich men never. There have been seven PRESIDENTS; two of them *died insolvent*, and were insolvent at the time they were PRESIDENTS.' The man to choose for Parliament should therefore be a man 'with no very great regard for riches. Industry, sobriety, moderation in his expenses, no fondness for luxurious living'; a man with 'a good store of knowledge, some talent and great resolution'. A man like William Cobbett, in other words.

Before standing for Parliament yet again, Cobbett had his own personal celebration to attend to, to commemorate the passing of the Reform Bill, 'which had in fact pronounced the fall of the rapacious, the insulting, the cruel and bloody-minded boroughmongers'. Lord Grey's final victory had been celebrated in much the same way as the battle of Waterloo and the acquittal of Queen Caroline – processions, bonfires, illuminations and dinners. Cobbett ignored it all, deciding to organise a special thanksgiving of his own. Turning a blind eye to the contribution that others might have made – among them the Birmingham banker Thomas Attwood, founder of the Political Union, and the tireless organiser Francis Place – Cobbett saw himself as the prime mover for reform and the man who had done more than anyone else to bring it about. But his natural egotism was tempered by the great respect he held for the agricultural labourers whose rising in 1830, he maintained, had triggered off the events that led to the passing of the Reform Bill:

> The general notion in London has been that the country labourers are ignorant creatures; that they have no sentiment at all relative to political rights and liberties; that, like cattle, they know when they are hungry and that their risings and committing acts of violence resemble, in point of motive the feelings which animate cows or oxen, when they break out of

a barren field to get into a rich pasture ... It has also been
fashionable, amongst even the working classes, to look upon
the country labourers, particularly those here in the South as
being totally ignorant with regard to public matters, and as
being utterly unable to be made to understand anything about
the political causes of their misery; and of course not knowing
the least in the world about Parliamentary Reform.[4]

It was to honour these farm labourers, and two in particular, that
Cobbett organised his 'Chopstick Festival'. It was to be held in the
Hampshire village of Sutton Scotney, chosen because it was from
there in November 1830 that a young farm labourer, Joseph Mason,
had set out to present a petition signed by 177 workers to the King,
then holding court at Brighton Pavilion. The petition was partly based
on one of Cobbett's recent lectures, but included a fine passage of
Mason's own composition which showed that he was not only a
religious man but also something of a poet:

> That many of us have not food sufficient to satisfy our hunger;
> our drink is chiefly the crystal element; we have not clothes
> to hide the nakedness of ourselves, our wives, and our chil-
> dren, nor fuel wherewith to warm us, while at the same time
> our barns are filled with corn, our garners with wool, our
> pastures abound with cattle, and our land yields us an abund-
> ance of wood and coal, all of which display, the wisdom, the
> kindness, and the mercy of a good creator.

After walking sixty miles from Sutton Scotney to Brighton, Mason
was kept waiting, then finally informed that the King could not accept
the petition, which should be handed to the Home Office in London.
Subsequently Mason and his younger brother Robert both took part
in the rising, and both were convicted of 'demanding money' from
farmers and parsons and sentenced to transportation to Australia for
life. Cobbett suspected, probably correctly, that in the absence of any

real evidence against them they were found guilty because they were shown to be subscribers to the *Political Register*, which they read aloud to regular meetings of the villagers.

The Chopstick Festival was intended as a counterbalance to the grand Reform Dinner which was about to be held in London, but also to draw attention to the fate of the Mason brothers, Cobbett pledging himself to campaign for their return along with that of all the others who had been transported. 'I shall give a dinner at SUTTON SCOTNEY,' he announced, 'to all the hundred and seventy-seven men who have not been transported and who signed the petition. When I was at Nottingham I purchased a ham that weighed *seventy two* pounds, which I have had properly cured. This ham with two or three fat sheep which I will have killed, shall be the meat for our dinner. I will have bread baked for the occasion; and I will have half a gallon of good strong beer for each man: MR ENOS DIDDAMS, whose name stands at the head of the petitioners, shall be our chairman; and we will drink to the health and speedy return of Joseph and Robert MASON: and we will say and do all those other things which, on such an occasion, will be most meet.' There was only one minor snag: 'Knives and forks will be the most difficult things to provide,' he wrote; 'each man must bring his own I believe.'

The date of 7 July was chosen, it being the anniversary of Cobbett's famous acquittal in the Guildhall libel action in the previous year. 'Everything was right,' he wrote, 'everything was pleasant. *The weather*, a bright sun and a gentle breeze, after a shower in the night, which had laid the dust.' At least seven thousand people, he estimated, flooded into the small Hampshire village from all over the country. They included most of his farmer friends, who brought their contributions for the feast:

A farmer from WERWELL sent, probably thirty pounds of bacon. Mr STARES of TICHFIELD sent a quantity of cooked bacon and some bread. Mr Budd [see page 209] came with his wagon from BURGHCLERE: stopped all Friday night at *Whitchurch* and had his sucking pig roasted, weighing *only thirty pounds*. He would take up nobody after he got to WHITCHURCH unless they brought their own provisions with them. He brought two geese, which he had roasted here for dinner and which he had hot; also some veal pies ready cooked, and some boiled bacon and some roasted veal. To these he added a good lot of plum-puddings ready cooked, and some immensely large gooseberry puddings: the gooseberries mixed in the batter, baked in milk pans, turned out when cold so that they could be cut up in solid pieces and handed about . . . There were altogether about two hundred and fifty pounds of puddings.

A tent (or 'booth') had been erected the previous day, with two long tables capable of seating about three hundred people. Pride of place was given to the men who had signed Robert Mason's petition – 'every one dressed in his smock-frock and with a blue riband to his hat'. Cobbett sat at the end of the table handing out food and observing with pride the good behaviour of all present: 'The goodness of the farmers and tradesmen who were present I can never sufficiently admire – They seemed to care nothing but supplying the people.'

In contrast to Earl Grey's Reform Dinner there were no toasts, 'or any of that disgusting stuff, which, if the mind be sound, makes the best of dinners sit uneasy on the stomach; Quite willing to leave a monopoly of that nasty rubbish to the guttlers and guzzlers who are to swallow three thousand pounds of our money next Wednesday'.

Overcome with the heat of the tent, Cobbett later adjourned to the village inn where he took off his coat and shoes and lay down for half an hour. At about three o'clock he got up and came down to the front of the inn, where a wagon had been provided by his friend Mr Blount. The word went round that he was about to make a speech: 'People soon flocked to the spot and I got into the wagon . . . positively stipulating that the persons nearest me while I was speaking should be the men, in honour of whom the festival was held. Some man put his little boy, about five years old, dressed in a smock-frock, and having a blue riband in his hat into the wagon. I sat him down upon some grass that had been brought for the horses; and there he remained all the time.'

Cobbett's speech touched on the usual themes – the excellent men who had signed the petition, his determination to secure the return of those who had been transported, the duty of the farmers towards their labourers, the unjust burden of tithes and taxes. When it was over those who had come furthest began to set off for home while the rest remained: 'dancing and singing and drinking occupied the time until Sunday morning'. Cobbett himself, as was his habit, went to bed early and got up at half past three the following morning, 'when the hamlet was as still as it ever had been since the first day of its creation':

> The booth was taken down completely, and gone. The morn-
> ing was rather wet, but very pleasant; and thus ended one of
> the pleasantest things that ever was seen in this world; forming
> a contrast, wide as that between heaven and hell, with the
> guttle and guzzle which will take place on Wednesday next
> in London [the Reform Dinner]; for here the provisions for
> the entertainment were a voluntary gift, there they are to be
> taken from the pockets of the people, who are to be excluded
> from participating in the feast. Here it was the generosity of
> men of property contributing to the means of giving pleasure
> to meritorious labourers; and there it is a set of impudent
> guzzlers and guttlers, swallowing the earnings of working
> people, which they have no more right to swallow than they
> have to take the skins off our bodies. Here there was no time
> wasted in toastings; there the nasty fulsome, lying, insincere
> rubbish vomited out upon one another reciprocally, will be
> even more disgusting than to behold the voracity of the
> guttlers and guzzlers, while they, straining and staring and

swelling, send down our turtle and turbot and turkey into those bottomless vaults which they call their stomachs. Here there will be no after-claps; there we shall have to pay for '*summer excursions*' for the guttlers and guzzlers, in order that they may take the salt-water to recover the tone of their voracious maws. Lord GREY would confess, I know, the truth upon this occasion, but if he have strength to resist the effects of what he will see and hear, I would bet my life that when he has left CHARLEY and FIGGINS and TAYLOR and the rest, and got safe into his carriage, he will exclaim 'By G-d, I wish I had been at COBBETT's chopstick dinner.'[5]

That morning being Sunday, Cobbett decided to go to church, and set out at six o'clock to ride to the nearby village of Micheldever. 'My practice,' he wrote, 'always is *to go to church*, which I always do in the country and never in town, because here, not only am I not offended by the sight of vanity and ostentation, but I have a very good opportunity of making an estimate of the condition of the people.' But there was another reason for Cobbett to ride three miles in the early morning to Micheldever, because it was there that the young plough-man Henry Cook, hanged the previous year for striking at Bingham Baring with a hammer (though not injuring him), was buried. It was a small pilgrimage on Cobbett's part, Cook being in his eyes a secular martyr to whom he wished to pay his final respects. This kind of gesture, similar in its way to his attempt to make amends to Tom Paine by digging up his bones, was important to him, his visit to Cook's grave alone on a quiet Sunday morning being the other side of the previous day's noisy celebration in the tent at Sutton Scotney. He soon found the grave, as it was covered with flowers, but there was no church service till the afternoon. He therefore adjourned to the inn, where he sat down and wrote about five thousand words for the *Political Register* describing the Chopstick Festival. He also wrote to his wife informing her that 'the whole ended without a single brawl though the parsons foretold "streams of blood"'.

The vicar of Micheldever, the Reverend Thomas Clarke, may not have recognised the tall, grey-haired gentleman in a red waistcoat who joined his congregation that afternoon and took his seat 'among the chopsticks'. Even if he did not, he might well have been alarmed by the keen attention with which the stranger seemed to be listening to his sermon, standing up while the rest of the congregation appeared to be lolling asleep in their pews. He would have been even more distressed to know that his words from the pulpit were about to be subjected to critical analysis by the most acerbic journalist of the day, a man whose invective at his expense would shortly be read by thousands of people all over the country.

'I was not disposed to expect anything in the sermon which would greatly delight me,' Cobbett wrote:

> I was not disappointed. I have never heard a discourse which I thought had less literary merit, and never one which I thought calculated to produce less effect. He took his text from the 10th chapter of the book of Numbers, and it consisted of the 29th verse, in the following words: 'And MOSES said unto HOBAB, the son of RAGUEL, the Midianite, MOSES'S father-in-law – we are journeying unto the place of which the LORD said, I will give it to you; come thou with us, and we will do thee good; for the LORD hath spoken good concerning ISRAEL' . . . I could not for the life of me imagine how the man would make it at all apply to any moral or Christian purpose. What was then my surprise when I found he had discovered . . . that the invitation from MOSES to HOBAB was meant that the latter was to abandon all earthly connections and all earthly goods; that he was all his life long to live sufficiently without wailing in order that, *after this life*, he might enjoy the kingdom of heaven!

It was unfortunate for Parson Clarke that he should have chosen to interpret his obscure text in this way, because it gave Cobbett an excuse once again to chastise verbally all those clergy who, along with the 'bishop in petticoats' Hannah More, sought to persuade their poor parishioners of the benefits of poverty and suffering: 'With regard to this doctrine of the necessity of worldly privations, sacrifice and sufferings, in order to ensure eternal life, it is at once the most absurd and the most mischievous that ever was held and that most at variance with the whole tenor of the holy scriptures.' If only Reverend Clarke had preached instead on the lessons he read from the Old and New Testaments:

> The first lesson was the 41st Psalm, which begins thus – *'Blessed is he that considereth the poor: the Lord will deliver him in time of trouble. The Lord will preserve him and keep him alive; and he shall be blessed upon the earth; and thou wilt not deliver him into the will of his enemies. The LORD will strengthen him upon the bed of languishing; thou wilt make all his bed in his sickness.'* What a sermon to a congregation of big farmers and miserable labourers might have been made from this exquisitely beautiful passage of scripture! I declare most solemnly, that this very passage which I have several times quoted in my writings, has *a great influence upon my conduct.* It is so just that a man should be blessed and protected: that he should be delivered from the grasp of his enemies; that his bed of sickness should be rendered less painful in consequence of his generous consideration of the poor: this is so just and natural, that, especially when expressed with the force and solemnity and simplicity of this passage, that the passage must make an impression on any man who reads it.

It was not only the parson that Cobbett found wanting at Micheldever:

> Fifty years ago it was the universal practice in all the villages and in all the country towns, for psalms to be sung by *singers*, consisting of persons belonging to the parish, who sang while the rest of the congregation sat silent. When PITT and his villainous paper money had introduced a mass of luxuries theretofore unknown in England, boarding schools sprang up

among the other toadstools of the system. Music became part of education and the farm-houses out of which the men and boys had been driven to make way for the music-master and the piano, became scenes of refinement in which the nose was turned up at the homely singing of the church. Organs were introduced; the general singing of the congregation, in imitation of the tabernacles of LONDON, crept about from church to church; hymns took the place of the psalms, but all this did not nearly equal what was going on in the meeting houses.

In hundreds and in thousands of instances the church congregation has been absolutely broken up by the musical ears of the parson's wife and daughters being too delicate to endure the choristers of the gallery.

About twenty years ago there was the common psalm-singing at MICHELDEVER; and I remember that my second son, who was there a little while at school with the parson of the parish, used to describe to me with great delight, the singing at MICHELDEVER, of which we had none at BOT-LEY. Old FRANCIS BARING had too much sense to suffer this order of things to be disturbed; and the parish used, as far as I can judge, to be a very happy one; but TOM BARING, having succeeded with his great stock of piety and with his curate (for he himself is the rector) of apparently the new caste, the psalm-singers are banished, and the hymn book is introduced; the parson stands up in his pulpit as lead singer and there is a bawling and squalling that admits not of adequate description. To be a singer in a parish used to be a little feather in a chopstick's cap; even that is now too great an honour for him; he is to be nothing but a hewer of wood and a drawer of water.[6]

Continuing his travels in Hampshire later that month Cobbett went to church at Havant, where he heard 'a heap of blundering stuff as one would wish to hear, doled out under the name of a sermon by a man, who, I am told, was an officer in the army during the late war'.

But at the village of Firle near Lewes in Sussex he was delighted to find the parson delivering 'some very wholesome instruction and in a very unaffected manner and what I have not seen since my return from AMERICA in 1800 – the *psalm singing* was in the old fashion, by a group of chopsticks assembled in a gallery'.

The following month, August, Cobbett travelled north to Birmingham, where he took part in a marathon and inconclusive two-day debate with Thomas Attwood, founder of the Political Unions and a major figure in the reform campaign. His main purpose however was to visit Oldham and Manchester. A number of reformers in Manchester had already invited him to stand as a parliamentary candidate, but he had also committed himself to stand at Oldham alongside the wealthy cotton manufacturer John Fielden. Born in 1784, Fielden had worked as a child in his father's cotton business based at Todmorden in Lancashire, the largest textile factory in the country, employing about three thousand workers. A nonconformist, Fielden had long been a disciple of Cobbett's, sharing his concern for the working man and his views on the paper money and the national debt. He first met Cobbett in 1830 when the latter was on a lecture tour of the north and showed him round his huge factory, the first Cobbett had ever visited. Though lacking political ambition himself, Fielden was eager for Cobbett to be elected, and was prepared to stand alongside him to assist the campaign.[7]

In the meantime Cobbett travelled north on a triumphal lecture tour through Northumberland, Durham and the lowlands of Scotland. Wherever he went he was greeted by crowds of supporters, bands, presentations and lengthy dinners involving countless speeches and toasts. Although it was his first visit to the north-east, Cobbett never wavered far from his traditional interests when describing his travels in the *Political Register* – the quality of the soil, the crops, the size of the turnips, etc. He saw coal being mined, and the railway between Carlisle and Newcastle under construction, but remained for the most part indifferent. 'I never liked to see machines,' he wrote, 'lest I should be tempted to endeavour to understand them. I constantly resisted all the natural desire which people had to explain them to me. As in the case of the sun and the moon and the stars, I was quite satisfied with witnessing the effects.'[8]

In Newcastle Cobbett lectured at the Playhouse to an audience of nine hundred people, and afterwards was presented with a two-volume history of the town elegantly bound in Morocco 'in the hope that when in after times (and may many years of happiness be in store for you) your eye shall meet these volumes, you will see them with no other emotion than that of a pleasing recollection of your visit and of your friends in this town'.

By way of reply Cobbett harangued the Newcastle worthies with an impromptu speech which included the following: 'For my own part, I have said before and I here repeat it in the presence of an audience of whose good opinion I set the highest possible value, that, rather than see the working people of England reduced to live upon potatoes, I would see them all hanged, be hanged myself, and be satisfied to have written on my grave "Here lie the remains of WIL-LIAM COBBETT who was hanged, because he would not hold his tongue without complaining while his labouring countrymen were reduced to live upon potatoes".'

In spite of his earlier disparagement of Scotland, and in particular the Scotch 'feelosofers' of the Whig journal the *Edinburgh Review*, Cobbett formed a most favourable impression of the country, and especially of Edinburgh, where he arrived in early October, announcing that 'it is the finest city that I ever saw in my life . . . I think nothing of *Holyrood House*; but I think a great deal of the fine and well-ordered streets of shops; of the regularity which you perceive everywhere in the management of business, and I think still more of the absence of all that foppishness, and that affectation of carelessness, and that insolent assumption of superiority, that you see in almost all the young men that you meet with in the fashionable parts of the great towns of England.'

Cobbett delivered four lectures in the Adelphi Theatre, to an audience, he estimated, of a thousand people. His themes were reform and the duty of the electors to secure good MPs, as well as traditional subjects like the iniquity of tithes and the paper money system. A correspondent for the *Edinburgh Magazine* who saw him speak gave this picture of Cobbett:

> His thin, white hairs and high forehead, the humour lurking in the eye, and playing about the lips, betokened something more than the squire in his gala suit; still, the altogether was of this respectable and responsible kind. His voice is low-toned, clear, and flexible, and so skilfully modulated, that not an aspiration was lost of his nervous, fluent, unhesitating and perfectly correct discourse. There was no embarrassment, no flutter, no picking of words; nor was the speaker once at fault or in the smallest degree disturbed by those petty accidents and annoyances which must have moved almost any other man . . . He is, indeed, a first-rate comic actor, possessed of that flexible penetrative power of imitation which extends to mind and character, as well as to their outward signs . . . The humour of his solemn irony, his blistering sarcasm but especially his sly hits and unexpected or random strikes or pokes on the sore or weak side of the Whigs, told with full effect. To oratory, in the highest sense of the term, Mr Cobbett never once rises, but he is ever a wily, clear and most effective speaker.[9]

There was intense interest in Cobbett among local Scottish journalists. Another correspondent writing in the *Fife Herald* reported how his host in Edinburgh had got up at five o'clock to see that his guest was provided for, only to find Cobbett already up and busy writing, with the fire lit. He spent only four minutes at the breakfast table before returning to his desk, and worked all day with an amanuensis, with another four minutes at dinner, which for him consisted of 'a very spare slice of mutton'.

> Among those who approached the great journalist, the first impression of him was akin to that given by Fearon [see pages 144–5], but further intercommuning has made the impression give way to a more pleasant one; they now speak of the takingness of his manner, his straightforward bluntness, *want* of pretension, and that companionable kind of quality, termed by the French, *bonhomie*. He took great delight in the children of the family in which he was an inmate.

On leaving Edinburgh Cobbett went via Dunfermline – 'a good solid town' – to Glasgow, where he was driven round the city in a carriage and pair and once again entertained at a lavish dinner at which toasts were drunk to no fewer than twenty-six parties, including Mrs Cobbett, Lord Grey, the electors of Manchester, the French nation, the Poles and the Belgians. (No one was tactless enough to remind Cobbett of what he had written only a few weeks previously about Lord Grey's Reform Dinner and all the time-wasting toasts – 'disgusting stuff'.)

He returned from Scotland just in time for the election at Oldham on 13 December. He had previously withdrawn from Manchester, where the Whigs were fielding strong candidates against him. But at Oldham he and his ally John Fielden were triumphant, the poll being as follows:

> Fielden 670
> Cobbett 642
> Bright 153
> Burge 101
> Stephen 3

Thus, at the age of sixty-nine, Cobbett achieved his long-standing ambition to become a Member of Parliament. He was convinced, mistakenly, that in this capacity he could achieve far more for his

A silhouette of Cobbett, cut with scissors without drawing
at the house of Mr David Bell, Glasgow, 1832,
by Alexander Blaikley, aged sixteen

country than he could as a journalist, and had even considered for a time closing down the *Political Register*. But his victory was also, for him, of symbolic importance. He was the farmer's son who had started life as a little boy in a blue smock and clogs scaring the crows on his father's fields. Yet now he had proved himself the equal of all the rich landowners and aristocrats who filled the benches in the House of Commons and who considered themselves the natural, rightful rulers of the country, and were accepted as such by the bulk of the population. To make the point clear, when he arrived at Westminster Cobbett, the new boy, did not slip quietly in at the back, but deliberately went and sat on the front bench next to the Whig ministers Lord Althorp and Edward Stanley, his opponent at the Preston election and, as Lord Derby, the future Prime Minister. The cartoonist John

Doyle captured the scene in a drawing of the top-hatted Cobbett, staring impassively ahead with a faint smile of triumph, Althorp furtively eyeing the newcomer and Stanley staring at him as if to say, 'Who let *him* in here?'

11

MEMBER for OLDHAM

FOR HIS FIRST APPEARANCE in the House of Commons Cobbett, who had rented a house nearby in Crown Street, ordered a new suit of clothes from his tailor, J. Swain of 93 Fleet Street, a regular advertiser in the *Political Register*, with detailed instructions of what was required:

> As you are disposed to have the goodness to clothe me for the perilous undertaking; and as you wish to know what sort of dress, I shall like to have, my decision is as follows to wit
>
> 1. A black coat, made *full* and like a black coat I have at home, or like the blue coat that I *wear now*, and not like the more fashionable ones.
>
> 2. A white washing waistcoat, of which, I suppose I have enough.
>
> 3. Black pantaloons, made not very, very long and big.
>
> In that dress, I shall, I think, be able to fight the devil, if he should come to meet me.[1]

Cobbett's arrival in the House of Commons created enormous interest. His name was better known than those of almost all the Members, but not many of them had set eyes on him before. Yet here he was on the Treasury bench, 'with one leg over the other, his head slightly drooping, as if sleeping on his breast and his hat down almost to his eyes'.[2] To many Members he was an almost legendary figure, as a fellow MP, Sir Henry Lytton Bulwer, wrote:

The world had gone for years to the clubs, on Saturday evening, to find itself lectured by him, abused by him; it had the greatest admiration for his obvious eloquence, the greatest dread of his scar-inflicting lash; it had been living with him, intimate with him, as it were, but it had not seen him.

I speak of the world's majority: for a few persons had met him at County and public meetings, at elections, and also in courts of justice. But to most Members of Parliament the elderly respectable-looking red-faced gentleman, in a dust coloured coat and drab breeches with gaiters, was a strange and almost historical curiosity. Tall and strongly built, but stooping with sharp eyes, a round and ruddy countenance, smallish features and a peculiarly cynical mouth . . .[3]

But if those Members who looked at him with such great curiosity were expecting Cobbett to rest on his laurels as the Grand Old Man who had at last achieved his life's ambition, they were soon to be disillusioned. Cobbett had assured his Oldham constituents that he would continue to fight for reform, the reduction of taxes and all those causes that he had supported throughout his career. He plunged into the proceedings of Parliament with the energy of a man half his age, making long speeches on a variety of subjects: tax reduction, the suspension of Habeas Corpus in Ireland, even the poor quality of the staff in the British Museum. On occasion he showed that he could be just as forceful on his feet as on the page, as when in 1833 he spoke in support of the great philanthropist Lord Shaftesbury (then Lord Ashley), who was promoting a Bill to reduce from twelve to ten the daily hours worked by children in factories. Shaftesbury's opponents argued that any reduction would threaten the nation's prosperity, Lord Althorp even contending that it would make famine inevitable. Cobbett replied:

> Heretofore we have sometimes been told that our ships, our mercantile traffic with foreign nations by means of those ships – that these form the source of our wealth, power and security.

At other times the land has stepped forward and bid us look to it and its yeomanry, as the sure and solid foundation of our greatness and our safety. At other times the Bank has pushed forward with her claims ... But, Sir, we have this night discovered that the shipping, the land and the Bank ... are all nothing worth compared with the labour of three hundred thousand little girls in Lancashire ... With what pride and what pleasure Sir, will the right-hon-gentleman opposite, and the honourable Member for Manchester behind me, go northward with the news of his discovery, and communicate it to that large portion of the little girls whom they have the honour and the happiness to represent!

Yet, although a good and fluent speaker, Cobbett was no more cut out to be an MP than a prisoner in Newgate. For years he had been accustomed to going to bed early, at eight or nine, and getting up at four or five. Now he was required to attend sittings that lasted well into the early hours of the morning. Then there was the cramped accommodation in the old House of Commons (burnt down in 1834), which made life even more difficult. 'Why are we squeezed into so small a space,' he wrote in a tone of exasperation,

that it is absolutely impossible that there should be calm and regular discussion, even from that circumstance alone? Why do we live in this hubbub? Why are we exposed to all these inconveniences? Why are 658 of us crammed into a space that allows to each of us no more than a foot and a half square, while at the same time each of the servants of the king, whom we pay, has a palace to live in, and more unoccupied space in that palace than the little *hole* into which we are all crammed ... squeezing one another, treading upon each other's toes, running about to get a seat; going to the hole at seven o'clock in the morning, as I do, to stick a bit of paper with my name on it on a bench to indicate that I mean to sit there for that day, and then to see us routed out of those places again, after a division has taken place, and see us running and scrambling for a seat in just the same manner as people do when they are

let into a dining room at a public dinner at the Crown and
Anchor or elsewhere.[4]

At his meetings and dinners Cobbett was used to being listened to in
respectful silence, but now he found he had to speak against a hostile
background of yawns, sneezing and shouts of 'ya ya ya'. 'The reader
is not aware,' he wrote, 'what it is to get up in the face of three or
four hundred men, nineteen-twentieths of whom are anxiously waiting
for an opportunity of picking some little hole or another in the coat
of him who so rises up; while every one of those same men begins
cheering the moment a Minister begins speaking against him. To take
your seat in that house,' he added, 'and to sit as constantly as you
ought to do requires in the present state of things not only perfect
health but great bodily strength.'[5]

Cobbett himself had enjoyed excellent health throughout his life,
without a serious illness of any kind. An observer who met him in
Manchester in 1830 noted his 'full head of very white hair' as the only
sign of change and decay – 'even his teeth remain entire and unusually
white'.[6] Yet now, under the stress of the parliamentary routine, his
health began to suffer. Three months into the session he was struck
down with 'flu and a cough that lingered on for weeks. Some years
later, in 1855, Macaulay, one of those young MPs who like Bulwer
had watched Cobbett with special interest on his entry to Parliament,
recalled in his diary: 'In truth his faculties were impaired by age and
the late hours of the House probably assisted to enfeeble his body
and consequently his mind. His egotism and his suspicion that everybody was in a plot against him increased and at last attained such a
height that he was really as mad as Rousseau – poor creature!'

A man as remorselessly energetic and egotistical as Cobbett, so
little given to doubts or uncertainty and so convinced of the rightness
of his opinions, would be particularly prone to mental instability.
Enough evidence survives to show that he was indeed, for a brief time
in 1833, in the grip of a persecution mania. On Christmas Day of that

year, for example, he wrote an extraordinary and quite untypical article for the *Political Register*, headed 'The Monsters', in which he maintained that a number of unnamed lawyers were putting it about that his many books had in fact been written by his children:

> It has been begun to be set about amongst the lawyers in those their dens called the inns of court that I have been an 'impostor' all my literary life ... and that, in fact, it is my 'CHILDREN' who have written the books ... This is the story that the ruffians with rusty camlet gowns on their backs, with brief bags as empty as their skulls and with skulls covered with old gray mares tails are circulating about in the streets in the neighbourhood of the Temple and other dirty holes in the vicinage of Chancery Lane ... You are not aware, my friends, that a man can be destroyed without publishing any-thing against him, if these mare-tailed harpies get to work upon him.

The conspiracy was not confined to casting doubt on the authorship of his books: 'I cannot swear that my opinion is correct but it is my firm belief that a scheme has been on foot for a considerable time by a crafty round-about hidden, damnable process to crush the Political Register and to drive me from my seat in Parliament.'

Cobbett was quite clearly deranged when he wrote this. Apart from the unnamed bands of lawyers plotting against him, the suggestion that he had not written his own books was so absurd that none of his readers would have taken it seriously. But if he suffered some kind of mental collapse at this time, it would not be surprising. He was old and overworked and ill, his finances were in a state of confusion and his marriage had broken down. Like Dickens, Cobbett presented himself and his family to his readers as the ideal of happy domesticity. In his *Advice to Young Men*, written only two or three years before in 1830, he had painted a glowing picture of himself as a devoted husband and Nancy as a devoted wife to whom he owed everything. But, as with Dickens, the reality was rather different from the version the public was given.

Nancy Cobbett, it is known, had had a breakdown of her own in 1827, when she attempted suicide at the age of fifty-three. It may well be, as George Spater suggests, that this breakdown coincided with the menopause, but in view of her history it was not to be wondered at that she should collapse. Unlike her husband and children Nancy was illiterate (a fact that does not seem to have bothered Cobbett), and so has left no personal record of her life. There is enough evidence to show that she had never been a docile, unquestioning wife. We know that she had very strict principles about certain things, and strongly objected to Cobbett's friendship with Henry Hunt – a man who 'lived in sin' with another man's wife, Mrs Vince. She also stopped her husband from going to a dinner to meet Mrs Clarke, the Duke of York's famous mistress (see pages 85–6). All this suggests that she had a mind of her own. But when, as a simple army sergeant's daughter, she married Cobbett at the age of seventeen, she cannot have imagined what lay in store for her. Apart from fourteen pregnancies she had survived her husband's imprisonment and bankruptcy, his exile in America, and several changes of home; she had for years endured the strain of being married to a man of fixed ideas and inexhaustible energy who expected his dependants to maintain the same level of activity as himself and to support him in all his various endeavours.

The immediate cause of her breakdown once again involved Henry Hunt, who quite apart from his irregular private life of which she disapproved, had made rude remarks about Nancy Cobbett in his recently published memoirs, suggesting that she was incapable of keeping her servants. In open defiance of his wife, Cobbett was none-theless prepared to ally himself with Hunt in order to do battle with Sir Francis Burdett and his fellow Member for Westminster John Hobhouse (later Lord Broughton), both of whom he now regarded as traitors to the cause of reform. Hunt and Cobbett caused havoc at a noisy Crown and Anchor dinner given in honour of Burdett – to the further distress of Nancy, who was later read a full account in the paper. Hobhouse recorded in his diary on 24 May 1827: 'It is certainly true that Mrs Cobbett made an attempt on her life the other day and is lying now very dangerously ill. She has been on bad terms with her husband for some time and told him that if he went to the Westminster meeting on 14th May she would destroy herself. On reading the account of that meeting in the Herald she tried to commit suicide.'

The crisis did nothing to restore relations between husband and wife, which, as Hobhouse reported, were already deteriorating. In a letter to Nancy only a month before, Cobbett had written: 'The truth is that the presumptuous talk about my "crotchets" has become so habitual that it seems to be almost impossible to eradicate the idea, or to prevent it from breaking forth into sarcastic criticism.' The Manchester reformer Absalom Watkin confirmed Hobhouse's report, writing that Richard Carlile had told him: 'It is reported that Cobbett is not on good terms with his family – that he does not eat with them but takes his meals in the seed-house.'

The following year (1828) Cobbett himself wrote in his book *A Treatise on Cobbett's Corn* that he was living on his farm at Barn Elm and only going home to his wife and family once a week. Typically, he put the blame for the estrangement on his wife and her bad temper, writing in 1832: 'Dean SWIFT says that when women behave like blackguard men, they are no longer to be considered as belonging to the sex of which they wear the ordinary apparel, but are to be considered as bullying men and are to be kicked downstairs accordingly.'

Although after Cobbett's death the family did their best to cover up all evidence of the quarrel, part of a letter written in September 1833 to his Norfolk patron Thomas Beevor survives which shows Cobbett in King Lear mode, railing at his ungrateful wife and children. He had returned at 2 a.m. from the House of Commons to find his home dark and deserted:

I had to creep to my bed without a bowl of warm milk and a little tea in it which I always wish for in such a case. I found neither bowl nor fire and nobody but the man to let me in, though there was wife, three daughters, two sons and two maid servants in the house, all in good beds of my providing. Too happy should I have been, however, if this had been *all*. But when I got into that bed which I so much needed for rest as well as sleep, that *tongue* which, for more than 20 years has been my great curse, and which would have worried any other man to death, suffered me not to have one moment's sleep, after my long fatigue and anxious labours and as I saw that this was a mere beginning of a month of it, she breakfasting in bed every day, and having the sofa to lounge on, and the park to take exercise in, to provide strength of lungs and the power of sustaining wakefulness at night . . . Therefore as soon as it was light, I called up my man, and decamped to Bolt Court and there I remained till the day when the King prorogued us.[7]

In his mad, Lear-like mood Cobbett fell out not only with his wife but with his children, who found his intolerance and conspiracy theories impossible to stomach. Cobbett was in debt to Sir Thomas Beevor to the tune of £6000, and there was a dispute over how to repay the loan, as well as over book royalties and the running of Cobbett's business, in which his sons had been heavily involved. In the end, such was his obstinacy that all his children were united against him, only his son William staying to help on his farm. The faithful Anne, who after his death made notes for a life of her father, writes nothing of the years beyond 1824, suggesting that from then on things had happened which she did not necessarily wish to be recorded for posterity. In April 1834 even William deserted his father, declaring that he 'would not live under such tyranny'. Cobbett was left to face the end on his own.

'No being,' he had written in his *Advice to Young Men*, 'is so wretched as an old bachelor.' Though still married, he was now in the same position himself. But Cobbett would never have thought of himself as 'wretched'. He valued his wife and children for their help and support, but he had no real need of them. He had no body of close friends. All his life he had been, from a psychological point of view, entirely self-sufficient. When he was not writing he was working on his farm or nursery. Other people did not impinge. Whether in Parliament, on his farm or at home, he went his own way, never looking for friends or seeking alliances. There is nothing to suggest that when his wife and children turned against him it made any difference to his well-being. He persuaded himself that they had formed some kind of conspiracy against him, that he was entirely in the right, and moved into his office at Bolt Court. He retained until the end a small body of loyal assistants: Jesse Oldfield, a former dealer in ivory who handled money matters; James Gutsell, his secretary; Benjamin Tilly, who worked as foreman of Cobbett's tailors Swain and Co.; and John Dean, who had been his steward at Botley and was now in charge of the farm he rented near Ash in Surrey.

If Cobbett was 'as mad as Rousseau' as Macaulay claimed, the madness consisted of a temporary breakdown which lasted only for a few months in late 1833 and early 1834. After the extraordinary 'Monsters' article there were no further signs of insanity in the *Political Register*. But his health, and in particular the cough, continued to frustrate and upset him. He retired to his farm, and in the *Political Register* issued regular bulletins on the state of his health. 'Wanting sleep is the great thing of all,' he wrote on 26 April 1834. 'I cannot go to sleep for fear that the cough will come . . . I dare not go out of doors, while the wind lasts . . . This cough is a source of great vexation . . .' A week later, however, he was feeling more cheerful:

> My cough is gradually leaving me, but I have to suffer a degree of lassitude and want of appetite, more difficult to get rid of than the cough. I think however that that is beginning to go. I have been able today to *think* about dining upon a sucking-pig on

Sunday next, and to think about it without loathing. I have tried very nice young chickens, very nicely roasted; and though I ate of them, it has been without relish. The only meat that I eat with anything worthy of being called an appetite, is a rasher of bacon, all fat, toasted before the fire and laid upon a thin bit of bread. Five or six times a day I have half a pint of very nicely made beef-tea, which has been the main-stay. Upon the whole, I think I am much better, and I feel stronger than four days ago.

In September 1834, after Parliament adjourned, he felt sufficiently restored to set out on a visit to Ireland. 'I have resolved to see this country with my own eyes,' he had written in July, 'to judge for *myself*, and to give a true account of it, as far as I am able, to the people of England.' Throughout his career Cobbett had taken a special interest in Ireland, and his study of the history of the Reformation had focused his concern particularly on the Catholics. The issue of Catholic emancipation (giving Catholics the same right as others to stand for Parliament, to vote, to be commissioned in the army, etc.) was one which provoked strong passions throughout the early years of the century. Cobbett, however, whilst supporting the campaign for emancipation, always insisted that it would benefit only a small number of people. Compared with the plight of the Irish nation as a whole, the issue was irrelevant, or what he called a stalking horse. 'It is the whole *state* of Ireland,' he had written as long ago as 1807, 'it is the *system of governing Ireland*, that all men, when they speak their minds, say ought to be changed.' Few of the politicians who argued so passionately about Ireland in the House of Commons would have agreed. Few had any personal knowledge of the country. Cobbett, as usual, was determined to see things for himself. He would travel through the country, he announced in the *Register*, going from inn to inn 'to mix as much as I can with persons in the middle rank of life and to see as much as I can of the real state of working people in the country'. Perhaps as a result of the many dinners he had sat through in Scotland, he told the Irish, 'It is my resolution *to be present at no public dinner.*'

In the event Cobbett found it impossible to keep his resolution. Wherever he went he was met with huge crowds, processions, and even, in Cork, a twenty-one-gun salute. The great nationalist leader and campaigner for Catholic emancipation Daniel O'Connell, with whom Cobbett maintained a typically quarrelsome friendship over the years, personally welcomed him to Ireland, invited him to stay at his home at Derrynane Abbey in County Kerry and urged his Catholic Association to give a dinner in his honour. 'He is really one of the most extraordinary men that the world ever saw,' O'Connell wrote, paying tribute to Cobbett's 'extraordinary and vigorous intellect' and saluting him as the master of 'the most pure English of any written of the present day'.

'The sole question,' Cobbett had written, 'is "Is Ireland happy?"' And he did not have to look very far to find the answer. He was used to scenes of poverty in England, but they did not begin to compare with what he found in Ireland. In Dublin, he reported, there were thousands of people living in conditions that were inferior to those of the pigs on his Surrey farm. In Limerick he saw 'more misery than any that I could have believed existed in the whole world'. A village near Kilkenny consisted of about seventy or eighty houses:

> the places which I call houses, were in general from ten to twelve feet square; the walls made of rough stone and mud, whited over, and about five feet high; no ceiling; rough rafters covered over with rotten black thatch; in some a glass window the size of your hat, in two or four little panes; in others no windows at all; but a hole or two holes in the wall; about a foot long, and four or five inches wide; the floor nothing but the bare earth; no chimney, but a hole at one end of the roof to let out the smoke, arising from a fire made against the wall of that end of this miserable shed; this hole is sometimes surrounded by a few stones put on the end of that roof a foot or two high; generally it is not, and in cold weather the poor,

ragged, half-naked creatures *stop up the hole to keep in the smoke to keep them from perishing with cold!* The fuel is peat, just such as that dug out of our moors, and never a stick of wood; and the people get the big dead weeds to light their fires and to boil their potatoes. One of these places costs the landowner about *four pounds to build it, and the poor creatures pay from thirty shillings to two pounds* a year rent for them, without any garden, without an inch of land, without any place for even a privy: WOMEN as well as men must go to the dung heap before the door.[8]

As always, simply by using his eyes Cobbett could see that this poverty existed in a country with great natural advantages. The land was fertile, the animals – in contrast to the humans – fat and well fed. 'I have now been over about 180 miles in Ireland,' he wrote in October, 'in the several counties of Dublin, Wicklow, Kildare, Carlow, Kilkenny and Waterford. I have in former years been to every county in England. I have been through the finest part of Scotland; I have lived in the finest parts of the United States of America. And here I am to declare to all the world that I have never passed over any 50 *unbroken miles*, of land so good on average during the whole way as these 180 miles.'

Various reasons, he told an audience in Dublin, were put forward to explain the wretched state of the Irish. Many people held that they themselves were to blame – 'the people are lazy, careless and wanting in trust-worthiness'. As for living on potatoes, one 'Irish gentleman' told him, 'Mr Cobbett, you do not think it, but really the Irish do not like meat. They like to have their cabins without a chimney.' Apart from pure racist prejudice, it was widely accepted that the backward-ness of the Irish was due to their Catholic religion. Yet anyone could see, as in England, simply by looking at the ruins of churches and monasteries and at the schools and libraries of Dublin, that Catholic Ireland had produced a long tradition of learning and a magnificent culture: 'They are not, God knows, wanting in literary acquirements, or in oratory. For if you were to take the one hundred Irish members out of the House of Commons, I wonder what sort would be the remaining 518.'

Absentee landlords were in part to blame, as was the obvious fact that almost all Irish produce – the corn, the meat, the butter – was being exported to England, leaving the Irish to live off 'the very worst sort of potatoes which they call LUMPERS' (near Kilkenny Cobbett saw an Irish family squatting on the floor of their hovel sharing the potatoes with their pig). Here were the conditions, the end result of a policy embraced by successive governments to promote potatoes as a staple diet, which in the next decade would lead to the terrible potato famine of 1845–46, the worst humanitarian disaster in Europe since the Black Death. Redcliffe Salaman, author of a definitive history of the potato, acclaims Cobbett as 'the only public man of his time to proclaim openly the danger society incurred by forcing its workers to adopt a standard of living based on the potato'.[9] Still, the poverty of Ireland could at least have been alleviated by public relief. But Cobbett harped on the fact that the Irish had no Poor Law, such as had existed in England since the reign of Queen Elizabeth – 'THE LAW, the *Christian* law, the *holy* law of England, which says that no human being shall, on English ground, perish from want'.

Yet it was this same Poor Law which the Whig government was now in the process of reforming – a reform which consumed so much of Cobbett's time and energy during the last two years of his life. The reform came after a lengthy investigation set up by the previous Tory administration into the workings of the poor relief system, which in turn resulted in a massive two-volume report. The commission, which included two bishops and a clergyman, was heavily influenced by the theories of Cobbett's most detested enemy Parson Malthus. The country did not have the wealth to support greater numbers. The poor were breeding faster than the rich, and as far as the rural labourers were concerned the fault lay mainly with the Speenhamland System of poor relief which encouraged them to breed in order to gain more assistance from the parish. Cobbett had always attacked Speenhamland because it was used by farmers to justify low wages and destroyed the self-respect of the labourer. But the trouble with the new Bill was that although it did away with Speenhamland, it had nothing to put in its place beyond a group of proposals designed to force men to look for work, the thinking being that there were always jobs to be had if only people were prepared to make the effort. And in the last resort there was the workhouse, where the sexes were to be separated to prevent any more breeding and where conditions should never be too comfortable in case they should attract loafers and the workshy. As Cobbett's life draws to its close we are entering the world of Dickens and *Oliver Twist* (the first instalment of which was published in 1837, only two years after Cobbett's death).

Enoch Powell famously stated that all political careers end in failure. Yet Cobbett represents a sort of exception to the rule. The last years of his life saw three major triumphs – his victory in the libel action of 1831, the passing of the Reform Bill, followed by his entry into Parliament at the third attempt. Cobbett however was never likely to be satisfied. The Reform Bill was not destined to usher the people into a promised land, as he in his more optimistic moments may have hoped. The Whigs under Lord Grey, having piloted the Bill through all the storms that it provoked, were happy to leave it at that. Grey himself retired shortly afterwards. The Bill, which had never been seen as the first step in a series of reforms, had achieved its most important object: to bring an end to the threat of revolution which had at one time seemed real enough to scare the King and the aristocracy.* The changes that Cobbett had hoped would follow reform – a reduction of taxes, an end to pensions and sinecures – these were postponed for a later day.

* Three Dukes had wheeled out cannon to guard their country seats.

Instead of the prosperity which Cobbett had promised the farm labourers a few years earlier, the Whigs were now busily bringing forward measures designed, in his view, to make them even worse off, measures which he had confidently predicted they would abandon once the reformed Parliament took control. 'Having got parliamentary reform in name,' he wrote, 'my resentment was becoming blunted – But the Poor-Law bill I could not stomach.' He focused once again on his old sparring partner Brougham, as the Bill's chief promoter. 'This man was a brawling lawyer for several years. He is the weazel, he is the nightmare, he is the indigestion . . .' A combination of Malthus and Brougham was enough to make Cobbett's blood boil. He noted how the lawyers framing the Bill had stated that one of the objects was to persuade the people of England to live on 'coarser food'. Realising that his readers might not be able to follow all the proposals put forward, Cobbett seized on this expression, and from then began to refer to the Whigs as 'the Coarser Food Ministry'. It did not take much for him to imagine English labourers reduced to the same state as those he had only recently seen in Ireland, squatting on the floor and sharing their potato supper with the pigs.

Opposition to the Poor Law Amendment Bill was widespread. The rick-burning and smashing of machinery broke out again, and as he neared the end Cobbett found himself becoming more and more revolutionary. All his life he had counselled non-violence and the need for peaceful change, but what good had reform produced, when the agricultural labourers were once again in revolt? In one of his last books, his *Legacy to Labourers* (1835), Cobbett was advocating the public ownership of land on the same lines as the Utopian socialist Thomas Spence, and when the old House of Commons was burned down in October 1834 he wrote his *Register* from Limerick, speculating publicly whether the fire had been caused by 'fire and brimstone from heaven or the less sublime agency of SWING my friend'.

According to the *Morning Herald*, whose report Cobbett relied on for his information, 'the mob when they saw the progress of the flames raised a savage shout of exultation'. 'Did they indeed!' he wrote:

> The *Herald* exclaims 'UNREFLECTING' people! Now perhaps the MOB exulted because the 'MOB' was really a reflecting 'mob'. When even a dog, or a horse receives any treatment that it does not like, it always shuns the place where it got such treatment; shoot at and wound a hare from out of a hedge-row, she will always shun that spot: cut a stick out of a coppice, and beat a boy with it and he will wish the coppice at the devil; send a man, for writing notorious truth, out of the Kings Bench to a jail, and there put him half to death, and he will not cry his eyes out if he happens to hear that the court is no more. In short there is always a connexion in our minds between sufferings that we undergo and *the place* in which they are inflicted, or in which they originate. And this 'unreflecting mob' might in this case have reflected that in the building which they saw in flames, the following, amongst many other things, took place. They might have reflected that it was in this House that the act was passed for turning the Catholic priests, who shared the tithes with the poor, out of the parishes and putting Protestant parsons in their place who gave the poor no share at all of the tithes.

Cobbett proceeded to list some of the pieces of legislation over the centuries that could justify the jubilation of the mob when they saw the House of Commons in flames:

> . . . the new treason laws, new game laws, new trespass laws and new felony laws.
> That it was in this same HOUSE that it was in 1819 voted that the House would not inquire into the massacre at Manchester . . .
> That it was in this same HOUSE that botheration

BROUGHAM, in 1820, defended the *employment of spies* by government.

That, it was in this same HOUSE, where CASTLEREAGH was the *leader*, for many years, up to the 6th August 1822 and he CUT HIS OWN THROAT, at North Cray, in Kent, on the 12th of that month, a Kentish coroner's jury pronouncing that he was INSANE and had been so for *some weeks*, he being the Secretary of State for Foreign Affairs . . . at the very time when he cut his throat . . .

That it was in this same HOUSE, that the BANK, the PAPER-MONEY, and the FUNDS were enacted . . . etc etc

Oh, God of Mercy! Might not those, whom the insipid and the time-serving wretch of the *Morning Herald* abuses; might not the people of London, whom the base crew of REPORTERS reeking with the heat of gin; might not the people of London, instead of being unreflecting, have DULY REFLECTED on the hundreds of things, of which I have, from the mere memory, mentioned only a *small part*? These things are always present to *my mind*. Why should they not be present to the minds of the people of London?

. . . I must say that those who talk of this matter as of a mere fire, do not, may it please their reporterships, reflect. It is a GREAT EVENT, come from what CAUSE it might, it is a *great event*. It astounds, it sets *thought* to work in the minds of millions; it awakens *recollections*; it rouses to remarks; it elicits a communication of feelings; it makes the tongue the loud herald of the heart; and it must in the nature of things . . . it is a great event! Say, the base, stinking *reporters* what they will, it IS a great event![10]

In the eyes of young, respectable Victorians like Macaulay such a passage could well read like the ravings of a madman. Even today there will be those who find something wild and distasteful about a writer, and a Member of Parliament at that, rejoicing in the destruction of a famous and historic landmark. But this was the Cobbett that his readers knew and relished, giving the lie to those like the *Morning*

Chronicle which had claimed (on 21 September 1833) that he had lost his touch, and that the *Register* had deteriorated. The same 'savage indignation' which had burned in his hero Swift's breast was going to be with him till his dying day.

12

END of the JOURNEY

S INCE 1824, when Cobbett published his *History of the Protestant Reformation*, he had been producing a string of books – a revised *French Grammar* (1824), *The Woodlands* (1825) and *Cobbett's Corn* (1828), *The Emigrant's Guide* (1829), not to mention assorted reference books, dictionaries and even a spelling book for children. In 1834, as he struggled with poor health, domestic difficulties and his duties as an MP, he managed to complete an entertaining *History of the Reign of George IV*. At the same time he had pursued his career as a farmer and a seedsman. Readers of the *Register* would find his political diatribes interspersed with advice on the planting of 'Cobbett's Corn' or advertisements for his mangel wurzel seeds.

He had been running a nursery farm in Kensington since 1823. Four years later, he boasted that what had been 'a rough and sour meadow' had been transformed. 'On about four acres of land, disposed in about four hundred and fifty beds, there stood, more than a million of seedling forest trees, and shrubs and about three thousand young apple trees.' But this, he claimed was 'insufficient to provide occupation for my leisure hours'. In 1826 he leased another 'walled in plot' south of the Thames in what was then open countryside at Barn Elm, not only to have more space for his plants but as an escape (partly, presumably, from his family). 'There I was as safe from the world as a monk of Latrappe. I positively shut all out, except the gardeners and one gardener's wife, who kept the key of the door. I did this not

287

Cobbett's farm at Normandy in Surrey

for the sake of secrecy; but because I would be certain of being uninterrupted when I was in that place.'

In 1832, as the Reform Bill was passing slowly through its final stages in Parliament, Cobbett gave up Barn Elm and rented a farm of 160 acres at Normandy, near Ash in Surrey. A visitor, Alexander Somerville, described the surrounding countryside in his book *The Whistler at the Plough* (1844):

> It is but a humble-looking place. The farm house and offices stand at the top of a common, removed from the farm land, which to a good farmer is a great annoyance and to any farmer is a loss. A wide range of heath variegated with furze, gravel pits and tracts of absolute sterility extends for many miles, behind the farm house; and on either side, right and left, the heath extends for several miles, variegated only with a few clumps of pine-trees, chiefly Scotch firs. In front lies a heathy

common, in complete disorder, as commons usually are, and beyond it, to the front, looking eastward, is the farm land, enclosed in small fields with very badly kept fences. There are trees in the hedgerows; and in some parts, more of them than should be upon a farm where there is a tenant bound to pay rent.

In this rather unpromising setting, Cobbett, living now with a few faithful helpers and a handful of chopsticks, embarked on an ambitious scheme of improvements, building a stable and cattle shed and experimenting with thirty varieties of grass seed. At the same time he thought about writing an autobiography, and even announced it in the *Political Register*: 'I shall entitle my book "The Progress of a Ploughboy to a Seat in Parliament", as exemplified in the History of the Life of William Cobbett, Member for Oldham, and I intend that the frontispiece to the book shall represent me, first in a smock frock, driving the rooks from the corn; and in the lower compartment of the picture, standing in the House of Commons addressing the speaker.'[1] The book was going to be published in numbers, like the *History of the Protestant Reformation*, and would begin with his childhood.

But Cobbett had already given an account of his early years when he was in Philadelphia, and it is not clear what he was going to add to the story, except perhaps to describe in greater detail what made him leave home in 1783 without even saying goodbye to his mother and father. He never did so, though many years later when he was riding through the village of Billingshurst in Sussex he saw a young farmer's boy in a blue smock frock who reminded him of his younger self, and said it was just an 'accident' that had led him to pursue his own path in life, implying that he could well have been a simple farm labourer like the other boys.*

There were times when Cobbett seemed to think that anyone who

* 'If accident had not taken me from a similar scene how many villains and fools who have then been well teased and tormented would have slept in peace at night and fearlessly staggered about by day' (*Rural Rides*).

applied himself could do what he had done. At others he was fully cons_cious of his extraordinary ability. More than once he harked back to his early meetings in 1802 with Pitt, Canning, Windham and others, reflecting that he could, if he had chosen, have been one of them. 'I am once more on a farm,' he wrote. 'I might have been, I am aware of it, possessed of bags of public gold or of landed domains, purchased with that gold. I trudge through the dirt and I might have ridden in the ring at Hyde Park, with four horses to draw me along in a gilded carriage with a coachman before me and footmen behind me. What I might have been, it is hard to say . . .' There had been a time, during the Windham years, when Cobbett had seen himself the confidant of great statesmen. What changed this forever was the prosecution in 1810 and his subsequent two years' imprisonment in Newgate. From that point on his course was clear. As Chesterton wrote in a typically purple passage: 'The man who came out of that prison was not the man who went in. It is not enough to say that he came out in a rage, and may be said to have remained in a rage; to have lived in a rage for thirty years until he died in a rage in his own place upon the hills of Surrey . . . The most terrible of human tongues was loosened and went through the country like a wandering bell, of incessant anger and alarm; till men must have wondered why, when it was in their power, they had not cut it out.'

In his old age, as he contemplated his memoirs, Cobbett comforted himself with the thought that the Cannings and the Liverpools would not be remembered for long: 'They are already rotten; and the Kingdom hardly recollects such men.' Every day as he entered the House of Commons he saw the newly commissioned statue of Canning. But what did that amount to? 'Plastered stuff, put upon canvas, or mortar moulded up together to look like a man – I despise these from the bottom of my heart.' It was his writing that would live on – his *Grammar*, his *Paper Against Gold*.

'I hate London,' he wrote, 'and neither can nor will live in it for a constancy.' But he continued to attend the House of Commons, now, following the fire of 1834, sitting in the Court of Requests, although his cough was again making it difficult for him to speak in debate. When Lord Chandos proposed the repeal of the Malt Tax in March 1835 Cobbett had been determined to rebut Sir Robert Peel's arguments opposing repeal. He sat on his bench from 2.15 in the afternoon until nearly one in the morning. He became hungry and thirsty at about ten o'clock, and a fellow Member kindly brought him a plum cake and two oranges. But when he finally got up to speak he had lost his voice, and had to sit down after making a few scarcely audible remarks.

In April 1835 his final little book, the *Legacy to Parsons*, was published, and all five thousand copies were sold within five days. Six editions were to be published during the year, and it was even translated into Welsh.[2] Appropriately it was one final blast at the clergy of the Church of England, and was dedicated to the Bishop of London, James Blomfield, the Chairman of the Poor Law Commission, whose proposals had caused Cobbett so much consternation. 'Bishop,' he began, 'About six and twenty years ago, you drank tea at my house at BOTLEY, when you were a curate of some place in Norfolk: or a teacher to the offspring of some hereditary legislator. How rugged has my course been since that time; how thickly has my path been strewn with thorns! How smooth, how flawless, how pleasant your career!' There followed a by-now familiar rehearsal of the history of the Reformation, an attack on the system of tithes, nepotism in Church appointments and absentee vicars (Bishop Blomfield was personally berated for procuring a living for a relative).

Cobbett considered himself easily the equal of any politician, and the same went for the clergy, of whom he had always held a low opinion ('Amongst all the qualities for which the Church, as by law established, is distinguished from every body of men in the world, the quality of cool IMPUDENCE stands very conspicuous,' he wrote). He had a wide knowledge of the Bible, as is evident from his book of *Sermons* (1821), and was always able to quote texts to support his views, especially on the Church's attitude to the poor:

> The poorer part of the people see the rich seated in pews, while they are compelled to stand about in the aisles, exposed to the draughts of the air, and to every possible inconvenience ... Those who have not money wherewith to purchase a seat are treated like dogs ... Great merit is taken by those who are teaching the poor people to read, and who are subscribing for Bibles to put into their hands. Probably very few of them, comparatively even read the books thus subscribed for; but those who do read are likely to tell others what they do read; and those who do read, read as follows in the 2nd chapter of the Epistle of St. James, who really seems to have been inspired with a foreknowledge of these very days in which we live and with the practice of this Church as established by law:
>
> 'My brethren, have not the faith of our Lord Jesus Christ, with respect of persons. For if there come unto your assembly a man with a gold ring, in goodly apparel, and there come in also a poor man in vile raiment; and ye have respect to him that weareth the gay clothing, and say unto him, sit thou here in a good place; and say to the poor, stand thou there, or sit here under my footstool; are ye not then partial in yourselves, and are become judges of evil thoughts?'
>
> One would almost imagine, that the Church-parsons had read this with all possible care; and had determined to act precisely in opposition to it ...

In the last weeks of his life there was no let-up in Cobbett's relentless activity. In April he announced the re-publication of his play *Surplus Population*. Cobbett quite frequently wrote satirical dialogues in his political articles, and had twice before attempted to write complete plays, but without any success. *Surplus Population*, which was far more successful, was a satire directed at his old favourites, the Malthusians seeking to impose 'moral restraint' on young villagers to stop them marrying and having large families. One of the villains of the piece, Peter Thimble, described in the cast list as 'a great Anti-Population philosopher', was based on fellow radical Francis Place, who despite having fathered fifteen children was a keen advocate of birth control:

> I think I see the slipshod critics of DRURY LANE and t'other place, the name of which I have forgotten, turn up their noses at this and express their astonishment that a clod-thumping politician like me should dare to think of writing a play! Let them read my play if they can read; and, if not, get their wives or mistresses to read it to them, but let them if they can beg their way down into Surrey or Sussex, come and see my play acted, and hear the country girls laugh till they are ready to tumble off the benches.[3]

Much to Cobbett's indignation, when his troupe of actors booked the Angel Inn in Tonbridge for a performance of *Surplus Population*, the authorities banned it:

> They had read it and their conduct and motives were like those of the King in HAMLET, when he, being at the play, rises hastily and cries 'Lights! Lights! Away! Away!' Well may they exclaim, with MACBETH, I think it is 'How is it with me, oh God! when every little noise alarms me!' How is it with them, when even the stirring of a mouse excites their fears; only think of their being alarmed at a mere piece of ridicule of the damnable Malthusian doctrine; only think of their taking fright, even at that! Why it would be better to go under ground at once, even alive, than to move about on top of it, in such constant dread.[4]

Cobbett vowed to get his revenge by writing a new play, to be called *Bastards in High Life*.

On 12 May he was again in the House of Commons, where he presented petitions for the repeal of the 'cursed' Poor Law Bill, launching a fierce attack on the Duke of Richmond. According to Hansard: 'The Hon-Member adverted to the situation of a parish in Sussex and censured the conduct of the Duke of Richmond who had induced a parish of Sussex to expend £2000 upon additions to the poor-house, one of the avowed objects being to put an end to the horrible system of bastardy. The noble Duke seemed to forget that he himself sprung from a bastard and he was noble because he had sprung from a bastard.'[5] Cobbett spoke again on 15 May in a long debate on the Civil Contingencies (the government's expenditures on embassies, committees of inquiry, etc.): 'I was upon my legs twenty times at the least – and came home at one o'clock in the morning half jaded with fatigue!' The next day, Saturday, he was filled with rage by the inadequacy of the press reports of the debate, and vowed to do something about it. Why should MPs like himself be misrepresented 'as a set of lazy or corrupt vagabonds whom the unfortunate people seem to have elected for the sole purpose of franking letters, or, at the most, for the purpose of strutting into the House of Commons to tacitly betray them?' He was determined not to stand for it: 'if the people be to pay for a gallery of the "gentlemen of the press", if there be privileged persons to be placed in that gallery, I will endeavour to take care that they shall not (as they did on Friday night) put their cheeks into their hands, and sit with their eyes closed, while the result of deep potations seemed to be coming from their mouths'. All this, while conscientious MPs like himself were bombarding the ministers with questions, querying the expenditure of taxpayers' money, such as the £7.70 put aside for ringing the bells of Christ Church Cathedral in Dublin 'for three days on the death of the late Duke of Gloucester, and muffling and preparing same'.

Even before he became an MP Cobbett had always been passionate about the reporting of parliamentary debates. Not only had he started the publication which is still known as Hansard, but he regularly devoted a proportion of the *Register* to the debates, particularly on important occasions like the passage of the Reform Bill of 1832. Now, at the age of seventy-two, he revived his idea of a daily evening paper which would report the debates in full, so that the public could be informed. And the paper would be written 'without the talents inspired by the contents of a pewter pot or of a gin-bottle'. In the same breath that he revealed details of his new paper, Cobbett announced that as well as his planned autobiography he was going to write *The Poor Man's Bible* and *The Legacy to Lords* – 'the last I have promised to have in the hands of SIR ROBERT PEEL by the next feast of St. Michael'. All this in addition to his play *Bastards in High Life* and a book based on his tour of Ireland, to be called *Ireland's Wars: A Warning to Englishmen*. And in the meantime he kept up his attendance in the House of Commons. On 25 May 1835 he made a long speech supporting a motion by Lord Chandos urging the government once again to relieve agricultural distress. It was to be his last appearance in the House, and having stayed up all night to vote he was left exhausted.

The following day he went back to his farm in Surrey, determined to rest and get rid of his cough. On 10 June he sat out in the garden and wrote his last ever *Political Register*, another attack on the reform of the Poor Law, the 'Coarser Food Ministries', and particularly his favourite Aunt Sally, Brougham, now described as 'Lord Crackskull', a very clever man 'though addicted to laudanum and brandy and with features none of the most human'.

An anonymous and very detailed account of Cobbett's last days was published in the *Political Penny Magazine* of 29 October 1836, only one copy of which is known to survive, in Columbia University, New York. It is violently hostile to Cobbett's children and must have been written by one of his two secretaries, Gutsell or Tilly, both of whom were with him throughout. After finishing the final *Register*, the writer reports:

Mr Cobbett retired early to bed, but was too ill to lie down owing to a sense of suffocation proceeding, no doubt from water on the chest; added to which he was severely attacked with a bowel complaint which greatly distressed him. On the following day he was worse and at length, and very reluctantly, he allowed Mr Gutsell, his secretary to send for medical aid. During the next night he became delirious for the first time, and discovered great bodily weakness, which was very distressing to those about him, his household consisting of Mr Gutsell, two maid servants and four or five chopsticks; not one of his own family, excepting his son William having spoken to him since September 1833! . . .

On the 12th Mr Gutsell got him down stairs at day-light. He constantly complained of heat and want of air, and was placed in every situation, and with the windows and doors open, but without getting any relief. The doctor attended early in the day, and administered some medicine to him that revived him a little but which left him very weak. This day he permitted Mr Gutsell to write for his son, William Cobbett to come down to him, and also for Mr Oldfield his publisher; and about mid-day on the following day the latter arrived, when Mr Cobbett asked him to whom he had told that he had been written for, 'To no-one' was the reply 'except to Swain and Tilly, and Dr. Lawrence.' 'You did not let them at Red Lion Court (his family) know of it?'

'No, Sir' said Mr Oldfield 'but, to tell you the truth, I put the information in train to reach them very soon.'

'Humph' said Mr Cobbett 'who told you to do *that*?'

He afterwards was got upstairs to bed, as he wanted to sleep, but he could not lie down, chairs and books were placed for him to recline a little, and in that way he got some sleep, but he slept very unsoundly, was light-headed, and talked about the currency, the poor-laws, and about his farm.

During the night his son William arrived:

When he entered his father's bed-room, his father said: – 'Ah! William! I have not seen anything of you and but rarely heard anything of you since February. Does my conduct towards you merit such treatment?'

Cobbett, supported by his retainers, remained convinced until the end that he was a wronged man, and showed no inclination to make peace with his children. 'On Sunday June 14th,' the writer goes on, 'he had violent spasmodic attacks; two medical gentlemen were in attendance, and they considered that he laboured under a complication of disorders.'

> . . . Towards the evening he seemed a little better, and sat in an easy chair out in his garden in front of his house conversing very cheerfully about the fields and their crops that he could see across the common; about the lettuces and cauliflowers that were growing just at his feet; and about the Cobbett-corn growing in a field at the back of his house, which he would go to look at, and which was then looking remarkably fine, he said he hoped that there were thousands of such crops in England. He was at length assisted up to his bed; but could not lie down; he again became delirious, and talked a good deal of the cruelty of his family towards him.

The next day Anne and John came to the farm, but Cobbett refused to see them, although the following morning he relented, but was in no mood to make his peace with them either:

> He told Nancy [Anne] that from her cruelty to him he no longer considered her his daughter . . . During the night he was very delirious and was almost incessantly talking of the conduct pursued towards him by his family . . . In the course of the night, whilst delirious he called for Mr Tilly to come and write at his dictation for the Register – after a while he fancied that Mr Tilly (who had often been his amanuensis) was seated ready to begin writing; he then began dictating an article, exactly as he used to; dictating, not merely the words, but the pointing [punctuation] too! The matter that he was dictating was on the subject of Lord Brougham, who, after having been almost literally kicked out of the Cabinet, had

297

gone to France, prancing about, and making a show of himself, being more than half mad.* After he had dictated a few sentences he concluded by saying: 'I shall say no more on this subject (comma), for the present (comma), for all ascends into the clouds (full point).'

The following day, Wednesday, 17 June, Cobbett was weaker, though his mind was clear. He asked to be carried round his fields to see what was going on. An easy chair was therefore 'fixed on a sort of hand barrow' and he was carried across the fields by his chopsticks. His son William, who recorded this incident, wrote: 'which being done, he criticised the work that had been going on in his absence, and detected some little deviation from his orders, with all the quickness that was so remarkable in him. As he was carried to see the fields, a little boy in a blue smock-frock happened to come by us, to whom my father gave a laughing look, at which I thought I should have dropped, I knowing what was passing in his mind. He seemed refreshed at the sight of the little creature, which he had once precisely resembled, though now at such an immeasurable distance.' On returning to the house after two hours in the open air he ordered a load of grass to be laid on the brick floor to make it cooler. Later in the day he dictated a letter to his son John, who had written on behalf of the family asking to be allowed to visit him:

> I think it right to inform you that you may inform the other five children and your mother, of my intentions as to certain family matters.
>
> First, I shall have no insuperable objection to see any of you at my farm; but it is to be on the express condition, that none of you ever attempt to sleep here; that none of you ever attempt to give an order of any sort to my servants and finally,

* 'His humour did not desert him to the last, if it be true that on his deathbed, on its being observed that the Whigs had "put Brougham on the shelf", he exclaimed "put him on a shelf? they might as well put a live rat there" ' (Lord Holland's Diary).

never interfere in any way whatever in my affairs near or remote.

That I regard your mother, as she stands upon somewhat different footing: but that, though I shall have no objection to her coming to the house in the day-time, I shall have an objection to her remaining in it all night; and, night or day, she shall never have the power of commanding, or giving an order to any human being in my house. All which is the smallest thing I can do when I consider the affairs of 1833 and 1834.

W. Cobbett.

At about three the following morning Cobbett's condition deteriorated rapidly, and one of his men was sent off to Farnham to fetch the doctor, who arrived at about six and persuaded him to drink some wine and water:

> After a while the doctor, seeing that life would soon close began very cautiously, and in a manner, that to Mr Cobbett, seemed rather affected, to enquire whether he wished to draw up any 'testamentary document' observing that, if he did, 'he may as well do it now as at any other time.' 'Not' continued he 'that there is any dainja [danger]' –. To which Mr Cobbett immediately replied – 'I have done everything that is necessary in that respect, and Mr Fielden knows all about it.' Before the doctor had quitted the room, Mr Cobbett happening to hear him cough and not being disinclined to a little sarcastic jocu-larity spoke to him with much apparent gravity, and in the same affected drawl saying – 'Doctor, do you take anything for that cough?' 'No! Sir' replied Esculapius 'then' continued Mr Cobbett 'I think you should' and looking very archly, he added 'not that I think there is any dainja'. The doctor looked rather blank at his humorous sally and as he was leaving the bed-side, Mr Cobbett added, with one of his arch laughing winks of the eye – 'There, take that, my buck!'

Before noon word came that Nancy Cobbett was waiting outside, but young William refused her entry:

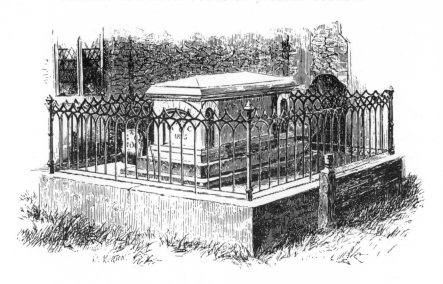

Tomb of William and Anne Cobbett at St Andrew's church in Farnham

However she was at length allowed to enter, and assisted in bathing his temples and moistening his lips; but this was at too late an hour in Mr Cobbett's life for him to be able to show either joy or displeasure at her presence . . . About a quarter before one (at noon) his eyes became dim; at about one they became fixed, his breathing was more difficult, his articulation gone, and at ten minutes after one o'clock he stretched forth one of his hands, as if bidding farewell; and then leaning back and closing his eyes, as if to sleep, he died without a gasp!

Cobbett was buried in the pouring rain on Saturday, 27 June 1835, next to his father in St Andrew's churchyard in Farnham. His four sons, William, John, James and Richard, acted as pallbearers, watched by a crowd of about eight thousand people. The vicar read Psalms 39 and 90, then led the way to the grave where he performed the burial service. The graveyard was packed, and as the coffin was lowered some people pressed forward to take a handful of earth or a clump of grass from the grave as a souvenir. Conspicuous in the crowd of mourners was the tall figure of Daniel O'Connell, wearing a green cap with a gold band.

The sole beneficiary of Cobbett's will was William, the only son who had stayed with his father after the family quarrel of 1833. The failure to make provision for Nancy and the other children was not thought remarkable, and remained unnoticed by biographers, who maintained that Cobbett had died surrounded by his faithful wife and children.* The Cobbetts successfully repressed nearly all evidence of the quarrels, and it was not until 1982, with the publication of George Spater's biography, that the full story was revealed.

---

* See, for example, Asa Briggs, *William Cobbett* (1967): 'He enjoyed his last years with his family on his leased farm.'

EPILOGUE

A NYONE WHO HAS followed the events of Cobbett's lifetime
through his eyes will inevitably feel a sense of loss when he is
no longer there. Things are happening, politicians are coming forward,
but we have lost that small twinkling eye watching the parade, and
the savage pen lashing the participants whenever they deserve it.
His contemporaries, his readers, felt that same sense of loss – even
those who least sympathised with his views. As Sir Henry Lytton
Bulwer wrote later: 'He left a gap in the public mind which no-one
else could fill, or attempt to fill up, for his loss was not merely that of
a man, but of a habit – of a dose of strong drink which all of us had
been taking for years, most of us during our lives, and which it was
impossible for anyone again to concoct so strongly, so strangely, with
so much spice and flavour or with such a variety of ingredients. And
there was this peculiarity in the general regret – it extended to all
persons.'[1]

Considering what the papers had written before about him, the
obituaries were surprisingly flattering. Even the 'Bloody old Times,
the most infamous piece of printing that ever disgraced ink and paper',
was complimentary: 'Take this self-taught peasant for all in all, he was
perhaps in some respects, a more extraordinary Englishman than any
other of this time. Cobbett was by far the most voluminous writer that
has ever lived for centuries. He has worked with incessant industry
for more than forty years, without, we may believe, the interruption

of so much as a single week from languor of spirit, or even from physical weakness.' The *Standard* paid extravagant tributes to the peasant whom it called 'the first political writer of his age . . . Undoubtedly Mr. Cobbett was a great man . . . gifted with the most extraordinary powers of intellect.' But here again the writer felt obliged to refer to Cobbett's inferior social origins, suggesting that he had changed course in 1807 because he had been snubbed by Pitt – something a gentleman would never have done, according to the paper. Yet one of the remarkable things about Cobbett was how little he had been influenced by personal rebuffs of this kind. The writer might have remembered that he had recently given his full support to Lord Grey, in spite of the fact that only a few weeks before Grey's government had prosecuted him for libel, and that he had stood in the Guildhall denouncing the Whigs and everything they stood for.

But the Whigs still maintained an attitude of condescension. Cobbett was indeed remarkable for a man of his social origins. The Whig grandee Lord Holland wrote in his diary: 'Cobbett a Man of Genius died on the 18th. He had been a common soldier and was entirely self-educated, then made himself the ablest and certainly the least scrupulous political writer of his time . . . the pride of the virtue of the Whig Aristocracy disdained in 1806 or in 1809 to admit a person of so low an origin, of such instability in principle, and of such scurrility in controversy to their councils or their society. Had they prudently acted otherwise, Cobbett would have probably felt the value of a decently honest character and laboured to preserve it.' How little he knew his man.

Holland's lofty tone was echoed in many of the tributes. Cobbett had had to battle against a poor background and a lack of proper education. There was no mention of all the obstacles that successive governments and their courts had put in his way – bankruptcy, libel actions and imprisonment – least of all of the continuous barrage of ill-informed abuse from the press itself. It was not only Cobbett's good health that had kept the *Register* going all those years, but an iron will, a determination not to be beaten by The Thing.

Another criticism which surfaced in the obituaries was the old one about inconsistency, a charge that had been made earlier by William Hazlitt, who in a much-quoted article originally published in *Table Talk* (1821) wrote that 'He changes his opinions as he does his friends . . . he has no comfort in fixed principles.' Cobbett had defended himself against the charge, pointing out that there was nothing wrong in changing your opinion once you realised you had been mistaken or misinformed. Quite apart from that, it could be argued that if anything, Cobbett was too consistent, rather than the reverse. He altered course over the Napoleonic War, but he never changed his views about the national debt and the paper money, he never admitted that he was wrong to think that the population was not increasing, or that it had been much larger in the Middle Ages. Even the commonly accepted view of him that he changed from being a Tory in his youth to a radical in middle age was a simplification. Cobbett was never a radical in the popular sense, that is to say a follower of Paine like Wooler or Carlile, who believed as Hazlitt did that kings and priests were responsible for the ills of this world. In spite of everything he knew about the Georges, especially George IV, he remained a monarchist just as he remained a faithful member of the Church of England whilst simultaneously denouncing the bishops and the clergy. 'We want nothing new' had been his recurring theme. He wanted the Poor Law of Queen Elizabeth, a Church that looked after the needs of the poor as in the Middle Ages. He wanted the farmworker to have bacon, bread and beer – not potatoes. He wanted gold coins in his purse. He wanted the farmer to look after his labourers. He wanted nothing new. It was the farmers and the politicians who had changed, not Cobbett.

The enormous influence of the *Political Register* can be compared to that of Tom Paine in an earlier age. Simply by the force of his writing Paine had inspired the Americans to rebel against British rule. In the same way Cobbett roused the working people of England to demand reform. There was nothing unique in his critique of the system or his proposals, most of which had been put forward many years before by Major Cartwright and others. But unlike Cartwright, Cobbett had the ability to express them in language that was instantly intelligible, entertaining and above all lacking in condescension. Cobbett instructed his readers, but he never talked down to them. He spoke to the working people as one of nature's democrats, who regarded the common soldier or the farm labourer as his equal, and himself the equal of Canning or Peel. As the Victorian economist and political agitator J.E. Thorold Rogers wrote, 'Cobbett familiarised the people with the most effective kind of popular education, that which criticises public events and public characters.' He continually stressed that it was the people, notably the chopsticks, and not Lord Grey or Lord Russell who had brought about political reform in 1832.

In the history of the reform movement Cobbett's achievement was not merely to educate the workers (which he did), but to identify more clearly than any other, and in phrases that were instantly memorable, the causes of complaint. This was his genius as a journalist, to label the targets and then belabour them incessantly, issue after issue – the borough-mongers, the tax-eaters, the fund-holders, the placemen, The Thing itself. In the end the radical pamphleteers and campaigners Hunt, William Hone, Carlile – even some of the Whigs – all used the same phrases as Cobbett.

Yet Bulwer's picture of Cobbett's arrival in the House of Commons, viewed as an object of curiosity by the young MPs, reminds us that by the time of his death Cobbett was already something of an anachronism. To men like Bulwer or Macaulay he belonged in a different world, a world of wars, riots and rebellions, where mobs roamed through London smashing windows, journalists were imprisoned and Jacobins hanged, a world of Gillray cartoons, of wild romantic characters – mad King George III, his dissolute son the Prince Regent, William Windham at the boxing ring, Admiral Cochrane surrounded by spitting parsons, Spencer Perceval assassinated, Castlereagh cutting his throat.

As the Victorian age dawned such scenes, such characters began to seem increasingly remote. Two of Cobbett's own sons, John and James Paul, personified the change. In spite of the quarrels that marred his last years they remained loyal to the memory of their father, keeping his books in print and editing a massive six-volume selection of passages from the *Political Register*. But in choosing their extracts they omitted almost all Cobbett's liveliest and most provocative articles, both of them being lawyers – John later became a Tory MP – as if aware that they represented a new, rather more respectable generation in which their father's violent language, his jokes and nicknames were out of place.

Cobbett himself had remained largely oblivious to the changes that were taking place even in the countryside. In 1834 there had occurred the affair of the 'Dorsetshire Labourers' (the Tolpuddle Martyrs, as they were later known), transported to Australia by Lord Melbourne for attempting to form a trade union. Though Cobbett referred to the story in passing in the *Register* it never aroused his indignation as the 'Captain Swing' events of 1830 had done. Yet it pointed towards a time when the struggle of the workers would become the struggle for the right to organise – a cause that never really engaged his attention. Despite his knowledge of Oldham and his close association with his fellow Member of Parliament the cotton manufacturer John Fielden, the Industrial Revolution had been passing him by. His world remained an agricultural one, just as it always had been. The workers, for him, are farm labourers, his beloved 'chopsticks'; when he thinks of children they are boys like himself, working on the land scaring crows or learning to plough. Only four weeks before he died he wrote a passionate attack on 'heddekashun' – the schemes for state education then being proposed by Brougham and other reformers. Because what use, after all, was the knowledge that would be taught in the schools 'by the unshaven, gin-drinking fellow called a parish schoolmaster'?

> The little buck, who has been frightening away the rooks from the cornfields, who has been weeding the corn with his mother: he has got some knowledge, he knows a rook from a crow, he knows cockle from barley, and the pea-blossom from that of the wild vetch. His mother can send him out into the hedges to get her some hop-tops, or wild marjoram; he knows a bee from a wasp; and if set to weed a bed in the garden, does not pull up the plants and leave the weeds . . .

As the years passed and the influence of the Whig aristocracy faded, Cobbett's genius came to be judged by less snobbish criteria than those of Lord Holland and his circle. His political influence lived on particularly amongst the Chartists, as was acknowledged by Karl Marx, himself an admirer of Cobbett. We can see it in the language of the Chartist leader Feargus O'Connor, who echoed Cobbett's cry for a Brave Old World: 'Here's that we may live to see the restoration of old English times, old English fare, old English holidays, and old English justice, and every man live by the sweat of his brow' – a typically Cobbettite manifesto.

The spirit of Cobbett survived most effectively in the works of his admirer Dickens, who took up his campaign against the new Poor Law and the workhouses and who set his novels in a pre-Victorian world partly inspired by Cobbett, a world in which honest labourers and benevolent gentlemen ('the good rich man handing out guineas', as Orwell described them) are set against The Thing, consisting of cold-hearted aristocrats, pompous lawyers and civil servants, and do-gooders of the Hannah More variety preaching the benefits of poverty whilst themselves enjoying the good life.

Although he lived through the colourful, raucous period of the

Regency, in some respects Cobbett had anticipated the Victorian age. He preached the benefits of sobriety, hard work, early rising and self-help. Even the Whigs like Brougham and Sydney Smith had admired his *Cottage Economy*, which advocated this way of life. His views on religion and the Church had an even greater impact, helping to encourage a new idealism in the Church of England, as exemplified in the Oxford Movement. William Morris, Matthew Arnold and Thomas Carlyle all admired his writings, and John Ruskin praised his *History of the Protestant Reformation.*

As far as recent historians are concerned, it is significant to find Cobbett being quoted and admired by the whole spectrum: Arthur Bryant (Tory), G.M. Trevelyan (liberal), A.J.P. Taylor (socialist), E.P. Thompson (Marxist), George Woodcock (anarchist).[2] This in turn suggests that his appeal transcends any political bias, being more emotional and specifically English in character. It was Margaret Cole who said of her husband and Cobbett's biographer, the socialist lecturer and historian G.D.H. Cole, that he was 'Conservative in everything except politics' – a description that could be applied just as well to Cobbett, or for that matter to A.J.P. Taylor, a member of CND who supported the 'Troops Out' of Northern Ireland campaign and who at the same time revered Dr Johnson and liked visiting old churches and reading Beatrix Potter to his wife in bed. Cobbett can be seen as the prototype of this species of Englishman, a man who combines radical opinions with conservative instincts, who believes that things are not as they once were, who hates London and loves the country, is suspicious of bankers and clergymen etc., the sort of person traditionally described as 'a mass of contradictions'.

Voltaire famously said that it was necessary to cultivate one's garden, as an alternative to engaging in politics. It was to Cobbett's great credit that he aspired to do both, devoting as much time to his turnips and his trees as he did to attacking the Whigs. From his writing on these subjects – *The English Gardener, The Woodlands* –

we see another side to the polemicist, but one which his contemporaries largely ignored. Heine portrayed him as a dog, Coleridge as a rhinoceros; neither realised that there were two Cobbetts, the crusading journalist and the lover of flowers and vegetables, of trees and landscape, a man who was as responsive to the beauty of nature as Wordsworth or Constable. The long obituaries, perhaps because they were written by Wen-dwellers, made little mention of this aspect of Cobbett's genius. Yet it had been in evidence since the publication in 1818 of his *A Year's Residence in the United States of America*, with its lyrical descriptions of the scenery of Long Island and his native Surrey.

'The great prophets of mankind,' A.J.P. Taylor once wrote, 'are remembered for a single book, even if they wrote many.' In Cobbett's case it was not his *Grammar* or his *Paper Against Gold*, as he himself predicted, that would keep his name alive. It was *Rural Rides*, a hastily-put-together collection of pieces from the *Political Register* to which he attached no special importance. The book survives because it gives a picture not just of England but of Cobbett himself, and not just Cobbett the political journalist but Cobbett the lover of the countryside, acutely sensitive to landscape and colour and the changes in the weather. Yet that combination in itself was not enough to ensure Cobbett's immortality. Dr Johnson once said of a book that it had not 'wit enough to keep it sweet', implying that there has to be a salt-like ingredient to preserve writing from oblivion. Amongst all the commentaries on Cobbett by critics and historians, many of them American, it is easy to overlook the fact that he was funny. It needs G.K. Chesterton, himself a brilliantly witty journalist, to emphasise that 'The man who does not find one of Cobbett's books amusing is doomed to find every book dull.' No one, not even Chesterton, who was almost as prolific as Cobbett, wrote as much that is still fresh and amusing. Yet, though many of his books have been occasionally reprinted in the years since his death, only one has kept its place as an English classic.

If the image of Cobbett the rural rider is the one that has survived, that is perhaps as it should be – a man on his horse alone, seeing things for himself. No one was more of an individualist, self-taught and self-sufficient. From his boyhood he had relied almost entirely on his own instincts, not needing his parents or his brothers, and at the end on his Surrey farmhouse with the brick floor, not needing his wife or children. However much he may have hankered after the life of an MP, Cobbett could never have been a successful politician because he could never collaborate or compromise. He hated meetings – frequented by people '*talking* about what they are to *talk* about next time'. He quarrelled with almost all his one-time colleagues or allies – Windham, Burdett, Place, Hunt, John Wright. It was said that Lord Folkestone was the only friend with whom he never fell out (though I can find no record of any estrangement from Admiral Cochrane). This self-sufficiency, or egotism, as his critics called it, was both his strength and his weakness. It meant that his reaction to public events was original, owing nothing to the thinking of others. But it also meant that he was hardly ever open to ideas from outside, and was unable to understand why so many people failed to agree with him.

Cobbett had envisaged the frontispiece of his proposed autobiography showing two pictures, one of him as a little boy scaring the rooks away from his father's fields, the other as an MP addressing the House of Commons. It is possible to imagine a sequence of such pictures illustrating the whole of his life. They might portray him in uniform poring over Lowth's *Grammar* by candlelight on his barrackroom bed, or imprisoned in Newgate writing his *Paper Against Gold*. Another might show him in his home-made tent on Long Island, or in the Guildhall giving Lord Grey and his colleagues a piece of his mind. Still, the picture that stays in the mind, as vividly as a scene in a film, is that of a young man on his way to the fair in Guildford in the company of three girls seeing the London coach coming down the hill, and there and then deciding to jump on it. Cobbett himself had seen that as the start of an adventure story, but even he could never have predicted all the upsets and excitements that would ensue, before he ended his life cracking jokes about his doctor and Lord Brougham only a few miles from where he had set out on that May morning so many years before.

REFERENCES

Chapter 1: A Sweet Old Boy

1. George Spater, *William Cobbett: The Poor Man's Friend*
2. William Hazlitt, *Table Talk* (1821)
3. Nuffield: James Paul Cobbett's biography
4. Anne Cobbett, *Account of the Family*
5. Nuffield
6. *Political Register*, 6 December 1817
7. Ibid.

Chapter 2: Off to Philadelphia

1. Agnes Repplier, *Philadelphia: Place and People* (1899)
2. Nuffield
3. Ibid.
4. Cobbett, *Advice to Young Men*
5. Ibid.
6. 'Peter Porcupine', Cobbett, *Works*, vol. 9, p.51
7. Thomas Rodney, *Diary* (1781)
8. *Dictionary of American Biography*
9. Benjamin Rush, *Travels Through Life*

10. *Letters of William Cobbett to Edward Thornton*, ed. Cole (1937)
11. Ibid.
12. Ibid.

Chapter 3: England Revisited

1. *Political Register*, 24 April 1819
2. Arthur Aspinall, *Politics and the Press 1780–1850*
3. L. Melville, *The Life and Letters of William Cobbett in England and America*, vol. 1
4. Ibid.
5. Granville, *Correspondence*, vol. 1, quoted A. Bryant, *Years of Victory*
6. Spater, *William Cobbett*
7. Melville, *Life and Letters*, vol. 1
8. Windham Papers, vol. 2
9. Quoted M.L. Pearl, *William Cobbett: A Bibliographical Account of his Life and Times* (1953)
10. Spater, *William Cobbett*
11. J.R. Spencer, *Criminal Law Review* (1977)
12. *Political Register*, 9 June 1804
13. Quoted Ian Dyck, *William*

Cobbett and Rural Popular Culture

14. *Political Register*, 16 June 1808
15. Cobbett, *Advice to Young Men*
16. Ibid.

Chapter 4: A Convert to Reform

1. Melville, *Life and Letters*
2. *Political Register*, March 1809
3. Quoted R.J. White, *Life in Regency England*
4. Spater, *William Cobbett*, vol. 1, p.193
5. Melville, *Life and Letters*, vol. 2
6. Quoted Spater, *William Cobbett*
7. J.L. and B. Hammond, *The Age of the Chartists*
8. Francis Place, *Autobiography*
9. *Dictionary of National Biography*
10. Melville, *Life and Letters*, vol. 2
11. *Political Register*, 1 June 1806
12. *Political Register*, 28 June 1806
13. Spater, *William Cobbett*
14. Melville, *Life and Letters*
15. *Political Register*, July 1810
16. *Political Register*, February 1809
17. Ibid.
18. *Political Register*, 11 March 1809
19. Aspinall, *Politics and the Press*, p.40
20. Bulwer, *Historical Characters*
21. *Political Register*, May 1809
22. Quoted in Draper Hill, *Life of Gillray* (1965)
23. Spater, *William Cobbett*
24. Cobbett, *A Year's Residence in the United States of America*, para 646
25. Quoted E. Smith, *William Cobbett: A Biography*, vol. 2

26. Cobbett, *Advice to Young Men*
27. Ibid.
28. Smith, *William Cobbett*, vol. 2
29. Gray, *Spencer Perceval*
30. Spater, *William Cobbett*
31. Wallas, *Life of Francis Place* (1918)
32. *Life of Lord Campbell*, ed. M. Hardcastle (1881)
33. Anon, *Life of Cobbett* (1835)

Chapter 5: Behind Bars

1. *The Autobiography of William Cobbett*, ed. William Reitzel
2. Cobbett, *Advice to Young Men*
3. Nuffield
4. Creevey, *Journals*, ed. Gore
5. L. Simond, *Journal of a Tour and Residence in Great Britain* (1817)
6. Anne Cobbett, *Account of the Family*
7. Nuffield
8. Pearl, *Bibliographical Account*
9. *Political Register*, July 1812
10. Cobbett, *History of the Regency and Reign of George IV*
11. *Autobiography of Cobbett*, ed. Reitzel
12. Cobbett, *History of the Regency and Reign of George IV*
13. Quoted White, *Life in Regency England*
14. Aspinall, *Politics and the Press*
15. *Autobiography of Cobbett*, ed. Reitzel

Chapter 6: America Revisited

1. *Autobiography of Cobbett*, ed. Reitzel
2. Cobbett, *A Year's Residence in the United States of America*
3. Cobbett, *The American Gardener*
4. *Political Register*, 24 November 1818
5. *Political Register*, 22 January 1820
6. *Political Register*, 13 November 1819
7. *Letters to Grenville*, 14 November 1819
8. *Letters of Sydney Smith* (1953)
9. *Political Register*, 27 January 1826

Chapter 7: Queen's Counsel

1. Handbill in author's collection
2. Cobbett, *History of the Regency and Reign of George IV*
3. Ibid.
4. Ibid.
5. Melville, *Life and Letters*, vol. 2
6. Hazlitt, *Collected Works*, vol. 2
7. *Political Register*, 8 July 1820
8. Ibid.
9. Coupland, *Life of Wilberforce*
10. White, *Life in Regency England*
11. Cobbett, *History of the Regency and Reign of George IV*
12. Melville, *Life and Letters*, vol. 2
13. *Political Register*, 18 November 1820
14. Ibid.
15. Melville, *Life and Letters*, vol. 2
16. *Political Register*, 18 November 1820
17. Quoted Wickwar, *The Struggle for the Freedom of the Press* (1928)

Chapter 8: Rural Rider

1. Quoted Dyck, *William Cobbett and Rural Popular Culture*
2. *Political Register*, 3 January 1835
3. *Political Register*, 23 March 1816
4. Nuffield
5. Melville, *Life and Letters*
6. *The Trial of the Unfortunate Byrne etc to which is annexed the opinion of that great political writer Mr. Cobbett on the late abominable and disgusting transaction* (Dublin, 1822)
7. *Political Register*, 17 August 1822
8. Quoted E.I. Carlyle, *William Cobbett*
9. Anne Cobbett, *Account of the Family*
10. *Political Register*, 19 January 1822
11. Quoted J.L. and B. Hammond, *The Village Labourer*
12. Spater, *William Cobbett*
13. Quoted Smith, *William Cobbett*, vol. 2
14. Cobbett, *A History of the Protestant Reformation*
15. Quoted J.L. and B. Hammond, *The Age of the Chartists*
16. *Political Register*, 31 December 1825

Chapter 9: The Final Prosecution

1. Melbourne Papers
2. *Autobiography of Cobbett*, ed. Reitzel
3. Ibid.
4. Henry Brougham, Introduction to *Collected Speeches* (1838)
5. *The Trial of William Cobbett Esq.* (1831)
6. Ibid.
7. Ibid.
8. Ibid.
9. Ibid.
10. *Twopenny Trash*, 1 August 1831
11. Charles Greville, *The Greville Memoirs* (1888)

Chapter 10: A Great Event

1. *Twopenny Trash*, 1 April 1831
2. *Political Register*, 19 May 1832
3. *Twopenny Trash*, 1 June 1832
4. *Twopenny Trash*, 1 July 1832
5. *Political Register*, 14 July 1832
6. *Political Register*, 4 August 1832
7. See S.A. Weaver, *John Fielden and the Politics of Popular Radicalism* (Oxford University Press, 1987)
8. Quoted Smith, *William Cobbett*, vol. 2
9. Quoted *Cobbett's Tour in Scotland*, ed. Daniel Green (1984)

Chapter 11: Member for Oldham

1. Spater, *William Cobbett*
2. J. Grant, *Recollections of the House of Commons* (1836)
3. Bulwer, *Historical Characters*
4. Huish, *Life of Cobbett*, vol. 2
5. Spater, *William Cobbett*
6. *Diaries of Absalom Watkin*, ed. Goffin (1993)
7. Spater, *William Cobbett*
8. *Political Register*, 11 October 1834
9. *The History and Social Influence of the Potato* (Cambridge University Press, 1949)
10. *Political Register*, 25 October 1834

Chapter 12: End of the Journey

1. *Autobiography of Cobbett*, ed. Reitzel
2. Pearl, *Bibliographical Account*
3. *Political Register*, 11 April 1835
4. *Political Register*, 6 June 1835
5. Melville, *Life and Letters*, vol. 2

Epilogue

1. Bulwer, *Historical Characters*
2. See Introduction to *Rural Rides*, ed. G. Woodcock (Penguin, 1967)

BIBLIOGRAPHY

A complete bibliography of Cobbett's journalism, pamphlets and books is contained in M.L. Pearl, *William Cobbett: A Bibliographical Account of his Life and Times* (OUP, 1953). Cobbett's principal books are as follows:

Paper Against Gold and Glory Against Prosperity (1815)
A Year's Residence in the United States of America (1818)
A Grammar of the English Language (1818)
The American Gardener (1821); revised as *The English Gardener* (1828)
Cottage Economy (1821)
A French Grammar (1824)
A History of the Protestant Reformation (1824)
The Woodlands (1828)
Rural Rides (1830)
Advice to Young Men and (incidentally) to Young Women (1830)
History of the Regency and Reign of George IV (1830)
Cobbett's Tour of Scotland (1832)
The Progress of a Ploughboy to a Seat in Parliament (1933), republished as *The Autobiography of William Cobbett* (1947, ed. William Reitzel), in which all Cobbett's autobiographical passages are joined together to make a continuous narrative.

BIOGRAPHIES OF COBBETT

Prior to 1982 the standard life of Cobbett was that by G.D.H. Cole published in 1924 (republished in a revised edition, 1947). Cole also, with his wife Margaret, edited the definitive three-volume edition of

Rural Rides (1930), as well as editing *The Opinions of William Cobbett* (1944), a collection of extracts from the *Political Register*, and *Letters of William Cobbett to Edward Thornton* (1937).

George Spater's massive two-volume biography *William Cobbett: The Poor Man's Friend* (1982) contained a great deal of new information, including the first detailed account of Cobbett's death and the family disputes that preceded it. A number of books have been published since, including two biographies, by Daniel Green and Anthony Burton, and two accounts of Cobbett's visit to Ireland in 1834: *Cobbett in Ireland*, ed. Denis Knight (1984), and Molly Townsend, *Not by Bullets and Bayonets* (1983). In 1999 the Cobbett Society published Anne Cobbett's reminiscences of her father, *Account of the Family*.

Of academic works the most valuable is Professor Ian Dyck's *William Cobbett and Rural Popular Culture* (1992). Professor Dyck also edited the most recent edition of *Rural Rides* (Penguin, 2001) as well as contributing the entry on Cobbett to the new *Dictionary of National Biography* (2004).

OTHER WORKS

Henry Lytton Bulwer, *Historical Characters* (1868)
E.I. Carlyle, *William Cobbett* (1904)
G.K. Chesterton, *William Cobbett* (1926)
L. Melville, *The Life and Letters of William Cobbett in England and America* (2 vols, 1913)
E. Smith, *William Cobbett: A Biography* (2 vols, 1879)

HISTORICAL BACKGROUND

Arthur Aspinall, *Politics and the Press 1780–1850* (1949)
A.J. Ayer, *Thomas Paine* (1988)
Samuel Bamford, *Passages in the Life of a Radical* (1893)
J. Belchem, *'Orator' Hunt* (1985)
Arthur Bryant, *The Years of Endurance* (1942)
Arthur Bryant, *Years of Victory* (1944)
Arthur Bryant, *The Age of Elegance* (1950)
J.R.M. Butler, *The Passing of the Great Reform Bill* (1914)

G.D.H. Cole, *Persons and Periods* (1938)

Thomas Creevey, *Journals*, selected by John Gore (1948)

J.R. Dinwiddy, *From Luddism to the Reform Bill* (1986)

Henry Fearon, *Sketches of America* (1818)

Denis Gray, *Spencer Perceval* (1963)

Elie Halevy, *The Liberal Awakening 1815–1830* (1949)

J.L. and B. Hammond, *The Village Labourer* (1911)

J.L. and B. Hammond, *The Town Labourer* (1917)

J.L. and B. Hammond, *The Skilled Labourer* (1919)

J.L. and B. Hammond, *The Age of the Chartists* (1930)

William Hazlitt, *The Spirit of the Age* (1825)

Draper Hill, *Mr Gillray the Caricaturist* (1965)

E.J. Hobsbawm and G. Rude, *Captain Swing* (1969)

Lord Holland, *Holland House Diaries*, ed. Kriegel (1977)

Henry Hunt, *Memoirs* (1820)

H. Montgomery Hyde, *The Strange Death of Lord Castlereagh* (1959)

R.W. Ketton-Cremer, *Felbrigg: The Story of a House* (1962)

C. Lloyd, *Lord Cochrane* (1947)

John Michell, *Eccentric Lives and Peculiar Notions* (1984; includes a chapter on Father O'Callaghan)

Mary Russell Mitford, *Recollections of a Literary Life* (1859)

Chester New, *The Life of Henry Brougham to 1830* (1961)

J.W. Osborne, *John Cartwright* (1972)

The Poor Law Report of 1834, ed. S.G. and E.O.A. Checkland (1974)

D.W. Roberts, *An Outline of the Economic History of England to 1952* (1960)

R.N. Salaman, *The History and Social Influence of the Potato* (1949)

John Stanhope, *The Cato Street Conspiracy* (1962)

E.P. Thompson, *The Making of the English Working Class* (1963)

G.M. Trevelyan, *British History in the Nineteenth Century* (1923)

Charlotte M. Waters, *An Economic History of England* (1925)

R.J. White, *Waterloo to Peterloo* (1957)

R.J. White, *Life in Regency England* (1963)

INDEX